6-06

Daimler & Benz: The Complete History

The Birth and Evolution of the Mercedes-Benz

Daimler & Benz: The Complete History

The Birth and Evolution of the Mercedes-Benz

Written and with Photographs by
Dennis Adler

⟡ Collins
An Imprint of HarperCollins*Publishers*

To Jeanne who keeps asking why I can't keep the Mercedes test cars,

my friend and agent Peter Riva, and everyone at Mercedes-Benz

and DaimlerChrysler for their continued support over the years

---

DAIMLER & BENZ: THE COMPLETE HISTORY. Copyright © 2006 by Dennis Adler. All rights reserved. Printed in the United States. No part of this book may be used or reproduced in any manner whatsoever without written permission except in the case of brief quotations embodied in critical articles or reviews. For information address HarperCollins Publishers, 10 East 53rd Street, New York, NY 10022.

HarperCollins books may be purchased for educational, business , or sales promotional use. For information please write: Special Markets Department, HarperCollins Publishers, 10 East 53rd Street, New York, NY 10022.

Designed by Keith Betterley

Library of Congress Cataloging in Publication data applied for.

ISBN-10: 0-06-089026-6
ISBN-13: 978-0-006089026-1

06 07 08 09 10 WOR 10 9 8 7 6 5 4 3 2 1

Contents

6-06

34.95

By **Sir Stirling Moss**

It is a privilege once again to write the Foreword for Dennis Adler's latest work on Mercedes-Benz. It seems that both he and I have made the marque a significant part of our lives.

Even as a young lad in the 1930s, I knew of Mercedes-Benz and their indomitable racing team. Whenever the Silver Arrows had raced they had been the leader in design and engineering and this left a lasting impression, one that would later lead me to their door as a young racecar driver in the 1950s.

Both of my parents were motor sport enthusiasts and having caught the bug at such an early age there was perhaps only one goal I could have set for myself and that was to become a professional racing driver. I know my parents would have liked me to adopt another profession but they supported my ambitions in every respect and my father became my manager.

In 1948, I competed in my first racing season in Formula 3, racing in 15 competitions and winning 12 of these – a good start. In 1949, 1950 and 1951, I clinched the British Champion's title in Formula 2, and in 1954, raced highly successfully in Formula One, driving my own Maserati. I had done well enough, in fact, to become part of the Maserati factory team, and on occasion we ran those new Mercedes cars close, but we always knew that it would take the most enormous slice of luck for us ever to beat them. I would imagine, in my particular case, the old adage, "If you can't beat them, join them," truly applies. I was in New York on November 22, 1954 when I was told that Mercedes' racing manager Alfred Neubauer had offered me a test drive in preparation for the 1955 season.

Dad and I flew to Cologne, Germany, where I was met and taken to *Hockenheim* racetrack to try one of their new 2-1/2 liter desmodromic-valved Formula 1 cars for the first time. On the damp track where I eventually equaled Karl Kling's lap record, I was very impressed with the straight-eight engine, though not so much with the car itself, which seemed rather hefty. But it also gave the impression it would be totally unbreakable. It was, after all, a Mercedes-Benz, and I never saw one lose a wheel!

On that rather unseasonable day at *Hockenheim* I was covered in road grime, as was often the case after a race, and as I clambered out of the car, rummaging in my pockets for a handkerchief or rag to wipe away the oil haze and road film, I was met by a Mercedes-Benz mechanic in impeccably clean coveralls, who presented me with a bowl of hot water, soap, a face flannel, and a towel! I was amazed. Out here, in the middle of the desolate *Hockenheimring*, was this forethought I could scarcely imagine. At that moment I thought, to be associated with such an organization, one capable of thinking of *everything*, could not be half bad.

After *Hockenheim* Mercedes-Benz offered me the opportunity to drive on the same team as double-World Champion Juan Manuel Fangio, and I was not about to say "No" to what seemed a dream come true. They engaged me to drive for them in both Formula 1 and sports car competition. With the great Fangio as my team leader, I knew I might not be able to win the Championship, at least not just yet, but whatever else might happen, I should certainly to able to learn following Fangio – the absolute master in my view.

I can only describe driving for the Mercedes-Benz team as my all-round master class in life. I learned very quickly that while Juan was a truly great racing driver, he was an even greater man. In fact, he proved to be one of several personalities that I met and worked with during that memorable season that would influence my life enormously. Fangio was the most impressive of men, not only fantastic behind the wheel of a Grand Prix car, and stupendously successful, yet faultlessly modest, tremendously determined and competitive, and remarkably gentle and understanding. Despite being the standard-setter of this era in Grand Prix racing he always remained accessible to everybody. Prince or pauper, he treated literally everybody exactly the same, with grace, and charm and open affability...and I hope some of that rubbed off on me.

I also enormously respected and liked Mercedes' legendary team manager, Alfred Neubauer. While his public image was loud, tough and authoritarian, to us, he was immensely warm, endearing and often tremendous fun. While one moment he could rap out orders like a sergeant major, he was also capable of great sensitivity and understanding, and in relaxed moments could have us all rolling with laughter. He was also a consummate strategist, confronting the rules that might take away any advantage for the team and directing a race from behind the scenes like it was theater. This too, rubbed off on his drivers and in May 1955 my friend Denis Jenkinson, a brilliant automotive journalist and motorcycle racer, was teamed with me in the Mille Miglia. After methodically pre-running the course, Jenks and I had it down to the extent that I would later rely on him to tell me by hand signals how to approach every turn, which he had mapped out, condensing the critical points of that 1000 mile course into a hand-written paper roller of route notes 15 feet, 6 inches long! On May 2, we won the Mille Miglia in the record time of ten hours, seven minutes and 48 seconds with the new Mercedes-Benz 300 SLR.

On July 16, 1955, I was the first to cross the finishing line in the British Grand Prix in Aintree, driving a Mercedes-Benz Formula One racing car, type W 196. I have to say there was nothing easy about driving the world's finest racing cars that year. In the W196 my feet were splayed wide apart, with the massive clutch housing between my shins, two pedals to the right, and the clutch pedal way to the left. The car rode very comfortably but everything about it felt heavy. The gear change was difficult because it was an unconventional layout, and although the cars were always very strong, and very fast, they were quite difficult to drive in the wet, and prone to weaving under power, wet or dry. The W196 always demanded, and was given, immense respect.

I won my first Grand Prix, my home event at Aintree circuit, Liverpool, in one of the "Silver Arrows" and at Monza, in the Italian GP, I vividly remember settling into my rhythm behind Fangio in our streamliners, when his car flung up a stone, which smashed my aero screen. I found myself badly buffeted in the air stream, so I had to make a pit stop to see if anything could be done. To my astonishment (I should have known better), the team had a replacement available, which the mechanics whipped onto the car and sent me away again in 36 seconds! Next time out, if the screen was broken, I just had to press a button and a standby would pop up in its place, without needing to make a pit stop! *That* was Mercedes-Benz.

Unfortunately, this was also to be a tragic year for Mercedes-Benz. Racing the 300 SLR roadsters across Europe in 1955 we won five out of six events entered, and only failed to win the sixth, at LeMans, after the company board ordered us to withdraw in the aftermath of Pierre Levegh's tragic crash, which claimed not only his life but that of more than 80 spectators. The decision had come eight hours after the fatal collision of his 300 SLR into a retaining wall, which destroyed the car and sent burning wreckage into the crowd. A telegram was delivered to Neubauer at the pits. It was from Fritz Nallinger in Untertürkheim. Wrote Nallinger: The pride of designers and drivers must bow to the grief suffered by countless French families in this appalling disaster.

As a token of Mercedes' respect, the remaining two cars were withdrawn. At the time, we were running first by three laps. That October, Mercedes-Benz retired from active racing to transfer the technical capacity hitherto used for motor sport to passenger car development. In the following years, I drove different cars and proved in each season anew what I had learned with Mercedes-Benz.

Mercedes' investment in their racing programs was typical of their approach, not only to competition but any objective upon which the company might set its mind. Regardless of cost, they were entirely engineering led...and it showed...and it was an absolute privilege to have been part of it. The commitment Mercedes-Benz has made to engineering excellence, to forethought, to preparation throughout the last 120 years, whether building a sports car, a grand prix race car, or a luxurious touring car, has never wavered.

Author and Mercedes-Benz historian Dennis Adler has written about, and photographed, some of the finest automobiles. This latest effort, commemorating the merger of Germany's two greatest manufactures, Daimler and Benz in June, 1926, is a long-awaited addition to his collective work that will surely find its place on the bookshelves of Mercedes-Benz enthusiasts the world over.

During his career, Stirling Moss competed in 495 motor sport events, driving 84 different cars, reaching the finishing line in 366 races and winning 222 of these. He missed the World Champion's title by a hair's breadth several times, clinching the runner-up position four times between 1955 and 1958, three times behind the great Juan Manuel Fangio and once, 1958, behind his compatriot Mike Hawthorn. His record of success also boasts 16 pole positions and a total of 19 fastest laps in World Championship races. In recognition of his achievements, he was knighted by the Queen of England.

— Dennis Adler

Preface & Acknowledgments

My relationship with Mercedes-Benz USA and Daimler-Benz AG (DaimlerChrysler) goes back more than a quarter of a century, much of which I have spent as Senior Contributing Editor to *The Star*, the official publication of the Mercedes-Benz Club of America. Over the years I built lasting friendships with many of the people who guided Mercedes-Benz, both in the United States and in Germany since the late 1970s. And it is those lasting friendships, which have afforded me the privilege of writing four books about this historic company.

The focus of this book, though covering the very beginning of both Daimler and Benz as independent manufacturers in the late 19th century, deals with the merger of Daimler Motoren Gesellschaft and Benz und Cie. in June of 1926, thus creating the company most have come to know as Mercedes-Benz.

Since the patent for the first Motorwagen was granted to Carl Benz in January 1886, these two legendary names, Mercedes and Benz, have given the world a whirlwind ride down countless roads, from the rough macadam paved streets of Europe and the British Isles in the early 20th century, to the high-banked curves of the Nürburgring racing circuit, from the grueling mountain roads of the Targa Florio and Mille Miglia, and the vastness of the Mexican desert, to the Autobahn, the interstates and Blue Highways of America, and from every corner of the globe where the Silver Star has left its indelible mark.

Gottlieb Daimler had a motto: "*The best or nothing,*" a difficult ideology to live by. In this book I have tried to live up to that axiom by offering one of the most comprehensive historical retrospectives of the marque, complete with a wealth of rare, archival imagery that has rarely been published, and some of which is being seen in these pages for the very first time.

As with any historical undertaking, research is a key element and no contemporary book on this subject could be written without paying respect to those authors and historians who have traveled this road before me. Most notably, *Mercedes-Benz, The Supercharged 8-Cylinder Cars of the 1930s,* by Jan Melin, Nordbok International Co-Editions AB, Gothenburg, Sweden 1985; *The Star and The Laurel*, by Beverly Rae Kimes, Mercedes-Benz of North America, Montvale, New Jersey 1986; *Mercedes-Benz Personenwagen 1886-1984* by Werner Oswald, Motorbuch Ver-

lag Stuttgart 1985; *Mercedes-Benz 300SL Art & Color Edition,* by Jürgen Lewandowski, Südwest Verlag GmbH & Co. KG, München, Germany, 1988; *Mercedes-Benz Illustrated Buyer's Guide* by Frank Barrett, Motorbooks International 1998; *Fantastic Mercedes-Benz Automobiles* by Peter Vann, Motorbooks International 1995; *Mercedes-Benz, The First Hundred Years,* by Richard M. Langworth, Publications International, Ltd., Skokie, Illinois 1984; and my own previous works, *Mercedes-Benz 300 SL*, Motorbooks International 1994; and *Mercedes-Benz—110 Years of Excellence*, Motorbooks International, 1995. The latter was actually adopted by Mercedes-Benz as a primer for new employees in 1996.

In the production of this latest work on Daimler-Benz history I have once again had the excellent support of Daimler-Benz AG and DaimlerChrysler, as well as that of the Mercedes-Benz Museum Archives and Classic Center in Germany. I would also like to express my personal thanks to my good friend Frank Barrett, publisher and editor of *The Star*, the incomparable Beverly Rae Kimes, without whose efforts Mercedes-Benz history would be less than complete, Juergen Hoedel for providing the Daimler-Benz Art Archive featured throughout the book, my number one car guy Bruce Meyer; Ralph Lauren; restorers extraordinaire Paul Russell and Scott Grundfor; Dr. Frank Spellman, Arturo Keller; the magnificent Nethercutt Collection in Sylmar, California; my friend Dr. Joseph Ernst of DaimlerChrysler Classic for his tireless efforts on my behalf, half a world away; and my European associate Tomasz Szczerbicki, for uncovering some of the rarest archival images of pre-World War II Mercedes known.

The level of cooperation and preparation I have had over the last 25 years working with Mercedes-Benz serves to further underscore the company's historic commitment to doing everything possible to ensure success in any endeavor it undertakes: to live up to Gottlieb Daimler's motto. As an author and photographer, I would have to say that the unprecedented help I have received from Mercedes-Benz for this, and every book I have written on the company, is my variation of Stirling Moss' bowl of warm water, soap, face flannel, and dry towel.

There is a reason that greatness endures.

— Dennis Adler

Carl Benz
The Inventor

This past January 29th of Twenty-O-Six we celebrated the birth of an idea put forward 120 years ago, that man should not be limited in his ability to travel by the constraints of steel rails or the shortcomings of horse-drawn carriages. To be truly free, one must not be encumbered by schedules and routes, or the stamina of horses. Thus a young German engineer named Carl Benz took to task the idea of motorized personal transportation in the mid 1880s.

The birth of the automobile, powered by an internal combustion engine, can be traced back to 1885 when Benz opened the doors of his small Mannheim workshop and rode around the yard in a three-wheeled carriage powered by a single cylinder engine of his own design. Of course, in 1885 the gasoline engine was not a new idea. Large, stationary engines had been in use since the latter part of the century to power industrial and farm machinery, and in fact Carl Benz had pioneered their development. It was his conception of a small single-cylinder version, however, that allowed him to create a phenomenon – the motorized carriage.

Having completed his first prototype single-cylinder three-wheeler, he went about applying for a patent, thereby making him the first to stake a claim for the design of a gasoline-powered motor carriage. German patent number 37435 was assigned to Benz on January 29, 1886. Shortly after, Gottlieb Daimler and his associate Wilhelm Maybach also applied to the patent office for their design. But Benz had been first.

His father Georg had been a railroad engineer, and Carl followed in his footsteps, graduating from the *Karlsruhe Polytechnikum* and beginning his career in the 1860s. His first job was in Mannheim, designing scales for Karl Schenck. Feeling less than fulfilled by the challenges at Karl Schenk, he moved to Pforzheim to build bridges for the firm of Benckiser Brothers, work in which the young Benz could take pride.

It was during his tenure with Benckiser that Carl met a beautiful, head-strong 20-year-old girl named Cäcilie Bertha Ringer. [1] In 1870 she accepted a proposal of marriage from Carl Friedrich Benz, almost five years her senior, at the Harmony social club in Pforzheim. At the time, she had no idea of the epochal role she would play in her husband's life or in the as yet non-existent history of the automobile. The vigor and decisiveness demonstrated by this young woman, as well as the determination with which she tackled her fiancé's problems and concerns, proved remarkable not only for that time.

After they were engaged, Carl went into business for himself, taking in a short-lived partner named August Ritter. They opened a machine shop in Mannheim, but Ritter soon departed when additional funds were needed to keep the doors open. This prompted the spirited Bertha to borrow against her dowry so her fiancé could buy out Ritter's interests in the new firm. From

Facing page:
It was 120 years ago this January (2006) that a motorized three-wheeler identical to this example claimed the right to be called the first motorcar. The 1886 Motorwagen pictured is one of a handful of reproductions built by Daimler-Benz craftsmen in 1985-86, using the same tools and materials as Carl Benz to commemorate the marque's 100th anniversary. *(Nethercutt Collection photo by Dennis Adler)*

[1] Some things about names. Many German texts spell Carl with a "K" thus Karl Benz. The same for Bertha, also spelled Berta and daughter Clara, spelled Klara. For the U.S. market we have chosen to use Carl, Bertha, and Clara for consistency.

In this recreation of Bertha Benz's historic drive from Mannheim to Pforzheim, a distance of more than 50 miles, she is shown with her two sons, Eugen and Richard. The dauntless trio made the trip in a single day, officially making Bertha and the boys the first motorists in history. Along the way they had to pull or push the Motorwagen up steep grades, and stop at a blacksmith's shop to repair the hand brake.

then on the business adopted the name Eisengiesserei und mechanische Werkstätte (Iron Foundry and Mechanical Workshop).

Owning a business and making it successful were to become two very different things for the new Mr. & Mrs. Benz, who were married in July 1872. In 1873 their son Eugen was born, followed by Richard in 1874. Their daughters Clara, Thilde, and Ellen were born in 1877, 1882, and 1884, respectively.

Success had continued to elude the young couple until 1880 when Carl introduced his first stationary engine. The "embryonic two-stroke engine," as christened by Carl Benz, finally came into being on New Year's Eve 1879 after many attempts, disappointments and privations, and for the first time, it continued to run smoothly. For Bertha and Carl it was a gift from heaven: "The more it hums, the more it enchants the pressing worries away from my heart," concluded Carl on that fateful evening.

The more troublesome two-stroke design had been his only choice. He had been prevented from building a four-stroke engine due to a patent granted to Nikolaus August Otto in 1877.

Around 1881 Carl took in a new partner to help finance the venture, Emil Bühler, a successful local photographer. Benz was responsible for building his stationary engines and Bühler for sales and marketing. He hired a sales agent named Otto Schmuck, who unfortunately spent more money promoting sales than he took in, requiring the small company to hastily apply for a loan. The first requirement of the local bankers was for Benz to form a corporation before any funds could be considered. Thus in October 1882, Gasmotorenfabrik Mannheim was established with a nine-member board of directors.

The harmony among the board was short-lived and within three months Benz had come to words with all of the investors over designs, most notably his plans for a small engine to power a motor-driven carriage, at which point several of the board's more outspoken members questioned Benz's sanity! In the fall of 1883 he resigned from the company. Wrote Carl, "During those days when disaster struck on the sea of life, only one person was waiting by my side. That was my wife. Fearless and courageous, she hoisted up new sails of hope."

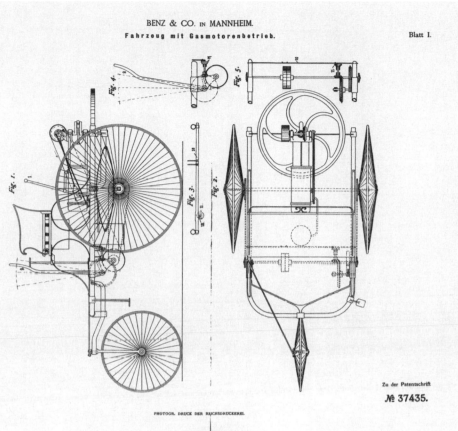

Still resolute in his plan to build a motorized wagon, and with Bertha's encouragement, Benz caught the ear and pocketbook of not one but two very successful businessmen, Max Kaspar Rose and Friedrich Wilhelm Esslinger, who jointly financed the creation of Benz & Cie., Rheinische Gasmotorenfabrik on October 1, 1883. Less than a month after leaving Gasmotorenfabrik Mannheim, Carl Benz was back in business.

The new company's primary trade would be the production and sales of the Benz stationary engine, which quickly brought riches to both Benz and his backers, leaving him the time to experiment and develop a motor suitable to power a "horseless carriage."

Benz had used coal gas to power his now very successful stationary engines and was wondering how to fuel his small, motorwagon engine, when the solution was provided by a local fire in Mannheim. It began when a bowl of benzene being used to clean work gloves was ignited by a spark. Benz reasoned that this highly volatile fluid could work in an engine, if the explosion could be controlled, and a proper spark provided to ignite it. His solution was a bat-

tery and trembler coil system with a spark plug, which he designed himself. Unknown to Benz, Daimler and Maybach had come to this same conclusion. There was a race on to build a motor carriage, and neither entrant in this race knew of the other's existence!

Benz, as well as his partners, Rose and Esslinger, was an avid bicyclist and though he had given the idea a great deal of thought, considering both four and three-wheeled designs for his motorwagen, he never considered the horse-drawn carriage as a basis for his design. A tricycle configuration, with power transferred to the rear wheels by a chain, appeared more logical, less complicated, lighter and easier to steer. This was the direction he chose when his concept for the motorwagen began to take shape in 1885.

A single-cylinder engine developing approximately two-thirds of a horse-power at 250rpm was placed on its side at the rear of the three-wheeler, with the immense flywheel running horizontally. The initial trial was in the fall, whereupon the very first motorized wagon built by Carl Benz stalled and, when restarted, proceeded to snap the drive chain!

The restored workshop of Carl Benz and his last home, in Ladenburg, were opened to the public in November 1985, one year before the 100th anniversary of Mercedes-Benz. On display is one of the reproduction Patent Motorwagens built for the celebration.

After making some minor improvements he was ready for another test run a few weeks later. Sitting proudly at the tiller, and with Bertha at his side this time, the engine was started by one of his assistants spinning the flywheel, and after engaging the chain drive Carl Benz proceeded to drive the Motorwagen straight into the brick wall of his shop, making this not only the first but shortest road test in history.

His next tests were conducted with his son Eugen running alongside the motorwagen carrying a can of gasoline. Benz had not yet equipped the Motorwagen with a fuel tank. On January 29, 1886 he received his initial patent. The Benz Motorwagen was powered by a water-cooled, single-cylinder, horizontal engine. The piston and cylinder were oriented fore and aft, and displacement was 954cc or 58cu. in. The choice of a four-stroke engine was rather daring on Carl's part, as the Otto four-stroke patents were not ruled invalid until January 30th. Benz received his patent the day before!

Still in the developmental stages, Benz was hesitant to begin production of the Patent Motorwagen. His testing had been confined to the road and yard surrounding his workshop. And while most would assume that the inventor of the motor carriage would be the first to actually take it out for a long distance trial, it was, in fact, Carl's wife Bertha who would go down in history as the first motorist. Yes ladies and gentlemen, the world's first driver was a woman!

In the summer of 1888 Bertha decided to "test drive" the second prototype Motorwagen on a journey from Mannheim to Pforzheim, a distance of more than 50 miles. With her two sons, Eugen and Richard, she set out at dawn and made the trip in a single day. Wiring her husband, who had been informed of her plans by the note she left for him on the kitchen table, "We're traveling to Pforzheim to visit Grandma," she wrote that they had arrived without any significant incidents. Even Bertha's father was extremely pleased about the first trip. "Father was so happy, we had finally achieved our goal," she wrote.

Bertha's trip had been *almost* uneventful, except for the fact that no one had ever seen a motor carriage, and the three-wheeler drew considerable crowds at every vil-

These three views of the 1886 Patent Motorwagen illustrate the layout of the single-cylinder engine and the massive flywheel. Steering was by tiller, and the only means of braking was the large hand lever acting upon a leather-covered block. The chain drive is also clearly shown in the rear close-up.

Left: The original 1885 prototype built by Carl Benz. The world's first motorcar is on display at the new Mercedes-Benz Museum in Untertürkheim.

Below:
Carl Benz is seen at the tiller of the improved model offered for sale in 1887. The "production" models could be ordered with a folding top and carriage lights.

lage along the route. They stopped in Heidelberg for a snack and then in Wiesloch at an apothecary to fill the radiator and purchase benzene for the fuel tank. The town pharmacy, which still exists today, prides itself as having been "the world's first filling station."

On the road they encountered two mechanical problems, which Bertha tackled with feminine ingenuity. A clogged fuel line was cleared with her hatpin, and when an ignition wire short-circuited she made an insulator out of one of her garters! The only other problem was the brake block, which she had fitted with a new piece of leather by a farrier in Bauschlott. They arrived in Pforzheim just as the sun was setting. And so the first step had been taken. In completing the very first long-distance journey in automotive history, Bertha Benz was not only able to prove to her husband, as was her original intention, but also to the many skeptics that a great future awaited the automobile. With her 50-odd mile journey, she was able to demonstrate the practicality of the motorcar. Without the daring courage of Bertha and that of her sons, as well as the decisive impulses it provided, the subsequent rise of Benz & Cie. as the world's largest automobile manufacturer would have been inconceivable.

While an improved Model 3 was being readied for exhibit in Munich, Bertha suggested one additional improvement to her husband's design, a low gear for hills, as Bertha and the boys had had to push the car up every steep grade

on their first trip. By year's end the improved Benz third version motorwagen was on the road, though not necessarily the road to success.

The horse and buggy was not so easily pushed aside as one's personal livery. First of all, just like a horse, a motorwagen needed fuel. Hay was plentiful, gasoline (benzene), on the other hand, was not. In the late 19th century no one had yet conceived of a gas station. Benzene had to be purchased at an apothecary and usually in small quantities, rarely more than five liters. The world was not quite ready for the Benz Patent Motorwagen, and it took until 1892 before any significant sales were recorded. But Carl and Bertha Benz were determined to succeed.

Back in September 1888, Benz had displayed the Model 3 Patent Motorwagen at the Munich Engineering Exposi-

Sitting in one of the later production versions of the Patent Motorwagen are Carl and Berta's three daughters (clockwise), Thilde, Clara and Ellen.

Top right:
By 1893 the Benz Viktoria had been introduced and the four-wheel model was another success for the Mannheim automaker.

Left & above:
The Benz & Cie. factory in Mannheim, c.1886-1908.

The smart little Velo was one of the most successful of the early Benz designs. This example from 1893 is being driven by Clara Benz.

Although commercial vehicles were more the interest of Daimler and Maybach, by 1895 Benz & Cie. was manufacturing a 5-horse-power Hotelwagen or Omnibus with seating for eight.

tion and offered test drives to anyone interested. Wrote one newspaper of the Benz's appearance in Munich: "Seldom, if ever, have passersby in the streets of our city seen a more starting sight." Another publication noted that "…without any sign of steam or other visible means of propulsion, human or otherwise, the vehicle proceeded on its way without difficulty…It was followed by a great crowd of breathless pedestrians."

The year 1888 was to be regarded as one of great historical and scientific significance in Europe. Heinrich Hertz succeeded in generating and proving the existence of electromagnetic waves, Fridtjof Nansen crossed Greenland on skis, European railroad connections finally reached Con-

stantinople and world exhibitions were staged in Barcelona, Melbourne, Moscow and Sydney. Carl Benz came home from Munich with a Gold medal from the Exposition, but not with a book full of orders. A year later Benz's first sales agent, French importer Emile Roger, displayed the Model 3 Patent Motorwagen at the Paris Exposition. By the end of 1892 he had sold almost a dozen and more were on order. The "production" models built from 1886 to 1889 were powered by a single-cylinder engine with a swept volume ranging from 1045cc to 1660cc and finally 1990cc. Power also improved from 1.5 to 2.5 and then 3 horsepower at 500rpm. A total of 25 were built.

Above: This picture of Carl Benz (in the left rear driver's seat of a Benz Vis-à-vis Viktoria) was taken in 1894. Seated next to Benz is Bertha and in the passenger seat daughter Clara and companion Fritz Held. One can see from this image the difficulty of literally being a back-seat driver!

Left:
A youthful Carl Benz posed for this portrait in 1860 after graduating from the *Karlsruhe Polytechnikum.*

In 1892 Benz & Cie. introduced the more advanced four-wheel Viktoria model, and in 1894 a third design known as the Velo (short for velocipede), the latter produced through 1900.

If there was indeed a race to see who would build the first production motorcar in Germany, it was Benz who would cross the sales finish line with the first successfully marketed horseless carriages in Europe. It was followed by the Benz Ideal, making Benz & Cie. one of the largest automakers in the world by 1900 with more than 1,250 motorcars sold since 1887. Of course by then Carl Benz had some serious competition from his neighbors some 60 miles away in Cannstatt – Gottlieb Daimler and Wilhelm Maybach, as well as other emerging motorcar builders throughout Europe and in the United States.

As the turn of the century approached, Benz could claim to have produced over 2,000 motorcars, along with commercial chassis and delivery trucks, and by 1899 there were various Benz & Cie. models on the road in England, France, North America, South Africa, Singapore,

Left:
Steering, braking, etc., were controlled by the driver of a Benz Ideal from the left rear seat.

Right:
Steering for the Ideal was still by tiller, although a more sophisticated version compared to the 1886 design.

The 1898 Ideal Vis-à-vis (face-to-face), was one of the last new models introduced before the turn of the century. It was a modern motorcar for the day, but Daimler would suddenly and forever change that in 1901, making the Vis-à-vis and all other Benz models obsolete almost overnight.

The Benz Ideal was powered by a single-cylinder engine developing 3 horsepower at 700rpm. Later versions had the engine stroke increased, boosting output to 4.5 horsepower at 960rpm and providing a top speed of around 22 mph.

New South Wales, and Germany. With a thriving business producing stationary gasoline engines for industrial uses as well, by 1899 Carl Benz had become the most successful automaker in the world. Unfortunately, it was a claim he would not be able to make for long.

By virtue of both an obstinate nature and having grown up poor, resulting in a tendency to be frugal in all things, Carl Benz had become his own worst enemy, failing to regard his early designs merely as stepping stones; the same error Henry Ford would make decades later by refusing to replace the Model T until the car was rendered virtually obsolete by his competitors. The boldest step Benz made prior to 1900 had been the introduction of the Velo, the aforementioned smaller version of the Viktoria. With half the horsepower it was what history might consider the world's first compact car. It was, for the time, an unparalleled success. At least 1,200 were sold between 1894 and 1901.

In 1898, Benz added the luxurious Ideal Vis-à-vis, (face-to-face), an unusual design that placed the driver in the rear seat facing the passengers. Originally powered by a single-cylinder engine developing 3 horsepower at 700rpm, a later version increased engine stroke, boosting output to 4.5 horsepower at 960rpm and providing a top speed of around 22 mph, but even these new Benz models resembled horse-drawn carriages without the horse, and had their single-cylinder engines mounted in the rear beneath the seats. What Carl Benz needed most was to invent a rear view mirror, so that he could see how close Daimler and Maybach were to running him off the road. In 1901 he would suddenly realize that his greatest weakness had been in failing to recognize their achievements. From his perspective, Benz had seen little reason to make sweeping changes. His motorwagens were reliable, proven designs, sales were brisk, and his stationary engine business was booming. But that was all about to change.

Facing:
With passengers seated in the front and the engine located beneath the rear seat, the Benz Ideal was anything but by 1901, when Daimler would introduce the world to steering wheels, front-mounted engines, and driver's seats.

Clockwise from top left:
This picture was taken in 1894 during an outing with the Benz family and Baron von Liebig.

Carl Benz watched his company regain market share in the early 1900s. He lived long enough to be present for the merger of Benz & Cie. with Daimler in 1926. He died three years later.

Vis-à-vis was a better idea when the driver was up front, as in this 1895 commercial Benz eight-seater. Richard Benz is at the tiller, his father seated in the rear flanked by V. Fischer and Julus Gauss.

In Munich, 1925, the elder Benz also appeared in a Jubilee parade driven by his son Eugen in an 1893 Benz Viktoria.

In 1925, a year before the merger with Daimler, Carl Benz, then 81 years old, posed with one of the original 1886 Patent Motorwagens at a festival in Munich. Standing behind the 1886 tiller is Bertha Benz, the world's first motorist.

Gottlieb Daimler & Wilhelm Maybach

Advancing on a Theory

They had been friends and associates for nearly three decades before Gottlieb Daimler and Wilhelm Maybach established Daimler Motoren Gesellschaft in November 1890. Interestingly, building a motorcar had not been their primary interest. Unlike Carl Benz who had dreamed of putting Europe on wheels, Daimler and Maybach had pursued more lofty goals, both figuratively and literally, designing internal combustion engines for a variety of purposes, including public transit, motorboats, and motor-powered dirigibles. This was the origin of the Daimler Motoren Gesellschaft emblem, a three-pointed star representing land, air, and sea.

Gottlieb Daimler (whose last name was originally spelled Däumler), began his professional career in the 1860s as Technical Director with Gasmotorenfabrik Deutz near Cologne. His chief engineer was Maybach. It was there that Maybach began studying the Otto four-stroke engine and its patent, later to be highly disputed and subsequently challenged in the German Court. Intrigued with the Otto concept, Maybach began his own development program, with Daimler's approval, to refine the four-cycle design. Ultimately both men found themselves in dispute with Nicholas Otto and Eugen Langen, the founders of Gasmotorenfabrik Deutz. This came as a result of improvements Maybach made to Otto's engine, which enraged both Otto and Langen. Even though the work had been approved by Daimler, the fracas continued

until the bitterness between the four men drove both Daimler and Maybach to resign in 1882.

In the early 1880s the steam engine was still king, and unless one could afford to ride the railcars, travel by horse-drawn carriage, or had invested in a bicycle, the only other means of personal transportation was your own two feet. Gottlieb Daimler and Wilhelm Maybach, like Carl Benz, were certain that the internal combustion engine was the answer, if one could be built that was light enough. The Otto engine had never been intended for anything except providing a source of power for machinery.

As is often the case when two brilliant men leave the employ of a company that inhibits their work, they start their own business. This was prevalent in the automotive industry from the late 1880s throughout the early 20th century and led to the creation of such renowned companies as Chrysler (now DaimlerChrysler), Audi, BMW, and for the record, Ford Motor Company, which resulted from the ousting of Henry Ford from his first automotive venture!

Daimler and Maybach pooled their finances and set up shop in a small greenhouse behind Daimler's villa in Bad Cannstatt. This is, of course, skipping over the trials and tribulations of many years at Deutz and the bitter conflicts that raged on between Nicholas Otto and Gottlieb Daimler, whose own temperament was none too receptive to criticism.

Main image: This seldom seen portrait of Gottlieb Daimler was taken a few years before his death at age 66. He was eulogized by Frederick Simms, the founder of Daimler Motor Company in England, as "Unquestionably the father of modern automobilism," an accolade that Carl Benz never earned despite having been the automotive industry's pioneering engineer.

Inset: Wilhelm Maybach was Daimler's closest friend and lifelong colleague. After Daimler's death in 1900 much of the responsibility for DMG fell on Maybach's shoulders. Coincidentally, he would pass away in 1929, the same year as Carl Benz.

Gottlieb and Emma Daimler, pictured here in the 1860s, had five children; Paul, born in 1869, Adolf, born in 1871, Emma in 1873, Martha in 1878, and Wilhelm (named after Daimler's associate) in 1881. The family group portrait taken in 1885 shows Daimler, wife Emma, sons Paul and Adolf, Emma's father, Daimler's son Wilhelm, Emma's sister Marie, and Daimler's daughters Emma and Martha.

As a team Daimler and Maybach developed and patented the world's first fast-running internal combustion engine in 1883. Daimler, never one to forget an antagonist, compared their new engine to that of the Nicholas Otto design as being "...like a rifle to a blunderbuss." He wasn't far off. Otto engines weighed as much as 750 pounds and operated at a mere 180rpm. The Daimler four-stroke design was light enough for a man to pick up, weighing less than 100 pounds, yet it could operate at speeds of up to 900rpm. With a lightweight engine, Daimler and Maybach began to examine other applications and within two years had built a motor-driven cycle or *Reitwagen* (riding car) powered by a single cylinder, four-stroke gas engine. (This came before the Otto patent was broken, but had not been considered for actual production at the time.)

The first motorized vehicle by Daimler and Maybach could best be described as a heavy, wooden-framed motorcycle with training wheels! It was, nevertheless, the first practical, motorized personal conveyance ever built, pre-dating the Benz Patent Motorwagen. Daimler's 16-year old son Paul was the test driver, taking the wooden-wheeled contraption from Cannstatt to Unter-türkheim and back, a total of roughly six kilometers. The year was 1885; at roughly the same time Carl Benz, some 60 miles distant, was breaking drive chains and running into walls with his prototype three-wheeler.

Gottlieb Daimler was a relatively wealthy man and his villa in Bad Cannstatt provided the grounds for his first independent workshop with Wilhelm Maybach, set up in the greenhouse behind the villa. In July 1992, the greenhouse was restored and turned into a museum.

Below:
The Daimler workshop in Bad Cannstatt has been restored and a reproduction of the 1885 Reitwagen put on display.

Little more than a test bed for their new, lightweight engine, the *Reitwagen* was built around the engine using a wooden frame with carriage wheels front and rear (no form of suspension) and fitted with a leather saddle seat. They applied for a patent which was granted on August 29, 1885.

Gottlieb Daimler was a comparatively wealthy man. He had been well compensated for his work at Deutz and was never hard pressed for operating capital. He had a magnificent home in Bad Cannstatt, and no shortage of patrons willing to support his efforts, among whom were Max Duttenhofer, commercial privy counselor and managing director of the Köln-Rottweiler powder factory (gun powder being very big business) and Duttenhofer's business associate Ailhelm Lorenz, who assisted Daimler in the financial backing to establish Daimler Motoren Gesellschaft.

A motorcar was still of secondary importance to Daimler and Maybach's research, and in the small greenhouse-workshop behind the Daimler villa, they were designing engines for a variety of conveyances, including the first motorboat, which they built in 1886.

While Carl Benz may have claimed the title as the maker of the first patented motorwagen, and the honor of building Germany's first commercial bus in 1894, Daimler and Maybach had gone from experimentation and development right into production and by 1896 were offering general purpose trucks, a handful of four-wheel motorwagens, the first motor driven fire engines, and had already made great strides in the design and develop-

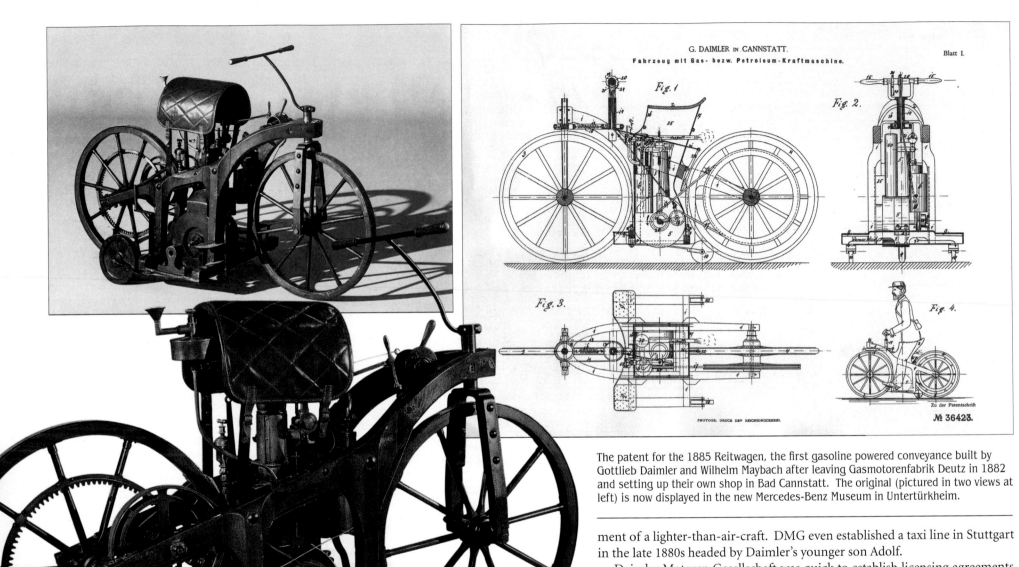

G. DAIMLER in CANNSTATT.

Fahrzeug mit Gas- bezw. Petroleum-Kraftmaschine.

Blatt I.

Fig. 1.

Fig. 2.

Fig. 3.

Fig. 4.

PHOTOGR. DRUCK DER REICHSDRUCKEREI.

Zu der Patentschrift

№ 36423.

The patent for the 1885 Reitwagen, the first gasoline powered conveyance built by Gottlieb Daimler and Wilhelm Maybach after leaving Gasmotorenfabrik Deutz in 1882 and setting up their own shop in Bad Cannstatt. The original (pictured in two views at left) is now displayed in the new Mercedes-Benz Museum in Untertürkheim.

ment of a lighter-than-air-craft. DMG even established a taxi line in Stuttgart in the late 1880s headed by Daimler's younger son Adolf.

Daimler Motoren Gesellschaft was quick to establish licensing agreements outside German borders, in France with both Panhard & Levassor and Peugeot, in Great Britain through Daimler Motor Company, Ltd. of Coventry, Warwickshire, as well as an Austrian subsidiary, Austro-Daimler, in Vienna. By the early 1890s, DMG had also become one of the first successful manufacturers of powerboats. In fact, Daimler motorboats generally outsold their motorcars, particularly in the United States where they were being marketed, along with Daimler stationary engines, through an arrangement with respected New York industrialist and piano maker William Steinway.

As early as 1888 Wilhelm Maybach had become friends with William Steinway, whose New York-based company produced keyboard instruments in the

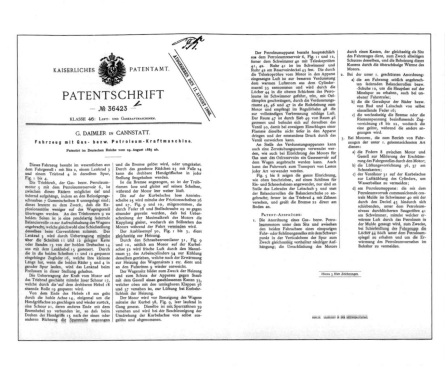

tradition of his German ancestors. During a stay in Germany in 1888, Steinway made the acquaintance of Gottlieb Daimler. Their conversations would always revolve around one thing: licensed production of Daimler engines in America. After Steinway's return to America, the plans quickly materialized. On September 29, 1888, Daimler Motor Co. headquartered in Long Island City, New York, was founded. Production on behalf of Daimler Motor Company was taken over by National Machine Company in Hartford, Connecticut, in 1891, and it was this company which engaged in license production of America's first operational vehicle engine based on Gottlieb Daimler's original design drawings. The company also manufactured gas and petroleum engines for stationary and marine applications. These early years were not easy but from 1895, orders began to arrive in ever-increasing numbers. The two entrepreneurs started considering production of automobiles in America at an early stage. Daimler was, after all, keen on developing new markets for his vehicles, and Steinway believed a bright future lay ahead for the automobile.

In a newspaper interview in 1895, William Steinway outlined his ideas of motorizing America: "The cars which we intend to produce for the American market will be capable of carrying between two and four people and will be driven by engines with between 2.5 and 3.5 hp. Each car will have four different speed ranges: 3.5, 6, 9 and 14 miles per hour. The fuel – petroleum – costs about one cent per hp an hour, making the automobile considerably less expensive than horse power. … We already had a horseless vehicle here in 1893 but it was too lightly built for the rough cobblestone streets we have in this country. We will therefore create a model that will be adapted to conditions in America."

This image of the 1886 Daimler shows the massive gear train required to transfer power to the rear wheels. While Carl Benz had decided to build his motorwagen based on a three-wheel design, Daimler and Maybach built a true horseless carriage.

Left:
In 1887, Daimler and Maybach built the first motorized public transit system in all of Germany in Bad Cannstatt.

Below:
Although they had already built motorwagens, Daimler, with his pocket watch in hand, and Maybach (pictured at his right) were proudest of their large commercial vehicles such as this immense truck.

This sounded like a very concrete plan being in existence and indeed, car production was started in the Daimler Motor Company factory on Long Island in 1895. But Steinway died in November 1896, and his heirs were not as convinced as he was that they could make money by selling motor vehicles. They sold off their shares in Daimler Motor Co. to General Electric Company; from 1898 and after a restructuring, the production facility was called Daimler Manufacturing Company.

The American Mercedes were produced from 1905 until 1907, when a disastrous fire razed the entire Long Island City factory in February, bringing an end to the American-made Mercedes.

Daimler and Maybach had always been very secretive about their work and as the 19th century came to a close they were about to make the single greatest advance in automotive history. In the late 1890s they had made a quantum leap in automotive design, developing and patenting a vee-twin engine,

By 1896 Daimler Motoren Gesellschaft in Bad Cannstatt was the most important automotive and commercial vehicle manufacturer in the world with an entire line of motorized products ranging from motorwagens, an omnibus, fire trucks and commercial wagens, to a complete series of small pleasure craft. The picture at top was taken at the factory in 1893.

followed by a four-cylinder engine, a 4-speed gearbox with gated linkage, a jet-type carburetor (still the basis for most modern carburetors), and in 1897 built the first motorcar with the engine mounted in front. Known as the Phoenix, the DMG motorcar was a bit ungainly in appearance but nonetheless a significant step beyond the hackneyed styling of the Benz motor carriages which continued to literally put the cart before the horsepower.

The concept was Gottlieb Daimler's legacy. Troubled by a serious heart condition throughout his later years, he passed away on March 6, 1900 at age 66. He had been, as one close associate, Frederick Simms, the founder of Daimler Motor Company in England, eulogized him, "unquestionably the father of modern automobilism."

Following Daimler's death, management of DMG was passed to the company's board of directors, Daimler's eldest son Paul, and Wilhelm Maybach. And in a roundabout way, to a wealthy customer named Emil Jellinek.

A tempestuous Austrian merchant with a passion for fast motorcars, Jellinek would underwrite the creation of the first modern automobile in 1901 and change the course of DMG's history, the lives of Paul Daimler and Wilhelm Maybach, and that of Jellinek's young daughter, Mercedes.

Above right: In 1896 Maybach completed and tested a dirigible powered by a 2-cylinder Daimler Phoenix engine. Maybach's interest in lighter-than-air-craft would be his passion in later years.

Left: The front engine Phoenix design had already been well developed by 1899 when this Daimler Omnibus was being used for public transportation in England.

Left & bottom left:
As early as 1886 Daimler was manufacturing a complete line of motorboats. Shown here are two examples of the larger luxury craft.

Below:
Diversity was the Daimler edict as exemplified by the three-pointed star. Air, land and sea, and of the latter Daimler was an industry leader. Shown here is the patent for the Daimler motorboat.

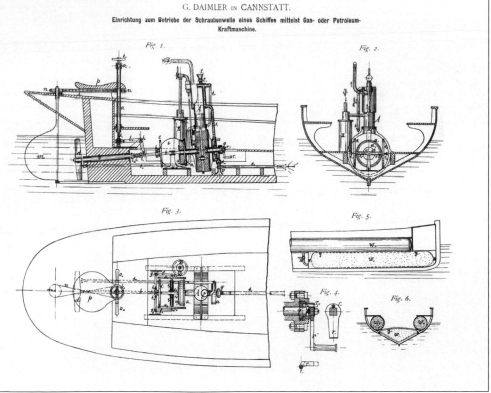

G. DAIMLER ɪɴ CANNSTATT.
Einrichtung zum Betriebe der Schraubenwelle eines Schiffes mittelst Gas- oder Petroleum-Kraftmaschine.

In celebration of their 1,000th motor in December 1895, Daimler decorated the garden behind his villa and displayed the first two vehicles he had designed and built with Wilhelm Maybach. Note the painting of the greenhouse where it had all begun in 1882.

Maybach took the tiller for this picture of an improved 2-cylinder, 1.5 horsepower model introduced in 1889.

28

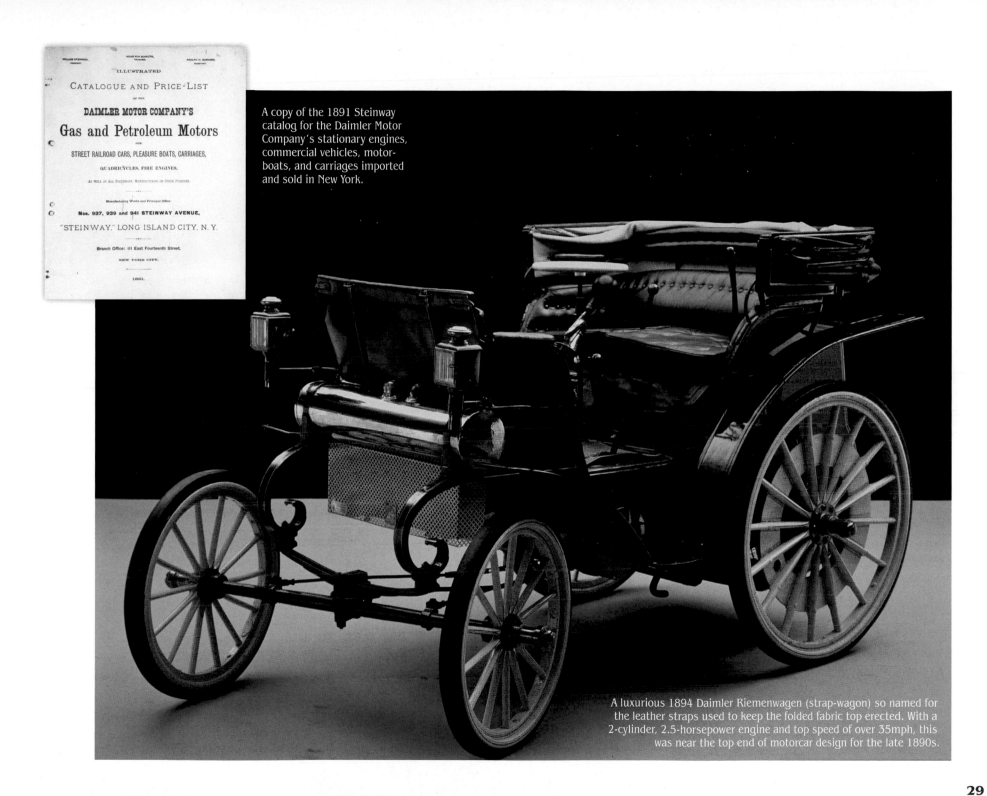

A copy of the 1891 Steinway catalog for the Daimler Motor Company's stationary engines, commercial vehicles, motor-boats, and carriages imported and sold in New York.

A luxurious 1894 Daimler Riemenwagen (strap-wagon) so named for the leather straps used to keep the folded fabric top erected. With a 2-cylinder, 2.5-horsepower engine and top speed of over 35mph, this was near the top end of motorcar design for the late 1890s.

Still as important, if not more so, than its motorcars, Daimler was advancing its design for commercial vehicles by the late 1890s. This 1898 Lastwagen (literally "truck") featured a 2-cylinder, 5.5-horsepower, 1526cc engine. The front end design was similar to that of the 1897 Daimler Phoenix, the first motorcar with an engine mounted in front.

THE AMERICAN MERCEDES

Is an exact copy—part for part—of the great car of international reputation, and is built here to save American buyers the heavy import duties.

The American **MERCEDES** is the car for speed, power and noiseless running.   It is the acme of reliability.

One size, 40-45 H. P.   One-horse power for every 50 lbs. of weight.   One price, **$7,500.**   *Our booklet explains all.*

DAIMLER MFG. CO., 931 Steinway Ave., Long Island City

New York City Garage, 10 WEST 60th STREET

Wilhelm Maybach is often considered the hyphen in Daimler-Benz, having been at Gottlieb Daimler's side throughout the company's founding years, and instrumental in the creation of the 1901 Mercedes. Maybach was born in February 1846 and lived to see Benz and Daimler become one. He passed away in 1929 and was buried near his life-long friend Gottlieb Daimler.

Above: Cover of the American Mercedes sales brochure.

Top left: The very first Mercedes built in America was shown in 1906. This car still survives and it on display at Mercedes-Benz North America Headquarters in Montvale, New Jersey.

Mercedes
The Modern Motorcar Is Born

Wilhelm Bauer was dead.

When word reached Wilhelm Maybach that the beloved race driver and DMG factory foreman had been killed in the April 30 Nice-La Turbie hillclimb, it was almost too much to endure. Maybach was still anguished over the loss of his closest friend in life, Gottlieb Daimler, who had died of heart failure only a month before. And now this. Maybach blamed himself.

It all began late in 1899 when Emil Jellinek, a wealthy Austrian aristocrat and Daimler distributor in Nice, asked Maybach to build a 28-horsepower Phoenix to enter in the April 1900 Nice Week competition. Gottlieb Daimler's worsening heart condition had forced him to leave the day-to-day operations of DMG to Maybach, and although feeling unsure of his decision, he took it upon himself to build the more powerful Phoenix model with the help of Daimler's eldest son, Paul.

Several years earlier, Jellinek had slipped into private life at his villa in Nice, and it was there, comfortably ensconced on the Côte d'Azure among Europe's wealthiest families, that he stumbled into a new career after a visit to the Daimler factory in Cannstatt and the purchase of a new 2-cylinder model.

The new motor carriage caused quite a stir along the French Riviera, and thus inspired, Jellinek wired the factory and ordered four more, but with the stipulation that they be so equipped as to reach a top speed of 25 mph, a blistering 10 mph faster than the example he had purchased in Cannstatt. Gottlieb Daimler and Wilhelm Maybach complied, although against their better judgment, as both men considered such an engine too powerful for the motorcar's carriage-like design.

Jellinek was a crafty businessman and he had a plan to sell most of the cars ordered to just one customer, another auto enthusiast who spent his winters vacationing on the Riviera, the Baron Arthur de Rothschild.

The Baron raced his French Panhard motor carriage up to the top of La Turbie hill almost every morning, winning his imaginary race consistently until the day Jellinek was waiting for him behind the tiller of a Daimler. Driving the 15 mph model, he sped past the Baron's car, which at best could do little more than 10 mph. Rothschild was so exasperated by the incident that when he caught up with Jellinek he jumped from the Panhard and stormed around the Daimler looking at it from every angle. After a brief conversation with Jellinek the Baron was the owner of a new Daimler.

A few weeks later, Rothschild was once again overtaken by Jellinek, who was driving one of the new 25 mph Daimlers. This too resulted in a sale. In fact, before long the Baron was the proud owner of three of the four 25 mph cars Jellinek had ordered. At this point he decided to become a dealer and purchased another six cars, these to be equipped with the new, more power-

By the late 1890s Daimler and Maybach had advanced the design of the horseless carriage into something that was beginning to resemble an automobile. Examples like this 1898 Phoenix Motorwagen had enthused Emil Jellinek into becoming a DMG distributor for Nice.

Inset: The Phoenix motor was originally a vee-twin.

From his villa in Nice, Jellinek started purchasing small quantities of Daimler motorwagens, which he quickly sold. Each order, however, was for an even more powerful car, until the late 1890s, when he finally asked DMG to build a Phoenix powered by the larger four-cylinder engine.

Emil Jellinek was a retired merchant who had made his fortune in the 1880s and slipped away from public life in Nice. Somewhat aristocratic, he fancied himself as sportsman, and when he purchased his first Daimler motorwagen, he found a passion that truly changed his life.

ful Daimler four-cylinder engines and built in the style of the latest Phoenix and Daimler-engined Panhards. These newer models had their motors mounted in front, which as Jellinek noted in his order, "…is where they should be, as the horse pulls the wagon."

The Phoenix or "N" engine was developed during a brief period when Gottlieb Daimler and Wilhelm Maybach were forced to withdraw to the "garden-house workshop" of the Hotel Hermann, having fallen out with the board of the Daimler-Motoren-Gesellschaft in the autumn of 1892. "N" stood for "new model," a two-cylinder engine with adjacent cylinders developed by Maybach in 1892. It was new in that it superseded the two-cylinder "V" engine, which had powered Daimler's "wire-wheeled car" of 1889. A further innovation was that both its cylinders were cast in one block, thus giving it a considerable weight advantage. Furthermore, with this design the torsional movements acting on the crankshaft – which was mounted on only two bear-

ings – were significantly lower as a result of the reduced distance between the cylinders. The cylinder block was screwed onto a roughly spherical crankcase, and for the first time the exhaust valves were operated by the camshaft. The "curved groove control" system developed by Daimler and Maybach had served its time.

Of course, in place of the bulky "surface" carburetor, the "N" had a Maybach spray-nozzle carburetor, which was more compact, occupied considerably less space, and allowed for quick and precise adjustment of the fuel-air mixture as circumstances required.

When the engine was unveiled it caused a sensation. The first 1.5-liter model had an output of 5.8 horsepower at 720rpm. An improved version was fitted with Robert Bosch's low-voltage solenoid ignition from 1897 suitable for use in automobiles. Together with its considerably more effective cooling system, the design greatly impressed European automotive manufacturers – most of all the French, who provided the name by which it became so famous: the "Phoenix" engine.

This sobriquet – a marketable asset in itself – was to attach itself to a whole series of Daimler models. And once and for all the automobile had acquired a front-mounted engine, at least at DMG.

During the Phoenix era a tight rein had to be kept on engine output, since for the longer journeys (which were now feasible) there was still no reliable cooling system for engines of 10 horsepower and above. Given the enormous quantities of water required, the reservoirs of the earlier cars were simply not adequate.

In 1897, Maybach – resourceful as ever – came up with a solution. His description for the patent of his "tube radiator" – that distinctive rounded cooling system mounted on the front end of the various Daimler "Phoenix" cars – read as follows: "Device for cooling the water circulating around the cylinders of combustion engines, consisting of a flat receptacle having a large number of tubes passing through it, whereby heat is extracted from the water coolant by means of a constant flow of air around the tubes supplied by a dedicated ventilation system."

From there it was but a small step to the "honeycomb radiator" patented in March 1900, which allowed the "Mercedes" cars built from 1901 onwards to achieve such success.

This 1899 Phoenix is similar in design, but not power, to the racecar built for Jellinek. At the time, this was the most modern automobile in the world. This example is now displayed at the Mercedes-Benz Museum.

By 1900 the Daimler factory in Bad Cannstatt was turning out motorcars in record numbers, many of which were of the new front-engine Phoenix design.

The Phoenix four-cylinder had been developed for larger vehicles demanding greater output. Gottlieb Daimler achieved this by doubling the number of cylinders. The Phoenix four-cylinder was built on the same principle as the two-cylinder, i.e., each pair of twin-cylinder blocks rested on a common crankcase. And with the four-cylinder, the crankshaft was mounted on a triple bearing. But otherwise its components were identical with those of its baby brother.

Over time, it was developed as an engine with 6, 10, 12 and 16 horsepower variants, the final ones from 1899-1900 even reaching 23 horsepower – and each version with ever larger displacements.

The Phoenix engines were coupled exclusively to a four-speed mechanical transmission – another of Maybach's inventions, first introduced in the wire-wheeled car of 1889. This formed a block with the differential acting on the chain sprocket shaft. Chain-drive to the rear wheels was still obligatory, with a conical leather clutch serving to ease gear shifts.

The early Phoenix cars, such as those first delivered to Emil Jellinek, were built on a straight U-section iron frame with a remarkably short wheelbase of 1753 millimeters (70.1 inches), and rigid axles suspended from longitudinal leaf springs. The double-pivot steering was turned either by a steering lever or a steering wheel. The foot brake used an outer shoe brake on the drive shaft to slow its rotation, while the handbrake operated via outer shoes acting on the rear wheels. In addition there was a "hill-support" – a sturdy pole attached to the rear, which as its name suggests was used when the vehicle was at rest on an uphill slope and could be kicked into position in the relatively soft road surfaces of the day. Automotive history was still years away from the concept of front-wheel brakes.

The wooden-spoke wheels – which normally varied in size front to back – were initially fitted with solid rubber tires. From 1899 onwards, however, pneumatic tires became standard. In total, the Phoenix tipped the scales at around 1400 kg., roughly 3,080 pounds.

As with other brands of automobile, the design of the Daimler Phoenix was remarkable for its very high center of gravity. This gave rise to an alarming rolling motion on rapid cornering, but for the gentlemen drivers of the day this was nothing unusual – at least until April 30, 1900.

Jellinek's order for Phoenix models equipped with four-cylinder engines troubled Maybach and Daimler. The engines had been designed to power commercial trucks. The Phoenix had been designed for a small vee-twin. On the other hand, both men knew that Panhard had already mounted a Daimler four in their similarly designed front-engine models and had experienced no ill effects. So, once again DMG built what their dealer in Nice requested. These were sold to residents living along the Côte d' Azure with not as much as a whisper of a problem. Late in 1899 Jellinek finally submitted his request to Maybach for the 28-horsepower Phoenix racecar. By then Gottlieb Daimler was bed-ridden. Maybach knew a 28-horsepower engine was far too powerful, but in a moment of doubt and wishing to avoid concerning Gottlieb with the matter, he made the decision to build the car. This time the results were disastrous.

The 28-horsepower Phoenix was completed and delivered to Jellinek shortly after Gottlieb Daimler had passed away on March 6, 1900. A little over a month later at the Nice-La Turbie hillclimb Wilhelm Bauer took the tiller of the Phoenix at Jellinek's request, and began his last race. The 28-horsepower model was unmanageable at speed and Bauer lost control of the unwieldy Phoenix in the first curve, spinning the high-centered racecar into a boulder. His mechanic was thrown clear but Bauer died of his injuries the following day. Jellinek laid blame for the accident not on Bauer but on Maybach and the design of the Phoenix, which he said was inadequate for the engine power. Maybach knew he was right. It was as if he had killed Bauer by his own hand.

Jellinek, though deeply affected by the tragedy, persisted with new demands for even faster cars than the 28-horsepower Phoenix, cars with better engineering and more modern coachwork. He had a vision of an automobile that would be built on a longer wheelbase, with a lower center of gravity and a

Emil Jellinek (far right) became friends with William K. Vanderbilt, Jr. (center) in Nice. It's interesting to note that Vanderbilt, an avid motorist and Daimler owner, was riding in a horse-drawn carriage when this photograph was taken around 1899.

The Phoenix that didn't rise from its own ashes, the 28-horsepower racecar Maybach and Paul Daimler built for Emil Jellinek. In the April 30, 1900 Nice-La Turbie hillclimb, factory driver Wilhelm Bauer was killed when the overweight Phoenix spun out of control at the first turn. Bauer's riding mechanic was thrown out of the vehicle, and Bauer himself into the rocks as the racecar slammed backwards into a boulder.

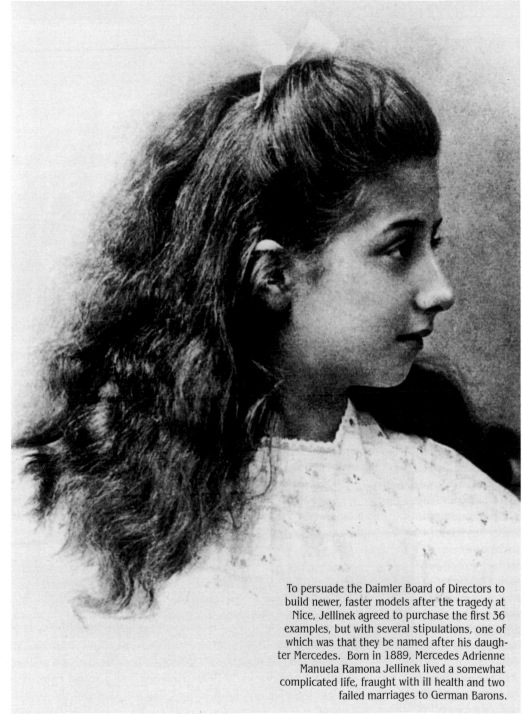

Mercedes with her first husband, the Baron Schlosser, and her stepsister Andrée Jellinek in 1910.

To persuade the Daimler Board of Directors to build newer, faster models after the tragedy at Nice, Jellinek agreed to purchase the first 36 examples, but with several stipulations, one of which was that they be named after his daughter Mercedes. Born in 1889, Mercedes Adrienne Manuela Ramona Jellinek lived a somewhat complicated life, fraught with ill health and two failed marriages to German Barons.

It is doubtful that Mercedes ever enjoyed having a motorcar named after her, as he father had hoped. She was divorced from Baron Schlosser and in 1923 married again, this time to Wiener Bildhauer Baron Weigl. She died in 1929 at age 40.

The maestro, Wilhelm Maybach took the wheel of his latest version of the Mercedes introduced in 1903, the Mercedes-Simplex Phaeton. Seated directly behind Maybach is Adolf Daimler.

Far right:
The success of the '01 Mercedes guaranteed the future of Daimler-Motoren-Gesellschaft. Pictured is the new Untertürkheim factory in 1908. It was very modern compared to the old Cannstatt werke, as was the Mercedes to the earlier front-engine Phoenix.

An elegant 1904 Mercedes-Simplex Tourenwagen.

This 1902 Mercedes 40hp is similar to the design of the '01 model delivered to Jellinek for Nice Week in March 1901. The model pictured is regarded as the oldest existing Mercedes motorcar in the world, one of only 35 built by Daimler-Motoren-Gesellschaft at the original Cannstatt factory. Originally owned by William K. Vanderbilt, Jr., it has since been re-restored and painted dark blue. It is now on exhibit at the new Mercedes-Benz Museum in Untertürkheim.

Maybach's improvements to the 1902 models finalized many innovations, including the honeycomb radiator, 4-speed gated transmission, and water-cooled rear brakes. Chain drive was still the only means of delivering power from the engine to the wheels.

Left:
Original wheel lug has taken its knocks over the last century, but still clearly denotes the Daimler name and Cannstatt werke.

Far left:
The fuel tank on the Mercedes had to be pressurized, and this stylish brass pump at the front of the driver's seat was necessary to keep fuel flowing. It would be necessary to pump up the pressure while driving, and this task was often delegated to the passenger.

Below:
This rarely seen photograph from the factory archives shows Mercedes race driver Wilhelm Werner and the young Baron Henri de Rothschild at ceremonies following the '01's total domination of the races in Nice.

The meteoric success of the Mercedes spelled disaster for Benz, whose entire model line had been rendered obsolete virtually overnight. Sales plummeted in 1901 and again in 1902, yet Carl Benz was hesitant to make such radical changes in the design of his vehicles, believing his little belt-driven cars would prevail. They would not. By late 1902 and into 1903 change was at last on the horizon at Benz und Cie. with the introduction of the new Parsifal model and Benz Spider, designs remarkably similar in most respects to the latest Mercedes but with far smaller engines. This marked the beginning of a rivalry between the cars from Mannheim and those from Stuttgart, a battle between men and machines that would be waged on both road and racetrack for more than two decades, turning the 1910s and early 1920s into one of the most exciting periods in the story of the automobile.

Having built the most advanced motorcar of the new century and named it Mercedes, what DMG needed next was a suitable trademark to compliment it. Paul and Adolf Daimler, who were now managers at their late father's company, recalled that he had once sent a picture postcard to their mother on which a star marked the house where they lived outside Cologne during his years as technical director at Gasmotorenfabrik Deutz. He had commented that, "eventually this star would rise and shine out over his work." DMG considered both a three-pointed star and a four-pointed star as their new emblem and applied for trademark protection on both. Originally placed at the front of the car as a radiator emblem, over the years the star acquired various additions and refinements, being placed inside a circle in 1916, thus creating the first Mercedes badge, and evolving after World War I into the three-pointed star surrounded by a ring, which in countless variations over the decades has become the marque's eternal symbol.

William K. Vanderbilt, Jr. at the wheel of his 1902 Mercedes-Simplex. A mechanic starts the 40hp motorcar with the starting crank.

The extent to which motor racing was attracting crowds is conveyed in this 1903 photo taken at the Gordon-Bennett race in Ireland. The car dashing down the dirt road towards the turn (and the spectators!) is a '03 Mercedes.

The 1907 Mercedes-Simplex Touring was one of the largest models, with seating for up to six. Note the individual front seats with the style and comfort of easy chairs. Leather upholstery and deep horsehair padding made the driving experience more comfortable, which can not be said for the stiff suspensions of the era.

New models were no less complicated to operate and this 1907 Mercedes-Simplex instrument board and steering wheel reveal the numerous controls which had to be set correctly for both starting and running. Also note the four pedals on the floor, used for breaking, declutching and throttle.

By this period the Mercedes name had been adopted and was a fixture on the honeycombed radiators. Also note the three-pointed star, already in use on the grille shell of this '07, two years before DMG received trademark protection for the now famous emblem.

Five emblems and 120 years of history.

Benz & Cie. vs. Mercedes
Building Motors and Motorcars

As the world raced headlong into the 20th century there was growth in virtually every area of industry. DMG and Benz were now heatedly competing for sales, not only in Europe, but in the United States, which was becoming a lucrative market for imported motorcars.

At Daimler, the animosity that had been increasing between Paul Daimler and Wilhelm Maybach had convinced the 60-year-old engineer that it was time to leave. Following a lengthy disagreement with Paul over the design of the 1906 Daimler racecar, on April 7, 1907 Maybach left the company he had helped bring into being with Paul's father. The problems that had arisen between the two were perhaps more politically motivated than a clash of personalities. After all, Paul had learned at Maybach's side. But now the older Daimler brothers, Paul and Adolf, sought to gain top management positions within the company, Paul having returned to Stuttgart after a brief tenure in Austria as chief engineer for Austro-Daimler. With Maybach's departure Paul was certain to ascend to the top engineering position at DMG, which is exactly what happened after Maybach "retired." Younger brother Adolf, who had always been close to Maybach, stepped into the position of factory manager. Meanwhile, over at Austro-Daimler, the engineering position vacated by Paul Daimler was being filled by another promising young engineer named Ferdinand Porsche.

As for Maybach, his retirement was short-lived. Having pioneered the development of the first motor-powered dirigibles in the 1880s, he was asked to join forces with Count Ferdinand von Zeppelin in the development of a new aero engine for the Count's giant airships. Since 1900 they had been powered by Daimler engines. What a slice of luck for Maybach, a new job and retribution all at once.

A separate company, Luftfahrzeug-Motorenbau GmbH (changed in 1912 to Maybach Motorenbau Gesellschaft), was established to produce Zeppelin engines. Maybach was given responsibility for overseeing the construction of all-new aero engines. His son Karl, fast becoming a gifted engineer in his own right, was appointed as technical director.

Other things at DMG were changing as well. Herr Jellinek-Mercedes soon found himself on an outbound road as well, having fallen in great disfavor with company management (read Paul Daimler) over his boasts of being the designer of the Mercedes. Wrote Jellinek in a letter to the esteemed German motoring publication *Allgemeine Automobil-Zeitung*, "…not only the whole business, but also the whole construction of the Mercedes car, was and still is entirely built on my plans." That was in 1906. A year later he was no longer a Mercedes distributor. His name and integrity, though, were well intact, at least for the moment. Archduke Franz Ferdinand, heir to the Austrian throne

Inset: After the death of his father, Paul Daimler became a chief designer working alongside Wilhelm Maybach. Soon a rivalry would develop between them and Maybach would ultimately be forced out of the company he had helped found.

Maybach was closer to Daimler's younger son Adolf (right), shown here with Maybach in the late 1890s. After Maybach's departure in 1907, Adolf became DMG factory manager.

Changes in design and engineering were taking place at breakneck speed. By 1910, the styling of Mercedes motorcars was setting the standard for the world. This is a 4-cylinder, 5.6 liter 22/40 PS Phaeton. In 1910 this massive touring car was capable of reaching 50 mph.

Below: The imperious Emil Jellinek-Mercedes posed for this formal portrait after being appointed Austria's honorary vice-council in Monaco by Archduke Franz Ferdinand. By now he was no longer permitted to be a Daimler dealer thanks to his self aggrandizing remarks about having designed the 1901 Mercedes.

(whose assassination in Sarajevo on June 28, 1914 would ignite World War I), had Jellinek-Mercedes appointed honorary vice-council in Monaco, a title and position suitable to his pompous nature. Unfortunately for Jellinek, his quasi-political status landed him on the wrong side when the battle lines were drawn and he was accused of espionage by the French. He fled to Switzerland where he would remain in exile. In his absence, the Villa Mercedes, Jellinek's personal properties, yachts, and automobiles were confiscated by the French. Everything was gone. In January 1918, Emil Jellinek, the man who, if nothing else, had bankrolled the Mercedes, died in Switzerland, never to know the outcome of the War to End All Wars, or the future of the motorcars which bore his daughter's name.

Before the war, as the first decade of the new century neared its end, Ransom E. Olds and Henry Ford were building automobiles for the masses – Henry's Model T put America on wheels, and would drive the price of most models below $1,000 by 1910. The Mercedes and the Benz, on the other hand, were among the most expensive motorcars one could buy in America, and it was here, in the United States, that Benz had established a solid footing by the early 20th century.

Benz chassis prices ranged from $3,250 for the 18hp model up to an astounding $8,500 for the sporty 60hp versions. In comparison, a new Model T sold for $900, and that was a complete car, not a bare chassis still in need of a body! To put that price in even greater perspective, 28 years later, when Duesenberg introduced the Model J, then the most expensive American car on the road, a bare chassis was priced at $8,500, the very same amount Benz had asked for a chassis in 1910!

Through the Benz Auto Import Co. of America, in New York City, the entire Benz model line was offered with a selection of four different chassis and 16 coachbuilt bodies. They were, in the opinion of many, the best motorcars of the era, from either side of the Atlantic – better than the Cadillac, Pierce-Arrow, or Packard. Better than a Rolls-Royce. Better than a Mercedes.

Benz & Co. had earned its stripes with American buyers in 1910 with a double victory in the U.S. Grand Prix at Savannah, Georgia, with David L. Bruce Brown and Benz factory driver Victor Héméry finishing 1-2 in their 150-horsepower Benz race cars. In 1910 Benz also set the world land speed record, with none other than American racing legend Barney Oldfield streaking across the hard-packed Ormond-Daytona Beach sand behind the wheel

Another 1910 Tourenwagen, which is in the new Mercedes-Benz Museum in Untertürkheim. Note the bold MERCEDES name across the front of the brass grille shell and the use of the star within a circle radiator mascot.

Daimler was heading in many directions in the early 1900s, building exemplary touring cars, marine engines, motorboats, commercial vehicles, and more importantly for building the company's national and international image, racecars. This is a 1908 Model 120 PS in which Christian Lautenschlager won the French Grand Prix with a top speed of 111.276 km/h (66.8 mph).

Below: Benz & Cie. was no less aggressively pursuing a reputation built upon racing victories by the early 1900s, and in 1910 American Barney Oldfield set a world speed record of 131.724 mph with a 200 horsepower Benz racecar at Daytona. The car, wearing the No. 19, was nicknamed the Lightning Benz, and later came to be known as the Blitzen Benz. Oldfield's record stood for only one year.

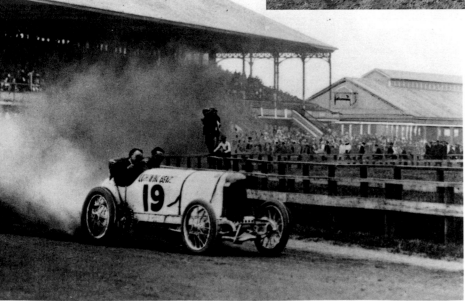

In 1915 American legend Ralph de Palma would win the Indy 500, driving a 1914 Mercedes Grand Prix car.

The competition between Daimler and Benz was not only on the race-track and showroom floor, but on the assembly line where workmen were putting in long hours to build the best cars in the world at the time.

of a 200-horsepower Lightning Benz (later known as the Blitzen Benz). Said Oldfield, who was never short of bombastic quotes, "A speed of 131 miles an hour is as near to the absolute limit of speed as humanity will ever travel." At the time it was very close to the truth. Wrote the *Florida Times Union* of Oldfield's official 131.724 mph record run, "The speed attained was the fastest ever traveled by a human being, no greater speed having been recorded except that made by a bullet." It was a record that would stand for only one year. In 1911, race driver Bob Burman piloted the Blitzen Benz to a top speed of 141.732 miles per hour at Daytona Beach, a full 10mph faster than Oldfield's record.

When this news reached Benz & Co., no doubt beer steins were lofted for the Blitzen Benz, but the exciting information failed to impress Carl Benz, who was generally opposed to motorsports and fast driving. The passion in Mannheim was being fueled by his sons Richard and Eugen, by company engineer and driver Victor Héméry, and chief engineer Hans Nibel, who quietly disregarded the "old man's" view of racing, or for that matter of building any car with a top speed greater than 50km/h, as "nonsense."

With an engine belting out 200 horsepower, the Blitzen Benz was the latest iteration of the 1908 Benz GP cars that had come in second and third in the Grand Prix de France, later known as the *Vingt-Quatre Heures du Mans*, crossing the finish line just moments behind a new Mercedes.

Benz & Co. had become a sleeping giant rudely awakened by Daimler, and now the Mannheim

This 1918 photograph shows the new Benz & Cie. factory in Gaggenau.

The competition between Daimler and Benz extended to every field of automotive and truck manufacturing. Shown here are fire engines built by Daimler (left) and Benz in the early 1900s.

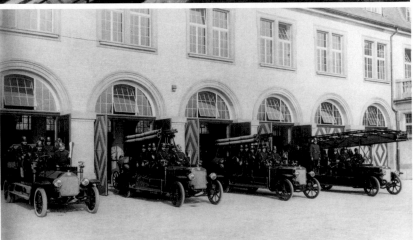

A contrast in concepts. Note the front end design and grille of both cars pictures. They are both 1911 Benz models. The sporty Runabout was equipped with a 100 horsepower, 4-cylinder engine. The same engine built for racing and, delivering 200 horsepower, was put under the hood of this stripped-down-for-racing model, which became the Blitzen Benz. Bear in mind that is 200 horsepower being delivered to the rear wheels by chain drive!

automaker sought to vanquish its antagonist. By 1910 Benz had its own branches in France, Belgium, Great Britain, Italy, Austria and Hungary, and was the majority stockholder in the Benz Auto Import Co. of America. Now it was DMG that had to continually look over its shoulder. In motorsports, wherever a Mercedes appeared, there was a Benz, with Mannheim claiming its share of victories on both sides of the Atlantic and setting speed and endurance records throughout the decade.

In reprisal DMG campaigned a Mercedes-Knight in 1913, piloted by the great Belgian race driver Théodor Pilette, in the Indianapolis 500. The car finished a respectable fifth. In 1915 American legend Ralph de Palma would win the Indy 500 driving a 1914 Mercedes Grand Prix car, which oddly enough belonged not to Daimler but the Packard Motor Car Company in Detroit! De Palma's winning Indy pit crew had been headed by none other Col. Jesse Vincent, Packard's chief engineer.

Throughout the 1910s Mercedes remained on the cutting edge of both engineering and design. With models like the 37/90 and 37/95, Daimler was further closing the distance with Benz & Cie. by 1911.

Produced from 1910 through 1914, the 37/90 was powered by a four-cylinder engine with a bore and stroke of 130mm x 180mm (5 x 7 inches) displacing 9530cc (approximately 400 cubic inches) and delivering 90 horsepower at 1300rpm. The inline engine had two blocks of two cylinders each with three overhead valves per cylinder and a single camshaft mounted high in the crankcase. Fuel delivery was through a single Mercedes sliding piston carburetor. A four-speed gearbox, with a gate change shifter mounted outside the body, delivered power to the chain-driven rear axle. Daimler Motoren Gesellschaft estimated the average top speed for the cars at 115km/h – roughly 70 mph – although it was reported that with lightweight coachwork they could almost reach the coveted 100mph.

The model 37/95 (thus 95 horsepower) was regarded as the most powerful production automobile in the world at the time. Produced from 1910 through 1914, the 37/95 was replaced in 1915 by an even more powerful 38/100 horsepower model. The actual output of the engines, incidentally, was always the second figure shown; the first was nominal output used solely for taxation purposes in Germany.

In the 1914 Grand Prix at Le Mans (the last prewar event in France), the Mercedes team scored an unparalleled first through third place sweep with Christian Lautenschlager driving the winning car, No. 28, Otto Salzer second in car number 39, and Louis Wagner third in car number 40. This was, for its time, the most exciting automobile race ever seen in Europe.

The car driven to victory by Christian Lautenschlager in 1914 is one of many on display at the Mercedes-Benz museum.

Mercedes models offered during this period were available either with shaft-drive, designed by Paul Daimler in 1907, or chain-drive, and while the latter was being phased out, in 1910 the factory introduced a new series of chain-driven cars, including the 37/90 and 37/95 models. The justification was simply that chain-drive had proven more durable in cars equipped with higher-powered engines such as the 37/95.

Daimler offered a total of 12 different chassis, four with conventional chain-driven rear axles and eight with shaft drive. Still, the most powerful car in the line was the chain-driven 37/95.

In 1913 Paul Daimler had also designed a six-cylinder model which was raced at Le Mans in August (not in the Grand Prix event, however), finishing third (with Pilette at the wheel), fourth, sixth and seventh, and then a brace of five new cars for the 1914 Grand Prix at Le Mans (the last race before the war), where the Mercedes team scored an unprecedented one-two-three finish, with Christian Lautenschlager driving the winning car, in what was for its time the most exciting automobile race ever seen in Europe.

By the late 1910s and early 1920s motorsports had become the greatest means by which a manufacturer could prove the mettle of its machines. At Le Mans, in the grueling Targa Florio (founded by Don Vincenzino Florio in 1906) and in motorsports competitions across Europe and the United States, Daimler and Benz were waging war.

Racing was also the inspiration for some rather remarkable road cars built by Mercedes in the early 1900s. This is perhaps one of the most remarkable of all, a wooden-bodied skiff created in France by Henri Labourdette on a Mercedes 37/90 HP chassis. The triple-layer body was created by crisscrossing tiers of mahogany over a ribbed frame, then applying a third horizontal layer atop the substructure. To preserve the rigidity, doors were kept as small as possible in number and size.

A strong right arm was necessary for driving the 37/90 and later 37/95 Mercedes models, with both the hand brake and shift lever located on the outside of the cockpit.

Bottom left & middle:
The 37/90 HP engine delivered 90 horsepower from a massive 9.5 liter (almost 600 cubic inch) 4-cylinder engine composed of two banks of 2-cylinders with the valve trains in each controlled by a single cam in the crankcase.

Dashboards were almost unheard of in 1911 when Labourdette built this 37/90 Skiff for American haberdasher Henry G. Stetson.

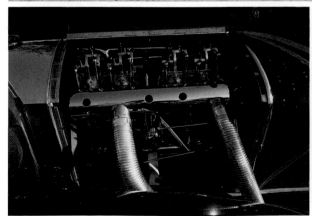

It wasn't what you could call a dashboard, but this 37/95 Mercedes had a full accompaniment of instruments mounted on the paneled firewall.

Luxury was defined by fine leather and wood in the 1900s, and few could rival the Mercedes.

The 95 horsepower output from the Mercedes 4-cylinder engine was adequate to carry a model with lightweight coachwork to nearly 100mph. The beautiful exhaust pipes were fast becoming a Mercedes hallmark.

The more powerful Model 37/95 offered coachbuilders an even better palette upon which to mix their designs. This graceful French-bodied model was commissioned in 1913 by the Mercedes Societié in Paris and bodied by Henri Labourdette. (Nethercutt Collection by Dennis Adler)

By the early 1910s the Mercedes prow had become an impressive sight with a towering vee-shaped honeycomb radiator. (Nethercutt Collection by Dennis Adler)

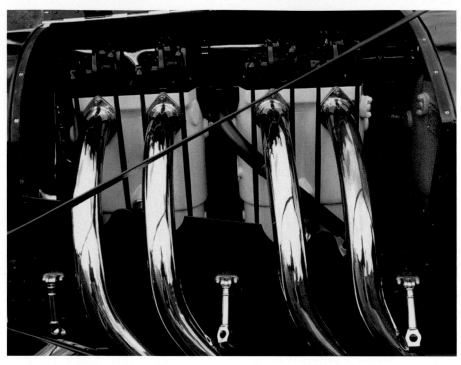

The Mercedes 37/95 engine was a mechanical and styling marvel. Bare exhaust pipes (without the corrugated flex pipe covering), such as this example, would glow red hot when the car was driven hard.

The real battle between Daimler and Benz, however, was for sales dominance, and in that competition Mercedes and Benz were nearly in a dead heat. In 1910 they both delivered more than 1,000 motorcars, a number that would double for Daimler within two years, but triple for Benz! Their respective commercial vehicle operations were also at capacity; Benz and Daimler trucks, buses, and fire engines (as well as aircraft and marine engines by the beginning of World War I) were in use the world over. With the beginning of the war in 1914, the fortunes of both Benz and DMG were to rise and then plummet with the defeat of Germany.

Throughout the period leading up to and after World War I, both Benz and Mercedes models grew in popularity with literally hundreds of different designs being created between them. It was an era of sweeping changes and technological achievements as the motorcar evolved from a turn-of-the-century curiosity into one of the most celebrated inventions of modern time.

Had French motor journalist Paul Meyan written another review in 1910 he would have had to make a slight change. *Nous sommes entres dans l'ere Mercedes et Benz.*

By 1916 styling was once again changing and automobiles were beginning to resemble those that would populate the roads after World War I and into the early 1920s. This Mercedes Tourer is an exemplary design, considering there was a war on at the time.

Facing page & main bottom: In comparison to the 1911 Mercedes 37/90, the 1911 Benz Victoria Touring was a far more conservative design. This example sold in the United States and bodied by A.T. Demarest & Co., New York, was specially equipped with a 50HP engine and cost nearly $10,000 as delivered. The owner was C.M. Hayes, president of the Chicago Grand Central Trunk Railway. Hayes was one of the men who gave up their seat (and life) to save the women and children on the maiden and last voyage of the Titanic in 1912.

Top facing page: The Benz was powered by a 4-cylinder T-head motor with one camshaft on the induction side, another on the exhaust side. A mechanical lubricator, driven by helical gears from the forward end of the inlet camshaft, oiled the motor by drawing oil from a box at the front of the engine. This was a "total loss" lubrication system with no seals, so oil simply dripped out the rear end bearing and the front main bearing as it went through the engine. This was not particularly popular with folks who had cobblestone driveways.

The Needs of The Few

Daimler and Benz after World War I

World War I brought significant changes to the European automotive industry and Germany in particular. It was during the war where the potential of the motorcar as a vehicle for combat was first realized. Renowned author and historian Beverly Rae Kimes noted in *The Star and the Laurel* that this "awakening" came in September 1914 when the French general Joseph Gallieni ordered the use of taxi cabs to ferry troops to the Marne front. In the midst of chaos the troop transport had been born. Something to think about next time you hail cab in Manhattan.

The development of armored cars soon followed, particularly those produced by Rolls-Royce, which were to play a significant role in battle. The advent of the tank, the ultimate armored car, gave British ground forces a marked advantage over the Germans, who found themselves sorely behind in the manufacture of military vehicles as the war waged on. Ironically, more than a decade before, Paul Daimler had tried to interest both the German and Austrian governments in armored military trucks, but neither showed any interest. Now DMG was racing to produce military vehicles for the war effort including staff cars and transports, as well as aircraft engines by the score, while the Benz plants were turned over largely to submarine and aviation engine work. It was all for naught. When the war ended on November 11, 1918, Germany had not only lost the confrontation, but its economy as well.

Following the Treaty of Versailles in 1919, the value of the German mark began to plummet. In 1914, before the war, the mark had traded against the U.S. dollar at 4.20 to one and both Daimler and Benz motorcars had become the import darlings of America. In 1919 it took 62 marks to equal one U.S. dollar and there were no sales of either marque in the United States. Tens of thousands of Germans were out of work, and both Benz and Daimler had been banned from any military production, including the manufacture of aircraft engines. The intent, at least immediately after the war, seemed to be to force Germany into becoming an agrarian society. Aside from fuel shortages and the general instability of the economy, Germany had been so destabilized by the outcome of the war that more cars were parked alongside the road than on it. The newest Daimler plant located in Sindelfingen was now being used to build furniture!

Before World War I, the German motor industry had always recorded high export surpluses; after the war, it was unable to come anywhere near its previous position. The possibilities of exporting cars were limited in view of worldwide protectionism. Evading customs barriers by setting up assembly plants or efficient organizations abroad were out of the question due to the

Main: Ferdinand Porsche stepped into Paul Daimler's shoes at DMG, assuming the chief engineer's position that Daimler vacated late in 1922. This was Porsche's official portrait taken in 1923.

Inset: In 1924, after firmly establishing himself at DMG, Ferdinand Porsche (wearing cap) was rebuilding Daimler's racing image. The rather intense-looking driver behind the wheel of this Mercedes racecar is Alfred Neubauer. In the late 1930s, a much heftier Neubauer would assume the role of racing manager for Mercedes-Benz, beginning a career with the automaker that would last well into the postwar Fifties and bring countless victories to the cars with the Silver Star.

Top: Race driver and factory engineer Max Sailer led the Mercedes racing effort in the years prior to Alfred Neubauer coming to Daimler-Benz from Austro-Daimler. Pictured in 1914, Sailer would lead the winning Mercedes team in the 1922 Targa Florio.

The Model 28/95 Targa Florio was the most famous Mercedes of the 1910s, as well as the early 1920s. Shown here in 1924, Alfred Neubauer (driving) and Porsche (at far right) before the start of the 1924 race in Sicily. Both men had worked together at Austro-Daimler before joining Daimler.

Built on a special, short 120.6-inch wheelbase, the 28/95 Targa Florio was fitted with a sports roadster body. The car's pressed steel frame was equipped with half-elliptic leaf springs front and rear, and friction-type shock absorbers. The center lock spoke wheels carry 33 x 6 inch tires. This is a road car, but it could easily be set up for racing by removing the fenders, folding top, and even the side mount spare. There were still two more tires mounted at the rear.

The silver radiator stars and star within a ring had become the established trademarks of Mercedes. Whether on the prow of a race-car or road car, this was a visage that commanded respect.

shortage of capital. As a result of the war, German motor manufacturers were also excluded from participating in international motor shows until 1927. In particular, this adversely affected companies like Daimler, and Benz & Cie., which had had export market shares of 50 to 60 percent before the war.

Daimler automobile sales were well under 1,000 units for the first year after the Armistice. The situation was much the same at Benz, which had faired slightly better than Daimler, but was still under 1,000 cars in 1919, an estimated 988 from the Mannheim werke, plus an additional 800 trucks from the new Gaggenau factory. Further compounding the difficulties was the loss of Benz and Daimler distributors in the United States. Both of these once thriving concerns would have to begin anew.

early postwar years. Paul Daimler had grown disenchanted with the managers of his father's company during the war and in 1922 he resigned and took a position as chief engineer with Horch, a direct competitor. This now left DMG without an engineering heir to follow in the footsteps of the company's founder. Daimler's younger son Adolf was a manager, not an engineer. A solution, however, provided itself, if not by sheer fate, than by circumstance. Ferdinand Porsche, who had followed Paul Daimler's departure from Austro-Daimler to become their new chief engineer, resigned from A-D around the same time Paul took his leave from DMG. Once more, he would follow in the vacated footsteps of Paul Daimler and in 1922 step into the position of chief engineer for Daimler Motoren Gesellschaft.

Porsche had new ideas, innovative if not unorthodox ways to get the most out of an engine, chassis, and suspension. The first of the great sports models created by Porsche was a supercharged racecar built in 1923, followed by a six-cylinder touring model and the Type 200 Stuttgart and Mannheim models, which, interestingly, were sold through both Daimler and Benz dealerships!

The nation's unstable economy had finally forced the hands of both Daimler and Benz management. Though they were still the two largest automakers in Germany, neither could sustain itself. Thus they

After the Great War, Germany was on perilous financial ground, restricted as a manufacturing nation in the production of aero engines, munitions, and other commodities that could be regarded as war material, and thus the automobile became a major focus of German industry. Unfortunately, there were precious few buyers for new cars in the early 1920s. Thus Mercedes went racing. Pictured in the 1922 Targa Florio is the incomparable Count Masetti driving a refitted 1914 Grand Prix Mercedes seemingly flat out in the world's toughest road race.

A hint of things to come from DMG was evident in the aerodynamic 1922 Teardrop-Rennwagen (racecar) powered by Paul Daimler's new 6-cylinder, 90-horsepower, 1.997 liter engine.

Below:
On a cool, overcast morning in March 1922, the Mercedes team cars prepare to leave Stuttgart for sunny Sicily and the Targa Florio. No car haulers back then – your team drove to the race. Seven Mercedes started the race and six finished. The results were 1st, 2nd, and 4th in the Race Class, 3rd in the Production Class, and a 1-2 sweep in Production Class of 4.5 liter, with Max Sailer and Christian Werner finishing in order.

agreed in principle to a mutually beneficial sharing of resources, and a year later, on May 1, 1924 the two struggling automakers entered into an "Agreement of Mutual Interest," a non-competitive and cooperative arrangement which combined some of their design, manufacturing and sales departments. It had, however, only come about after a hard fought series of compromises and corporate intrigue.

Looking back on the pre- and post-World War I era, Mercedes had managed to make the most of what was on hand, and that included their aircraft engines.

The prewar DMG six-cylinder aero engines had won second prize in the 1912 Kaiserpreis competition for the best aircraft engines produced by German manufacturers. The revolutionary overhead camshaft six displaced

a mammoth 7,250cc with a 105mm x 140mm bore x stroke, yet weighed only 388 pounds. Known as the D.F. 80, this engine, with only the necessary modifications made for automotive applications, went directly into a pair of Mercedes racing cars entered in the Sarthe Grand Prix at Le Mans in August 1913.

Modifying an aircraft engine to suit the needs of an automobile required mounting it to a chassis and linking it to a rear differential via gear-change transmission and driveshaft. In an aircraft, the vertical shaft drive for the camshaft and cross drive for the water pump and magneto were at the rear of the engine and opposite the propeller drive end of the crankshaft. Thus, unless the car was going to be propeller-driven, the engine had to be reversed, putting the cam and accessory drives next to

The 1922 Mercedes Targa Florio, named for the event in which the car competed, was actually the Model 28/95 Sport powered by a modified World War I Mercedes aircraft engine.

Not much to look at. Except for crankcase alterations required to fit an automotive chassis, the long-stroke, 7,250cc overhead cam, inline six in the 28/95 was nearly identical to the Daimler D.F. 80 aero engine. The supercharged versions of the engine, such as the one used in the Targa Florio by Max Sailer, developed 140 horsepower at 1,800rpm.

the radiator and the drive end of the crankshaft at the rear, coupled to a differential. With crankcase modifications necessary for fitting to an automobile, and the addition of a Bosch starter and generator, the D.F. 80 was otherwise ideally suited to its role as a racing car engine. While such modifications would not ordinarily lend themselves to the more practical needs of a passenger vehicle, the Daimler engineers managed to design the 28/95 (as it was known) as both a racing and a passenger vehicle! It was the fastest and most remarkable car of its day.

Although the factory had planned an entire range of models around the aero engine and chassis combination in 1914, few were actually built before the war, 20 in 1914 and just five in 1915.

The 28/95 was reintroduced in 1920 as one of Daimler's principal postwar models, with 40 completed by year's end. Both pre- and postwar series can be cited as good examples of how racecar design influenced and improved passenger car development at DMG from 1914 on.

The 28/95 chassis were originally available in two wheelbase lengths, 3390mm (133.5 inches) and 3555mm (140 inches). A 3065mm (120.6 inch) wheelbase Sport chassis, designed by Paul Daimler and DMG engineer and race driver Max Sailer, was added to the line in 1921. The cars were further differentiated by having radiators mounted lower and further back on the chassis behind a new dropped frame crossmember similar in design to the 1914 racecars. In addition, the radiator was positioned closer to the engine, a feat accomplished through the use of a smaller-diameter cooling fan placed within the hollow of the radiator's vee.

From the time of their introduction, Sport models were equipped with four-wheel mechanical brakes; not until later did they appear on the long wheelbase chassis 28/95. By the time 28/95 production resumed after the war, DMG had made numerous improvements to the engine. The

The 28/95 Sport Models had a lower driving position made possible by an angled steering column and shorter control levers.

original aircraft engines used in 1913-14 had exposed rocker arms and valve springs, with foot-operated "total-loss" lubrication, which was tolerable for an airplane but quite untidy on the road. The postwar model featured a new high-pressure lubrication system, operated via a gear-driven pump and a fresh oil supplementary pump, providing continuous circulation of fresh oil, and allowing only the requisite amount of oil leakage expected from a motorcar. In addition, a one-shot lubrication system, actuated by a foot pump, saw to the lubrication of the driveshaft, universal joint, and steering worm gear case. Back in 1914, the cars had required daily attention to 23 lubrication points and weekly servicing of ten more!

Although the cylinders for the postwar 28/95 were again made in pairs, they were now cast and surrounded afterward by a welded-on water jacket, with each cylinder pair encased by its own aluminum rocker cover. The valve-in-head six was operated by an overhead camshaft, driven by a shaft and bevel gear located at the front of the engine. Carburetion was either by two updraft Mercedes-Pallas, or Zenith carburetors, now with a balance pipe added between the two three-branch inlet manifolds.

With only four main bearings and an undernourished crankshaft, the 28/95 engines never ventured far above the vibration-limited revolution rates of their high-flying prewar ancestors. Maximum output at 1800rpm was estimated at 99 brake horsepower, with a virtually level torque curve of 315 pounds-feet up to 1400rpm. Paul Daimler and Max Sailer designed a supercharged version in 1922, developing 140 brake horsepower at 1800rpm.

Paul Daimler had developed the first supercharged automotive engine based upon his experience with the D.F. 80 during the war. His first attempt was to fit a Roots-type blower to the Knight sleeve-valve engine of a Mercedes16/50 HP model, which proved to be an unsuitable host. Continued experiments with the larger 7.3 liter six used in the 28/95 series were successful, and in 1922 Max Sailer drove the first supercharged Mercedes racecar to victory in the Targa Florio.

One might regard supercharging as creating "free horsepower." Driven by the engine's crankshaft, the blower was geared to rotate at a greater speed than the engine. Installed ahead of the carburetor, it forced the pre-compressed air to mix with the fuel. The net result was more horsepower; however, a supercharger could only be engaged for brief stints without causing damage to the engine, but in those ephemeral moments when a supercharged engine played its siren song, a Mercedes was glorious both in sight and sound.

Aside from competition cars, the 28/95 was offered with a long wheelbase suitable for limousine, town car, and dual windshield phaeton body styles. Roadsters, sport phaetons, and a Sport-Zweistzer (sport two-seater) such as the example shown in this chapter were on the short Sport chassis. In 1923, a rakish Rennsport-Zweistzer was introduced which closely resembled Sailer's Targa Florio car.

One thing a race-car needed in the grueling Sicilian Targa Florio, which was four laps of 67 miles each over terrain best suited to mountain goats, was plenty of spare tires. The 28/95 carried three, two on the rear deck and one side mount. Of the 42 cars starting the 1922 Targa Florio only 24 finished, of which one quarter were Mercedes.

Tires in the 1920s were narrow and tall like these Dunlops mounted on wire spoke wheels.

In 1921, Sailer had won the Coppa Florio (the racing division for production-based touring cars) in a 28/95, and finished second overall behind Count Giulio Masetti, driving a Grand Prix Fiat. Testament to the difficulty of the race, Masetti's winning speed was an average of only 36.2mph! Sailer, just moments behind, averaged 35.9mph. The difference, history records, was the time lost for a tire change.

The following year DMG returned to the Targa Florio with seven cars and a crew of 20. Driving the supercharged 28/95, Sailer once again completed the Medium Madonie Circuit behind Count Masetti, who was now driving a Mercedes. The Count's car was a former 1914 Grand Prix racer refitted by Paul Daimler with front wheel brakes. DMG veteran drivers Christian Lautenschlager and Otto Salzer also drove retrofitted 1914 GP cars. The remaining four entries in the 1922 Targa Florio were Sailer's supercharged 28/95, an un-supercharged 28/95 driven by factory mechanic Christian Werner, and two smaller supercharged sports cars which were assigned to Italian driver Fernando Minoia and to Daimler mechanic Paul Scheef. When the dust had cleared, Sailer had finished sixth overall and first in class, and Werner, making his racing debut, eighth overall and second in class – stunning validation for the 28/95 Sport model.

A short 120.6-inch wheelbase chassis 28/95, which came to be known as the Targa Florio model, was equipped without the supercharger for public sale. Coachwork for the sports version was very rakish. Exact production numbers for this model are unknown; however, only four examples are extant today.

One could view the period from the end of World War I until the merger of Daimler and Benz in June 1926 as an interim postwar era where survival was the prime motivator for everything DMG and Benz & Cie. chose to do. The cars were perhaps not as innovative as those which would come in the late 1920s and throughout the 1930s, yet those built from 1919 to 1926 marked exceptional advances in design and engineering at a time when such achievements should have been all but impossible.

The Merger of Daimler and Benz

A Titan Emerges

The creation of Daimler-Benz AG in 1926 consolidated the engineering and production capabilities of the two largest automobile manufacturing companies in Germany, neither of which would have been able to survive without the other in the aftermath of World War I. Though the two firms initially retained their individual identities, as time wore on the need grew for Benz & Cie. and Daimler Motoren Gesellschaft to become one and the same. The pathway to that crossroads, however, was a long, and at times, exasperating one.

The German automotive industry's crisis in the postwar 1920s had not only cyclical causes; it also signaled the reaching of relative growth limits and the associated structural changes that come after a war, especially when you lose. World War I and the economic orientation during the conflict, including the cutting off from foreign markets and the controlled distribution of resources to the wartime industry, accounted for an enforced break in passenger car development. That, however, was not the problem German automakers were facing in 1919. The real problem was that a substantial German passenger car market simply no longer existed after the war. The domestic market's meager volume, in turn, created an unfavorable condition for international competitiveness. For companies like Daimler and Benz it was as though a generation of prosperity had been wiped from the face of the earth. Even five years after

the war life was extremely difficult. "The changeover to peace-time business required a lot of time and many sacrifices," was how it was described in the annual report of DMG, and biographer Paul Siebertz described the difficult time of reconstruction as follows: "In industrial terms, it was not just a question of changing over from war production to useful peace-time production; the companies had to start from zero in every respect."

The histories of Daimler and Benz revealed many parallel developments. Before World War I, both companies pursued similar policies of diversification, resulting in very similar product ranges, from motorcars and commercial vehicles to boats. In the automotive sector, they operated in the same market segments or complemented each other ideally with non-competitive models in different price ranges. During World War I and after losing their foreign markets, both companies completely changed over to military production, and both were thrown back into automotive production by the outcome of the war and the Treaty of Versailles. Daimler and Benz were perhaps more heavily affected than other companies as excessive military production had left their respective automotive production facilities outdated. Conversion back to automotive production would take time and, as design work had also been discontinued, both companies restarted by launching outdated prewar models into a war-torn economy.

Left: Another of the early art pieces released by Mercedes-Benz is this rather alluring poster done in a style reminiscent of the popular French artist and illustrator Louis Icart.

Middle: One of the first posters produced to publicize the merger of Daimler & Benz in 1926, and the creation of Mercedes-Benz.

Right: The pre-World War I racing exploits of both Benz and Daimler were equally promoted in the 1926 merger with posters such as this example incorporating the Benz laurel around the Mercedes Grille.

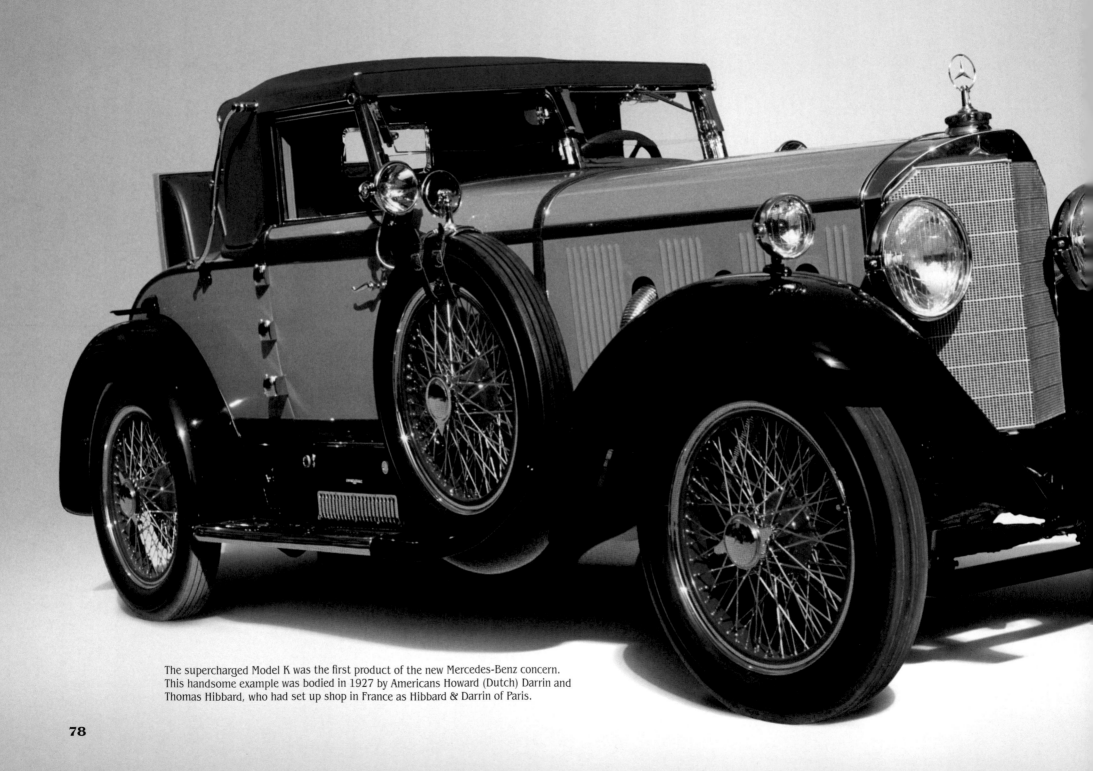

The supercharged Model K was the first product of the new Mercedes-Benz concern. This handsome example was bodied in 1927 by Americans Howard (Dutch) Darrin and Thomas Hibbard, who had set up shop in France as Hibbard & Darrin of Paris.

With the loss of foreign markets and licensees, the cost of production change-over rapidly depleted their reserves, but more than anything else, it was inflation that ruined the German automotive industry. With the devaluation of the currency, people's purchasing power dwindled. The excessive scale of price increases is illustrated by the example of operating costs at Benz & Cie., rising from some 500 million marks in October 1922 to 22,600 billion marks less than a year later. And since German money had also lost its worth abroad, the acquisition of raw materials was jeopardized.

While Benz tried to overcome unfavorable cost structures and excess capacity by combining or selling off unprofitable units (for instance, the stationary gas engine division upon which the company had been founded), DMG endeavored to master the crisis while retaining its property. The attempt to compensate for the losses, and to use the existing capacity more efficiently by branching out into mass products such as bicycles and typewriters, failed. The serious problems in the fields of procurement, sales, and financing soon encouraged DMG and Benz to enter into cooperative ventures – however, not initially with each other.

Daimler first sought an alignment with Krupp, the leading arms maker in Germany, but this proved unsuccessful. Benz aligned itself with the Otto Wolff Group in January 1922 but it was soon realized that such associations did not yield any significant advantages. It was becoming clear that the scale that could be created in a Daimler and Benz merger were each other's best hope for survival.

Plans for merging the two oldest motor manufacturers in the world had actually been considered during the war. In 1916 DMG was offered a large block of Benz shares by a third party, causing DMG board of management member Dr. Ernst Berge to consider a merger. In his opinion, a stock investment by DMG in Benz without the

Another of the great renderings created to establish the image of a combined Mercedes and Benz marque after the 1926 merger.

Far right:
Mercedes-Benz often catered to its feminine clientele and this early merger advertisement, showing a new Mercedes-Benz Tourer, was certainly aimed squarely at that audience.

On June 1, 1926, after a year of trial and error, the Daimler and Benz boards of management finally approved a merger of the two companies. The merger contract was finally approved by the two originating companies' stockholder assemblies on June 28 and 29. Shortly thereafter a series of advertisements were released showing the combined Daimler and Benz logo and publicizing the Mercedes-Benz brand name.

intention of merging the two companies would merely have resulted in a restriction in free competition without any advantages for DMG. By contrast, a full merger would yield savings in material purchasing, production and the sales organizations of the companies. In his considerations, Berge already envisaged a situation after the war where England and France could cut off the German motor industry from West European markets. And he was perfectly right in proceeding from that assumption. He foresaw difficult times ahead for DMG, which could most easily be overcome by a merger with Benz.

However, Berge's far-sighted plan met with grim resistance by the chairman of DMG's supervisory board, Alfred von Kaulla. The latter was convinced that it would be "…impossible to move Benz & Cie. by means other than irresistible pressure to permit its incorporation in DMG." He concluded, "The current rulers at Benz will give up their influence only when there's absolutely no alternative for them." The "current rulers," however, were not the Benz family. Those

in power were at Rheinische Kreditbank, Benz's principal bank, whose director, Dr. Carl Jahr, had been a member of the Benz supervisory board since 1910. Von Kaulla, himself a banker, and the representative of Württembergische Vereinsbank, DMG's principal bank, feared the influence of the competing bank on the company's management. His perspective was of a more short-term nature than Berge's when he concluded: "We are doing quite well right now, so the advantages to be gained would have to be quite significant for us to engage in an operation that would be so difficult to initiate and accomplish." With this unambiguous "no" the project was buried; more likely than not, the Benz family never found out about these activities at the time.

After the war it was Benz that voiced the idea of a merger. The difficulties feared by Berge had materialized; both companies faced tremendous problems in changing over to peacetime production. Therefore, on March 9, 1919 Dr. Jahr traveled to Stuttgart and suggested the foundation of a "community of interests," a customary cooperative-venture model in Germany at the time, close to being the

The Daimler assembly line c. 1925 with the Model 630 Mercedes under construction. This would be the platform upon which the first joint Mercedes-Benz design would be built in 1926-27.

equivalent to a merger. In particular, he insisted on a board of management with an equal number of members from both parties, and alternating supervisory board chairmanship by Richard Brosien (Benz) and Alfred von Kaulla (DMG). This, however, was unacceptable to von Kaulla. He insisted on the sole management of the company from Stuttgart, and above all rejected the idea of alternating supervisory board chairmanship. Additionally, von Kaulla saw only disadvantages for DMG arising from a realignment of the model ranges within the two companies. He feared that the large models with the low sales figures would be allocated to DMG while Benz would be able to benefit from the successful sales of their smaller models.

Despite von Kaulla's principal reservations, Ernst Berge saw the project in a more positive light. However, he had underestimated the economic situation of Benz, believing that Benz would have to accept Stuttgart's predominance

sooner or later. He therefore played for time. In many ways he had overlooked Benz's corporate self-esteem. In December 1919, the management and supervisory boards of Benz AG unanimously rejected DMG's proposal.

Since the fiercest opponent of a merger of Daimler and Benz had been the chairman of DMG's supervisory board, it was not surprising that immediately after Alfred von Kaulla's death, on January 14, 1924, Carl Jahr launched a new advance. As soon as early February, Dr. Jahr submitted a memorandum on the "merger of Messrs. Benz and Daimler" to all members of DMG's and Benz's management and supervisory boards. The aim of the merger was to be the retention of competitiveness vis-à-vis foreign motor manufacturers. Dr. Jahr hoped to achieve this by means of price reductions made possible by extensive rationalization measures in purchasing, production, and sales.

Left: The Model 630 chassis was redesigned by Ferdinand Porsche in 1926 and renamed the Model K.

The Model K was an ideal platform for a variety of body styles. This sporty convertible is actually a four-door model with center-hinged doors. The rear door, however, is remarkably small considering the K stood for short and the wheelbase was a scant 133-7/8 inches, long by today's standards but not in the 1920s.

Below right: Carrozzeria Farina in Italy created this regal body style for the Model K around 1927.

Foreign coachbuilders were quick to take advantage of the sporty Model K platform and its supercharged engine, creating dashing models such as this convertible sedan bodied in Paris by Jacques Saoutchik.

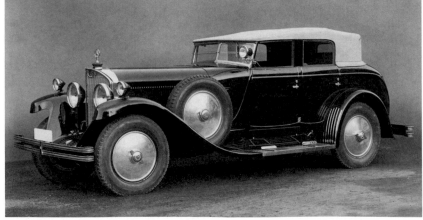

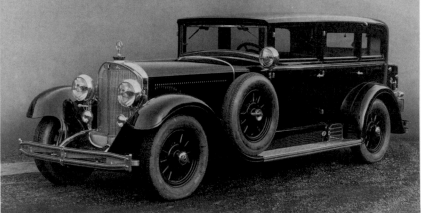

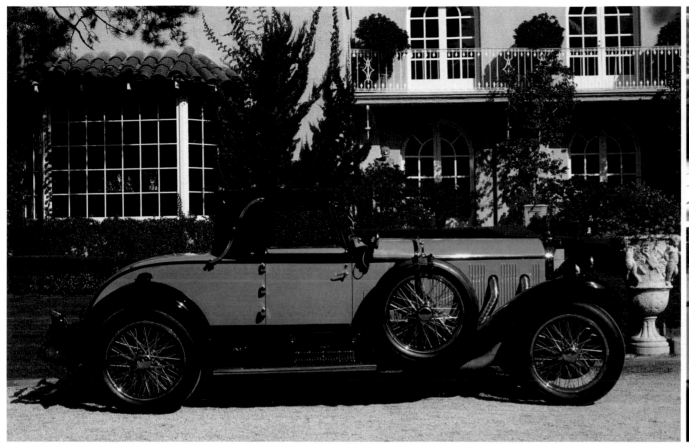

Model K interiors were provided in a standard version but each coachbuilder took a turn at adding their own distinctive touches. Hibbard & Darrin opted for this extraordinary hand-crafted wood dash panel with contrasting double inlays. The immense double ring steering wheel was standard on all Model K chassis.

Standard styling cues for the Model K included the side-mount spare.

This led to the "community of interests" or what we have also termed as an "Agreement of Mutual Interest," which for the short term bypassed the difficulties involved with a full merger. Those involved had learned from the problems encountered in 1919, and this time Jahr was not to be faced with major resistance; the situation had changed, and not only through the death of von Kaulla. In 1924, Württembergische Vereinsbank merged with Deutsche Bank. The latter had also been the majority stockholder of Rheinische Kreditbank (Benz's banker) since 1922. Through the merger Deutsche Bank emerged as an entity that now represented both Daimler and Benz! Alongside Carl Jahr, Emil Georg von Stauss, member of the board of management of Deutsche Bank, as well as a member of DMG's supervisory board, became the driving force behind the merger. Von Stauss was one of the few people who, at an early stage, had recognized the significance of the motor industry as a growth-promoting branch of industry. But time was pressing upon them.

Since 1922, Benz AG had permanently been forced to look over its shoulder because of a speculator, Jacob Schapiro, a dealer and coachbuilder born in Odessa and living in Berlin. Schapiro had bought large numbers of cars at a fixed price but paid for them much later when the money was almost worthless. With this trick, Schapiro earned so much money that he almost managed to secure the exclusive sales rights for Benz automobiles and could have bought more than 40 percent of the Benz stock. It took almost until the merger in 1926 before Schapiro could be forced to withdraw by means of a number of legal maneuvers.

This was the background against which Dr. Jahr's memorandum was developed into a syndicate contract, approved by the boards of management as early as May 1 and by the stockholders' assemblies of both companies on May 8. This contract went far beyond the conventional idea of a "community of interests," as indicated, above all, by the planned profit sharing in a ratio of 600 to 346 (DMG to Benz).

The combined management panel was empowered to "reorganize operations, departments, outposts, etc. of both companies completely or in part, to relocate individual units completely or in part, to integrate them or close

Main: The perfect body style for the Model K was a roadster with rumble seat. Perhaps the very best example, done in 1927, was this beautiful two-seater designed and bodied by Hibbard & Darrin of Paris.

Under the hood, no matter what the design, was Porsche's improved Daimler six with supercharger. Output with the blower engaged was a rousing 160 horsepower from the 6.24-liter (381-cubic inch) engine. Inside the car, and this is from first-hand experience, when the blower engages its sounds like a second engine kicking in and the road begins to pass more swiftly.

them down, to expand units that are inadequate for the purposes of the 'community of interests' and to add or establish new operating units." Over and above this, the contract obliged the boards of management of both companies to "specify the design plans and production ranges for all plants and to distribute manufacture of the agreed products to the individual plants." This prepared the ground for a much needed rationalization in production. Rationalization in sales was to be achieved by a uniform "corporate identity" in sales and advertising. The products of both companies were to be marketed under a new name – Mercedes-Benz.

Initially, it looked as if the syndicate program was going to progress smoothly. Contractual stipulations like joint management and joint sales were rapidly implemented in formal terms. Corporate management was unified through the formation of a syndicate committee chaired by Emil Georg von Stauss and by appointing the management and supervisory board members of one company as deputy members of the other company's respective bodies. To implement the joint sales tasks, Mercedes-Benz-Automobil GmbH was founded. This company was to be made up of the entire sales organizations at a participation quota of 600 to 346, and its management was to report directly to the syndicate committee. This realignment was discussed and finally agreed in a special meeting on May 30, 1924, and the details in terms

of every staff position and business process had been clarified by June 18. But then the integration process stagnated, with the exception of an agreement on the organization of purchasing functions for the syndicate's factories. The principal issues of implementation were left undecided because of differences of opinion and inadequate cooperation at the board of management level. It took until May 5, 1925 for the two automakers to outline an agreeable joint concept. The level of compromise on both sides clearly demonstrated the scope of different approaches between Benz and DMG management. The declared aim was the streamlining and distribution of the model ranges, with just one model being allocated to any one of the manufacturing plants. All other activities were to be consolidated or sold wherever possible to ensure undisturbed production processes.

Among other things, the merging and centralization of the design offices and bodywork manufacturing facilities of Daimler and Benz was planned. A special technical committee was to tackle the task of machinery modernization as well as diversification issues and both horizontal and vertical expansion of operating units, with the aim of setting up the syndicate's own steel works and coal mine and introducing American manufacturing methods.

The greatest differences of opinion had been with respect to diversification, in-house production, and the aforementioned manufacturing methods.

The Castagna Town Car was built on a lengthened Model K chassis. Fitted with a luxurious, hand-crafted interior, the car cost Charles Murray a total of $28,000 by the time it was delivered to the United States!

In Italy, a Mercedes-Benz chassis was a welcomed challenge for the leading Carrozziera. Castagna took this Model K to task, producing a remarkable town car for Oklahoma oilman Charles Murray and his wife Marion. They resided in the penthouse of the Waldorf-Astoria in New York and used the Italian-bodied Mercedes as their chauffeured livery around the city. The chauffeur, incidentally, was also imported from Germany.

The chauffeur's compartment was lavishly appointed. The round dial at the far right of the dash was a series of directions for the driver which could be illuminated from the passenger compartment with the touch of a button. The dial read: Left, Right, Quick, Slow, Stop, Turn Around, and Go Home. Presumably their German chauffeur read English.

Whereas the DMG board of management favored greater diversification (aero engines, marine engines) and wanted to introduce mass production rapidly, Benz & Cie. executives felt that it was imperative to first regain competitiveness in the automotive business. The Benz team therefore pursued what they regarded as a realistic policy of small steps, with the goal of gradually stepping up production. They favored improved designs and sales promotion measures to broaden the sales basis, thereby slowly closing the gap between manufacturing costs and sales revenues.

To reach principal agreement on the question of model range streamlining and allocation, and the ongoing merger and concentration of various functions, the Benz board of management had made considerable concessions in other areas where, as a consequence, DMG had enforced its own ideas to a major extent. Things were made even more difficult by the fact that rapid economic success failed to materialize: immediately after its founding, the "community of interests" stumbled into the deflation crisis caused by the German currency reform. Thus sales figures for Daimler and Benz continued to decline, gigantic product inventories built up, and both companies had to dismiss staff on a major scale. In March 1926, those in charge even considered closing down production entirely!

DMG was particularly hard hit by the crisis because in the distribution of models to the two companies, the large four- and six-liter luxury cars had been allocated to Untertürkheim - exactly as predicted by Alfred von Kaulla in 1919. This sales crisis caused conflicts in management to erupt on both sides. There were those who felt that the only way out was the complete merger of Daimler and Benz, while others were convinced that the "community of interests" had failed. It was then that a number of key players (bankers) attempted to force a different type of consolidation involving a quite different merger concept that would combine the automakers Hansa-Lloyd, NAG, Adler, and Daimler and

Ferdinand Porsche became the engineering figurehead at Daimler-Benz after the merger, but his tenure would be short. He left the company at the end of 1928, and was succeeded by his associate, Hans Nibel, the former chief engineer at Benz & Cie.

Right: The Mercedes was popular on both sides of the Atlantic. Zeppo Marx owned one, as did song and dance man Al Jolson, seen here with his wife at their Hollywood home with the new 1927 Model S.

Below: With an even sportier design, the Model SS Sportwagen (roadster) was another popular body style of the era. Equipped with the supercharged six, maximum output from the new 6.8 liter engine was 200hp with the blower engaged.

Benz in a giant conglomerate (a German version of General Motors). Fortunately a more realistic policy supported by Benz was arrived at, after which major conflicts did not arise at the board of management level. The situation was clarified and on July 29, 1925, the complete board of management met for its first meeting. Jahr specified the line to be followed: the focus was on sales policy, and investment was to be concentrated on development and marketing. The sales basis was to be broadened by attractive models and designs as well as by sales-promoting measures, and production was to be streamlined to increase profitability.

The most important task in product policy was to finally arrive at an agreement on model ranges. A compromise had to be found here, between the requirements of the market and production capabilities in terms of the type and number of models to be produced. On the one side, the sales basis was to become as broad as possible; on the other side, production costs had to be lowered. The focus had to be on a price dictated by the market, and this required a smaller car, an ideal situation for Benz. The original plan to produce one model per assembly plant could not be implemented due to market conditions. Thus those responsible agreed on three passenger car models for the time being, retaining their basic principle of building just one model as a "mass-produced car" at Benz. Finally, people settled down to take a closer look at American pro-

Above: The 1927 Model S, designed by Porsche, was the beginning of a new era for Daimler-Benz and the first all-new car to bear the Mercedes-Benz name. This sporty Tourer was typical of Model S designs. Note once again that the publicity photo from 1927 played up the feminine side of motoring.

Top right: The SSK had a domineering front end design created by Porsche and on the Boattail Speedster body it was even more prominent as the two-seat passenger compartment barely began ahead of the rear wheels.

Top left: This Model SSK chassis was shipped to California in 1928 and custom bodied by the Walter M. Murphy Company in Pasadena as a Boattail Speedster. It is regarded as the raciest design ever on an SSK, only outshone by the sporting SSKL race cars.

The Murphy coachbuilders fitted the car with a striking polished copper dash panel. The car was originally painted black, later painted red, and then the dove gray as shown.

In 1928 Daimler-Benz described this Model SS as a "sports car." Considering the power, up to 225 horsepower, generated by the supercharged engine, and the car's lower center of gravity, "sports car" may well have been an accurate description.

Racing was one of the features that distinguished the Models S, SS, SSK, and SSKL. Even the Model S two-seater was a racecar at heart, as evidenced by its victory in the 1928 Nürburgring with driver Otto Merz, pictured in the foreground. Third from the left (behind the garland) is designer Ferdinand Porsche.

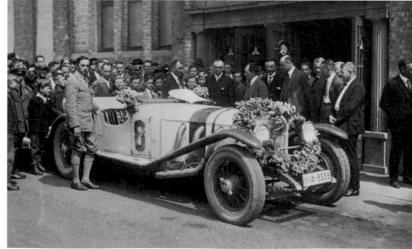

duction methods, resulting in decisions relating to the integration and concentration of individual functions, i.e., purchasing and marketing, as well as on in-house production.

On June 1, 1926, after a year of trial and error, the Daimler and Benz boards of management finally approved a merger of the two companies. Stock was to be exchanged at a ratio of 1:1. The merger contract was finally approved by the two originating companies' stockholder assemblies on June 28 and 29. Shortly thereafter a series of advertisements were released showing the combined Daimler and Benz logo and publicizing the Mercedes-Benz brand name.

During the "community of interests" stage, one man in particular had proved his mettle: Wilhelm Kissel. He was appointed to the new company's board of management and soon established himself as the leading figure at Daimler-Benz AG.

Unfortunately, the well-planned consolidation expected from the merger

A trio of Mercedes line up on the first row for the opening day event at the 1927 Nürburgring race.

This early 1927 Model SS was built for Daimler-Benz race driver Rudolf Caracciola. It was with this car that the great Caracciola surpassed 120mph in the 1927 Belgian Speed Trial, and won the opening event of the Nürburgring.

Below: This is another styling example of the Type SS. The convertible coupe features a single large door on each side, allowing access to both front and rear seating.

ran headlong into its first crisis, a postwar recession. At times, this meant that the policy of small steps degenerated into mere reactions to a declining market and into production at the lowest conceivable level. In this way the corporation survived the world economic crisis. The outstanding achievements of those involved in exerting all their energies and retaining the corporation's innovative strength under the engineering guidance of Ferdinand Porsche served to establish a foundation for recovery in the late 1920s.

The first model to bear the Mercedes-Benz name, aside from the little changed, traditional, lower-priced Mannheim and Stuttgart models, was the Model K, an update of the pre-merger 1924 Type 630 24/100/140 PS Mercedes. Introduced in 1926, the Model K was principally the work of Porsche and his predecessor Paul Daimler. Porsche improved upon Daimler's pioneering overhead camshaft six-cylinder engine design and Roots-type supercharger, giving the massive K unparalleled straight-line performance. Specified by Mercedes-Benz to attain a top speed of 90mph, it was billed as the fastest standard production model of its type in the world.

Supercharged engines had become the foundation for an entirely new and more powerful generation of cars that would emerge in the late 1920s and flourish up until the beginning of World War II. As Mercedes-Benz so poignantly noted in *The Fascination of the Compressor*,

The sportiest road car of the series was the SSK. Although the cars were equally suited for competition, many were built as sport roadsters, such as this 1928 example.

Bottom right: Legendary race driver Rudolf Caracciola is seen driving an SSKL in the 1931 French Grand Prix. (Tomasz Szczerbicki Archives)

Below: In the 1931 race at Le Mans, this Mercedes Model SS finished second with drivers Ivanosky and Stoffel. (Tomasz Szczerbicki Archives)

Here & right: One of the finest examples of the rare Mercedes-Benz SSK is on permanent exhibit at the new Mercedes-Benz Museum in Untertürkheim.

Here & left: The rarest of the S-Series cars was the 300-horsepower SSKL. Only seven were built, none of which have survived, though several SSK models have since been rebuilt to resemble them.

A masterpiece of power and aesthetics, the SSK six-cylinder engine had a swept volume of 7.1 liters and a maximum supercharged output of 225 horsepower at 3200rpm. Bore x stroke were 100 x 150mm.

a 1998 book on the history of the company's supercharged cars, "…the sound and appearance of the Mercedes-Benz engines were testimony to the raw power beneath the hood. This was innovative technology encased in the most elegant car bodies of the time. The high-gloss chrome exhaust pipes that peeked from the side of the hood became synonymous with superchargers, the symbol of power and glory. These mighty machines were like creatures from ancient legends. The only way to escape their beguiling melody, their aura, their fascination, was to hide yourself away and stop up your ears." Such was the image Mercedes-Benz had fashioned for itself in the late 1920s.

The "K" designation of the new Mercedes-Benz model stood for Kurz, German for "short," as Porsche had reduced the wheelbase of the Type 630 from 147.5 inches to a more compact 134 inch stretch. (The "K" designation

Of all SSK models, this is without doubt the most unusual and most striking of all. Built in 1932-33 for millionaire Italian race driver Count Carlo Felice "Didi" Trossi, the chassis was sent to England where this remarkable body was purportedly built from Trossi's own design drawings. The car is now owned by Ralph Lauren.

often leads to confusion because it has two meanings. A car with a "K" suffix can also denote a supercharger, which is the more common usage.) With less overall weight on a more responsive suspension, Porsche increased the output of Daimler's supercharged six, which had previously made 100 horsepower and an additional 40 horsepower when the supercharger was engaged by depressing the throttle pedal fully to the floor. Porsche's improvements enhanced output to 110/160 horsepower. The new supercharged models also marked a departure from the earlier method of differentiating taxable horsepower and brake horsepower. With the new models, dual figures (i.e., 110/160) represented the standard output and supercharged output of the engine. When three figures were shown, the first was used for tax purposes, as vehicle taxation was based upon an engine's output and a different formula was used.

Increased power came from a higher compression ratio (5.0:1, up from 4.7:1) and better ignition through Ferdinand Porsche's use of two spark plugs per cylinder. With a bore and stroke of 94 x 150mm (3-11/16 x 5-29/32 inches), the Model K engine displaced 6.24 liters (381 cubic inches). One of the few carryovers from the old 630 was the 4-speed gearbox with straight-cut gears and a 1:1 ratio in top gear. As a transitional model during the Daimler and Benz consolidation, the K proved to be an excellent luxury alternative to the sporting S, SS, and SSK series that Porsche would create in the latter part of the decade.

Porsche's new S series cars first seen in 1927 were to prove particularly successful in racing and, with drivers such as Rudolf Caracciola, Christian Werner, Otto Merz, Manfred von Brauchitsch, Adolf Rosenberger, and Hans Stuck, would reclaim the racing heritage of both Benz and Daimler by 1930.

Under the sleek hood of the Trossi SSK was the straight six-cylinder, supercharged Daimler engine designed by Porsche. The trio of polished exhausts was symbolic as well as functional. The output of the 7.1 liter engine in Trossi's car was 300 horsepower at 3400 rpm with 512 lbs.-ft. torque at 2000rpm.

The Model S and subsequent SS and SSK were built on a new drop-center frame with a 133-inch standard wheelbase. To improve handling over the Model K, Porsche moved the radiator and engine about a foot rearward on the chassis, resulting in better front to rear weight distribution and a lower center of gravity. The lower chassis also improved cornering and encouraged more rakish, open coachwork.

With the improved chassis also came greater output from the Mercedes-Benz supercharged inline six: now 120 horsepower under normal aspiration, 180 with the supercharger engaged. The updated engine in the Model S, the single strongest tie to Daimler, had its bore increased from 94mm to 98mm. With a 150mm stroke, this brought displacement up to 6,789cc, about 414 cubic inches. The SSK, powered by a 170/225 horsepower (increased to 180/250 horsepower in 1929) Roots supercharged inline six, was capable of reaching the magic century mark. Racing versions with higher-compression engines running on Elcosine – an alcohol-fuel mixture used for competition – were capable of speeds well in excess of 100mph. In one of these competition versions,

Left: Grilles on the Nürburg were prominently marked with the factory name.

Above right: Though a formal car, the Papler coachwork on this Type 460 Nürburg chassis is quite stylish.

The 460 Nürburg series provided a variety of coachwork almost as diverse as the S-Series cars. This sports two-seater was powered by the normally aspirated straight eight. The cars were named after the Nürburgring, where during their initial tests a 460 test model ran for 13 days (311 hours), stopping only for fuel and tire changes. The car traveled a total distance of 12,500 miles with an average speed of 40.5 mph, double the previous record for a factory stock automobile.

Top left: Further down the price scale from the SS and 460 was the Stuttgart Model 260 offered in the late 1920s. This 10/50hp model features sporty roadster body styling.

By the end of the 1920s and into the early 1930s, SS models went through several variations. This 1930 Model Type 710 SS was bodied in England by Forrest-Lycett as a competition sports roadster. The styling is quite different from German coachwork and in some respects more closely resembles an SS-100 Jaguar.

The British-bodied 710 SS is pictured at the Castle Solitude, an historic locale in Mercedes-Benz history and frequently the site of many original factory photographs.

Below left & right: No matter who the coachbuilder, the traditional trio of exhaust pipes was present on every S, SS, and SSK model.

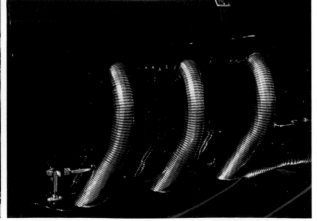

Rudolf Caracciola surpassed 120mph in the 1927 Belgian Speed Trial, and won the opening event of the Nürburgring.

The culmination of the S Series was the SSKL (K for short and L for lightweight) which appeared in 1931. A more powerful version purposely built for motor sports, the SSKL was also at home on the open road. Production of the supercharged S or Sport (180-horsepower) model was limited to 128 chassis. Another 111 SS or Super Sport (improved 7.1 liter engine, 200- to 225-horsepower) models were built, along with a scant 33 SSK (250-horsepower, short wheelbase) examples, and just seven SSKL (300-horsepower) competition versions were built, none of which have survived. This was the factory tally for the entire Model S series produced from 1927 to 1934: 279 cars.

Off the track, nearly all Model S body styles were of the open touring design, but they were very traditional, severe and upright in appearance. The majority of bodies were designed and manufactured by the Sindelfingen Werke, but S Series chassis were also fitted with coachwork designed in Germany by Karosserie Erdmann & Rossi or Karosserie Papler, and in Geneva, Switzerland by Zeitz.

Apart from the normal touring bodies were several sport-touring types with cut-down doors and more rakish bodylines. Sindelfingen built a stylish "tourenwagen" with dual rear-mounted spares instead of the traditional side-mounts, yet some of the best styling on the Model S chassis came from outside Germany. Exotic coachwork from cutting edge French stylist Jacques Saoutchik included a splendid convertible coupe; Van Den Plas of Brussels built a cabriolet, and an even more stylish cabriolet came from d'Ieteren Frérès in Belgium. The Model S chassis were also fitted with bespoke coachwork in England by Freestone & Webb in traditional British Saloon styling, and chassis delivered to the United States were mounted with coachwork by the Walter M. Murphy Company of Pasadena, California, a firm principally recognized in later years for its work on the Model J and SJ Duesenberg.

Although Porsche had started the supercharged revolution at Daimler-Benz, many of the later changes appearing on SS, SSK, and SSKL models was the work of Dr. Hans Nibel, who had been chief engineer at Benz and Ferdinand Porsche's successor in January 1929. Porsche had originally gone to work for Daimler prior to the merger, and decided not to renew his contract with Daimler-Benz in December 1928. He instead returned to Austria where he accepted a position as technical director at Styer. After a year there he resigned and moved back to Stuttgart where he established a design and engineering firm, Dr. Ing. H.c. F. Porsche GmbH. The rest, as they say, is history.

Although the Model S was the Mercedes flagship, it wasn't the only popular model offered. Below it, but not too far below, was the all-new 4-1/2 liter Straight "8" Nürburg 460. The 460 chassis measured 145 inches in wheelbase with a narrow 4-foot 9-inch track, and average overall length of 195 inches. Suspension was by semi-elliptic springs with Houdaille shock absorbers. The 460 also offered four-wheel brakes with a vacuum servo system, automatic central chassis lubrication, and a choice of wooden or wire spoke wheels with Rudge hubs.

Powered by a non-supercharged side-valve straight eight engine displacing 4592cc (80mm x 115mm bore x stroke), the 460 motor developed 90 horsepower at 3200rpm. The 460 Nürburg chassis (W 08 and 460 K supercharged) were manufactured through 1933, with a total production of 2,893. The pressed-steel drop frame platform was offered in two wheelbase lengths: the standard 3670mm (145-inch) model and a short 3430mm (135-inch) Kurz sport version, here once again "K" denoting a short wheelbase. The 1928-29 Type 460 models were primarily bodied as limousines, tourers, or cabriolets, while the supercharged 460 K was available with similar body choices and as a Sport-Roadster.

As the 1920s came to a close Mercedes-Benz launched another magnificent model known as the Type 770 or Grosser Mercedes. Introduced for 1930, the 7.7-liter passenger cars were the largest, heaviest, and most expensive vehicles to bear the Mercedes-Benz star. Available as a touring car, pullman, or sedan, and in several cabriolet versions, the 770 was intended for heads of state and affluent clientele desiring a prestigious, top-flight motorcar. The supercharged 770 developed 150 horsepower normally and, with the compressor engaged, a rousing 200 horsepower – capable of propelling these enormous 6000-pound automobiles up to 100mph.

As a new decade dawned, Mercedes-Benz had taken a commanding lead in engineering and technology, offering suspension, engine, and transmission designs which were to become the standard of the world in the 1930s. The greatest pre-World War II achievements in Mercedes-Benz history, however, were yet to come.

At the close of the 1920s Mercedes-Benz introduced the Type 770 (or Grosser Mercedes) for 1930. The immense 7.7-liter, supercharged eight-cylinder passenger cars were the largest, heaviest and most expensive vehicles to bear the Mercedes-Benz star.

The 1930s

Daimler-Benz Redefines the Automobile

The toughest competitors for the German motor industry were American automakers; despite customs barriers and transportation costs, mass production enabled Detroit to charge competitive prices on European sales. Imports and local assembly reached a maximum level in 1929 when American brands accounted for a staggering 38.5 percent of registrations in Germany! In spite of these adverse conditions, the German passenger car industry, and more specifically Mercedes-Benz, had regained international competitiveness by the early 1930s.

The merger of Germany's two largest automakers resulted in an era of momentous advances in design and engineering. In the 10 years between 1926 and 1936 Mercedes-Benz introduced and perfected four-wheel independent suspension, a supercharged straight eight that would rival America's mighty Model SJ Duesenberg, while at the Sindelfingen Werke, body design advanced beyond that of other European coachbuilders, with the exception of Figoni, Saoutchik, and Chapron, in Paris.

The first great breakthrough came in 1933 when Mercedes-Benz introduced the first production automobile in the world with a four-wheel, fully independent suspension. This new level of ride comfort was then fortified by a catalog of sensational coachwork that would soon be known by the name Sindelfingen, the city where Daimler had first established a factory for the production of aero engines and aircraft during World War I.

This was now the Daimler-Benz Karosserie, and under managing director Hermann Ahrens, the design and construction of custom bodies became its most important role. The first examples from Sindelfingen were shown on the 1932 Type SS Mercedes, Type 380 S, and 1933 Supercharged Type 380.

In addition to the Porsche-designed supercharged six-cylinder engines used in the S series, the engineering department also had the new straight eights, which had been introduced with the 1928 Nürburg models. This was also the year Ferdinand Porsche chose not to renew his contract with Daimler-Benz

In 1930 Daimler-Benz introduced the Grosser or "Grand" Mercedes. Because of its imposing appearance, the Model 770 was destined to become the vehicle of choice for heads of state, including the Japanese Imperial family and Germany's exiled Kaiser Wilhelm II, for whom this 1931 Cabriolet F was built.

Left: In a decade of both extraordinary and rare motorcars, the 1937 Mercedes-Benz 540K Special Coupe would be the ultimate embodiment of both.

Above: This 770 limousine was built for the Japanese Imperial family. It is seen here in a postwar photograph taken in 1959 with Emperor Hirohito, members of the Japanese government, and representatives from Daimler-Benz.

Above right: In the late 1930s the Grosser 770 Mercedes sedans with compressor were becoming popular with German dignitaries and government leaders. The later 770 models had the same improved suspension as the 540K and a five-speed gearbox. The long wheelbase limousines such as this 1938 model were capable of touring at over 100mph on the Autobahn.

Below: Although intended as the foundation for formal coachwork, the 770 could also be bodied in a style similar to the Type SS and SSK touring models. Such was the case with this regal phaeton powered by the Daimler 7.2 liter (7655cc) supercharged straight eight developing 200 horsepower.

after a heated debate on the design of a lower-priced economy model he wanted to build (and later would, with Hitler's support, develop the Kdf-Wagen, later to be known as the Volkswagen). Ironically, Mercedes-Benz would, in fact, produce such a car in 1934, the Type 130, and follow it with the Type 150 H and in 1936 the 170 H, which all too closely resembled the Porsche-designed Kdf-Wagen.

The next step in Mercedes' endeavor to expand into the European luxury market, which was occupied primarily by Rolls-Royce, had begun in 1930 with the introduction of the magnificent 770 Grosser (7.7 liter), shown at the Paris Salon. The largest engine in Mercedes-Benz history, it was intended for the great touring cars and limousines being created at Sindelfingen.

The most important design, however, was on a smaller scale, and with half the displacement, a supercharged 3.8 liter straight eight with a bore x stroke of 78mm x 100mm. This would power the most technologically-advanced model of the early 1930s, the Mercedes-Benz Type 380. What few people realize today is that the engineering and styling of the now legendary 500K and 540K were developed for this short-lived predecessor introduced in 1933 and discontinued the following year.

Daimler-Benz had already pioneered four-wheel independent suspension with the Type 170, utilizing a transverse leaf spring in the front and a swing axle design with coil springs in the rear. The engineering department under Hans Nibel refined this design in 1933 for the Type 380, which became the first production automobile in the world with independent front suspension by means of parallel wishbones and coil springs. The independent rear was a continuation of the proven 170 swing-axle design, but fitted with two coil springs per side.

The new front suspension vastly improved ride characteristics by allowing the front wheels to flex slightly to the rear on impact with a bump, further absorbing vibrations before being taken up into the chassis. The shock absorber was a lever-type which was carried on the outside, behind the spring and attached from the chassis to the top A-arm. In the rear, the revised swing axle design relied on two large coil springs per side, and in back (behind the fuel tank) two horizontal assist springs linked the two axle halves together. In the event one axle was forced up radically, the assist spring would pull the axle down tightly against the pavement. This minimized the tendency for the swing axle to tuck up under the car in tight cornering situations. Variations of this design would remain in use at Mercedes-Benz for the next 35 years! In 1933, however, a car equipped with a four-wheel, coil spring, independent suspension was nothing short of unconventional, considering that most of the automotive world was still riding on solid rear axles and leaf spring suspensions.

Thus the 1933-1934 Type 380 introduced virtually all of the features for which its successors are revered, including most of the coachwork created by Sindelfingen. Total production of the 380 (not to be confused with the 380 S, produced in Mannheim in 1932 and 1933) amounted to approximately 157 examples, according to historian Jan

Melin, with body styles ranging from open tourers to sport-roadsters, sedans, roadster-coupes, and convertibles in two and two-plus seating, known as Cabriolet A or Cabriolet B.

So what happened to this innovative automobile? The 380 had one major shortcoming: the 3.8 liter engine was insufficient in power, even with the supercharger. The car was built on a massive box-section frame, which with coachwork averaged well over two tons. At maximum output (120 horsepower) the beautiful 380 could barely get out of its own way. Even a handful of improved 1934 models with output increased to 140 horsepower and then 144 horsepower at 3600rpm remained inadequate. It was at this juncture that Mercedes-Benz embraced an American ideology – "There is no substitute for cubic inches."

Late in 1934 the new 5.0-liter 500K models were introduced. They were the same cars as the 380 but with a new, far more powerful supercharged straight eight beneath the hood. In fact, the early sales catalogs used the same photographs used in the 380 brochures.

Considered to be cars of uncommon quality, comfort, and style, the 500Ks immediately proved their mettle in the Deutschland Fahrt (roughly "Tour of Germany") endurance test in 1934. Covering a distance of 2,195.8 km (approximately 1,364 miles) from Baden-Baden, through Stuttgart, Munich, Nüremberg, Dresden, Berlin (Avus), Magdeburg, Cologne, Nürburgring, and Mannheim, and back to Baden-Baden, the factory 500Ks, along with privately owned Mercedes-Benz entries, virtually dominated a field of more than 190 vehicles.

Introduced in 1930, the Type 370 S was the top sports model produced by the Mannheim werke. Manufactured between 1929 and 1934, the "S" stands for "Special Design," for which chief engineer Hans Nibel chose a very pronounced dropbed frame in order to achieve a lower center of gravity and more stylish coachwork. Pictured is a 1931 roadster from the Mercedes-Benz Museum collection. (photos by Dennis Adler)

The 370 S interior was simple, with extensive use of steel plate for the firewall, driver's footwell, and transmission tunnel. The rear of the car was affixed with single spare and lighted number plate bracket.

The 500K became one of the most desired sports and touring cars in Europe from 1935 to 1937, when an even more powerful 5.4-liter supercharged straight eight was added. Both the 500K and 540K chassis offered an extraordinary platform upon which to build a custom body. It was comprised of two main frame rails, cross braced by one heavy front I-beam, which supported the radiator and independent front suspension mounting; a smaller bolted-in cross member, used to support the rear of the engine and transmission; a large box section cross brace located behind the transmission; and in the rear, two small cross members which served as front and rear supports for the differential.

As a styling cue, the frame was tapered at the front, allowing for the narrow radiator, which, along with the engine, was nestled behind the front suspension (with the exception of short-wheelbase chassis), allowing the frame rails, and therefore the bumpers, to extend well past the grille. This gave the cars a longer, leaner appearance.

Despite their tremendous weight the 500K could accelerate from a stand to 62mph (100km/h) in under 16 seconds, and in top gear effortlessly attain 100mph. In the 1930s, any automobile that could achieve triple digits was

On the occasion of the Berlin Motor Show in February 1933, the public had the opportunity to admire the beautiful shape of this car for the first time. The Type 380 was powered by an eight-cylinder inline engine, which had an output of 140 horsepower when supercharged. The following year the 380 would give way to the 5.0 liter 500K.

The 500K radiator was a masterpiece of workmanship in itself. One of the most complex radiator designs of all time, its magnificent appearance was also the source of its greatest problems—maintenance and restoration! The interior of the radiator was formed with individual soldered tubes. The chromed shell was also more than decorative – it held the water.

immediately legendary. With the addition of the 5.4-liter 540K, the mighty Mercedes had reached its zenith. Producing 115 horsepower, increased to a spirited 180 horsepower with the Roots compressor set in motion, Mercedes-Benz fashioned one of the most powerful production automobiles the world had ever seen.

To take full advantage of the 5.4 liter straight eight, 540Ks were equipped with a four-speed manual transmission. First gear was 3.90:1, second 2.28, third 1.45, and top gear 1:1. This was further improved upon in 1939 when 540K models became available with a new five-speed transmission offering a 0.80:1 overdrive, or Schnellgang.

Following the 540K's introduction, a right-hand-drive model (of which fewer than 200 were built in the 500K and 540K series) was reviewed by the editors of Great Britain's prestigious automotive journal *The Motor*. In the May 11,

The 1935 model 500K Special Sport Roadster pictured is one of the earliest of that body style built by the Sindelfingen factory. Approximately 12 of these true Roadster bodies (those having side curtains rather than roll-up windows) were produced in 1935-36. Chassis number 123778, this car appears to be the sixth Special Roadster built, although the Komm.-Nr. 202124 would make it the third 500K model built. Such contradictions in records are not unusual. One of the distinctive features was the folding split windshield.

The 500K engine was an in-line eight with Roots supercharger. Bore x stroke was 86mm x 108mm for a swept volume of 5.018 liters. Output of 100 normal and 160 horsepower blown was delivered to the rear by a three-speed gearbox with additional semi-automatic overdrive gear.

Double stacked rear spares were an early styling cue of the 500K which carried into the 540K series in 1937, being refined in the 540K Special Roadster.

1937 issue they put a 540K Cabriolet to the test and found the mighty new Mercedes "...extremely well built throughout, in the characteristic Mercedes-Benz fashion and the cabriolet coachwork is as robust and as beautifully made as the chassis." Interestingly, before making mention of the 540K's top speed, the editors were prompt to remark on the car's remarkable handling in London traffic. "On the quiet third speed it will amble along at 10 mph with the engine turning a modest 500 rpm. On the same gear the car will accelerate from 10 mph to 70 mph in 19 seconds and will reach 75 mph if the engine is taken a little beyond the recommended limit of 3,500 rpm." At the famed Brooklands race track the test car was then pressed to a speed in excess of 90 mph unblown and a rousing 106 mph with the supercharger engaged. Noted *The Motor*, "The latter figure was obtained by timing the Mercedes over a full flying half-mile along the railway straight in complete touring trim with the windscreen and foldable head erected." On the open road they discovered the 540K's superb balance and handling, even at higher speeds. "On a fast main-road bend one can hug the kerb at really high speeds in a way which can only be described as comparable to running on rails."

The 540K was unparalleled for its time, with the possible exception of the Model SJ Duesenberg and Hispano-Suiza J12. One European journalist described the 540K as having "aggressive styling and Teutonic arrogance." An astute observation, for that was exactly the image Mercedes-Benz had sought to achieve, not only in the world of production automobiles but in the world of motorsports as well.

Since the early 1930s Daimler-Benz had been dominating European motor racing with the incomparable W 25, W 125, W 154 and W 165 Silver Arrows. Even though the large supercharged Mercedes SSK and SSKL had scored victory after victory, their time seemed to be running out by the early 1930s as the international motor racing authority, AIACR, decided to introduce the new 750 kilogram formula (weight without fuel, oil, coolants, and tires). This weight limit was not to be exceeded. The officials intended to ban the ever

larger, more powerful and heavier cars from the racetracks for safety reasons, since their handling had become difficult especially with regard to brakes and tires. Although not directed specifically at Daimler-Benz, the marque with the most powerful race cars and most consecutive victories, when the new formula came into effect in 1934 it caused a moment of pause for everyone at Mercedes.

By 1934, the world economic crisis that began with the stock market crash in 1929 had severely affected sales of every automaker on both sides of the Atlantic, and money to start a new racing program was scarce. In spite of everything Daimler-Benz developed the W 25, a car soon to become legendary, to meet the formula. The W

The 5-passenger convertible touring car is one of the rare body styles offered in the 500K and 540K series. Taking both model versions together, only 28 examples were built, amounting to less than 4 percent of total 500K and 540K production. One of the distinguishing characteristics of this model is the location of the engine directly behind the front axle with the radiator on level with the front hubs. Most 500K and 540K sports chassis had the engine and radiator positioned further back on the frame.

Special Roadster interiors were lavishly upholstered with instruments typically surrounded by a mother-of-pearl fascia.

The 500K Special Roadster was introduced in 1934 and produced through 1936, after which a more streamlined version of the Sindelfingen body style became the 540K Special (or Spezial) Roadster. This was the sportiest model offered on either chassis.

Double stacked rear spares were standard on the 500K Special Roadster.

of the paint was exactly one kilogram! Thus the Silver Arrows were born in 1934 and von Brauchitsch went on to win the Eifelrennen in record time. A few years later, the German press invented the legendary name "Silver Arrow" for the Mercedes racing cars.

Strong competition from the Auto Union, whose new racecars, designed by Ferdinand Porsche and later nicknamed Silverfish (not quite as elegant as Silver Arrows), prompted the further development of the highly successful W 25. In the course of the years, the eight-cylinder's displacement increased from 4.0 to 4.7 liters, and the engine developed up to 494 horsepower, depending on the type of supercharger and fuel quality.

The 1935 season was extraordinarily successful for Mercedes-Benz. The company team won nine out of 10 races with the W 25 and scored five double victories: Rudolf Caracciola clinched the European and German champions' titles, and the battle with Auto Union for the world speed record attracted worldwide attention.

In the 1936 season, Alfred Neubauer's team found its masters in the company teams of Auto Union and Alfa Romeo in circuit racing. The W 25 only won individual races – it had clearly lost its dominance.

The experience gained with the newly fortified competitors led to a restructuring of the racing department – young Rudolf Uhlenhaut became the new Chief Engineer, and from his analyses of the W 25, the W 125 emerged. The chassis was modified more extensively than was the super-charged eight-cylinder engine. For weight reasons, the idea of a completely new V12 was abandoned again, and so the proven in-line engine was thoroughly revised in terms of displacement, carburetor, and supercharger. The engines now generated up to 646 horsepower from a displacement of almost 5.7 liters. With the

Below: Among the selection of factory body styles produced at Sindelfingen for the 500K chassis was the Special Sport Coupe. The design was first seen in 1935 and later was revised into the rare 540K Special Coupe.

25's eight-cylinder in-line engine with supercharger and four-valve technology developed 314 horsepower from a displacement of just 3.36 liters. Equally progressive was the car's four-wheel independent wheel suspension and hydraulically operated drum brakes.

The legend of the Silver Arrows was created in the W 25's very first race according to the 750 kilogram formula on the Nürburgring. Despite systematic lightweight design and careful attention to every detail, the W 25 tipped the scales at one kilogram above the limit. It was no longer possible to incorporate technical modifications during the night before the race on 3 June 1934. Faced with the certainty that the W 25 would not be able to qualify, driver Manfred von Brauchitsch whispered to racing manager Alfred Neubauer, "You'll just have to think up one of your old tricks, or else sitting here watching the race will be like watching paint dry!" It was that remark which prompted Neubauer to have all of the white paint scraped off of the W 25's body, and the car polished down to its bare aluminum finish. The weight

Aerodynamic styling was the vogue in the early 1930s, and at the 1934 Berlin motor show Mercedes-Benz previewed the 500K Autobahn-Kurier "streamline limousine." By 1935 the company would build a total of four such examples powered by the new 160-horsepower, 5.0 liter supercharged straight eight.

W 125, Mercedes-Benz was again a big step ahead of all other manufacturers in 1937. Rudolf Caracciola re-gained the German championship as well as the European champion's title.

The highlight in this ever so successful year for Mercedes-Benz was, without any doubt, the international Avus race. Hermann Lang, promoted from racing mechanic to company driver, reached an uncontested average speed of 261.7km/h (156mph) in the final heat; the top speed of 380km/h (228mph) in this race was not to be exceeded until 1959!

Ever more powerful and ever faster, in the course of just a few years, the 750 kilogram formula racing cars reached ever new heights – output ratings of more than 650 horsepower and top speeds of over 400km/h (240mph) in record runs called for another scaling down of engine performance. Thus a 3.0 liter formula limited the displacement of supercharged engines to 3.0 liters and that of engines without superchargers to 4.5 liters.

The taper-tailed streamlined design pioneered by the 500K was also used on the six-cylinder, 3.2 liter Type 320 chassis. This striking 1939 example was designated as a streamlined limousine or "Autobahn Courier" and was the largest of the 320 models. The 320 series also consisted of a four-door sedan, six-passenger touring car, a number of cabriolets, and a roadster.

Below: The 320 Series provided more affordable luxury than the much costlier 500K. The sacrifice, however, was not so much in styling as it was performance. The interior of this 1939 Autobahn Courier is quite plush for a mid-priced Mercedes-Benz model, what one might regard as an E-Class today.

Under the streamlined skin of the Type 320 Autobahn Courier was a 3.2 liter inline six, which in 1937 was increased to a swept volume of 3.4 liters (though the name of the car was unchanged) delivering 78-horsepower at 4,000rpm. The 320 engine employed a sleeve valve design with the camshaft in the block and the valves poking upward in "flathead" style. This mandated that the intake and exhaust systems were both on the same side of the head.

A symbol of Germany's dominance both on land and in the air was this special promotional photo taken in 1936 with a 500K Special Roadster and the Graf Zeppelin Hindenburg hovering overhead. The Hindenburg went on to make its first transatlantic flight to the U.S. that year, powered by Daimler Type DB 602 16-cylinder diesel aero engines. A year later disaster would strike when the gigantic dirigible exploded while landing at Lakehurst, New Jersey. To commemorate the 70th anniversary of this historic union, the author created this three-panel art deco print from an original 1936 black and white photograph.

In response, Daimler-Benz again did something quite unexpected – they abandoned the straight eight. While retaining the supercharger, Uhlenhaut and his staff developed the W 154, a car based on the W 125 but powered by a completely new V12 with a cylinder angle of 60 degrees. The new V12 developed 430 horsepower from just 2962cc in its initial form. It is interesting to note that all the new 3-liter cars were faster than the clearly more powerful racing cars entered the previous year!

The first major triumph with the W 154 was accomplished by the Mercedes-Benz team in Tripoli, Libya: Hermann Lang, Manfred von Brauchitsch, and Rudolf Caracciola scored a fantastic triple victory. Against strong competition from Maserati, Alfa Romeo, Bugatti, and Auto Union, Caracciola won the 1938 European champion's title for the Stuttgart-based team. After winning six races, the W 154 was systematically redesigned for the 1939 season. In its further improved chassis, the V12 now developed 480 horsepower. It was another electrifying season with numerous team victories, culminating in three titles: the European champion and German hill-climb champion titles both went to Hermann Lang, and Rudolf Caracciola won the 1939 German road race championship.

The Tripoli Grand Prix, won by Mercedes-Benz in 1935, 1937, and 1938, was to everyone's surprise staged exclusively for 1.5-liter racing cars the following year. Rumor had it that the organizers wanted to give the Italian manufacturers a chance to win; the marked dominance of Auto Union and Daimler-Benz in the 3.0-liter formula races is not unlikely to have played a role. To everyone's dismay, in the unbelievably short time of eight months the Mercedes engineers developed a new 1.5 liter car for this race: the W 165. Its supercharged V8 engine developed a remarkable 254 horsepower. After just a single test a few days before the race, team manager Alfred Neubauer sent Rudolf Caracciola and Hermann Lang out to race against a superior line-up of 28 Italian and British racing cars. Daimler-Benz succeeded in impressively proving its excellence with a splendid double victory. Lang won the race ahead of Caracciola; the third-ranking Alfa Romeo was one lap behind when it crossed the finishing line! The W 165 was not entered in any other races in 1939 because those responsible held the view that it would otherwise devalue the regular 3-liter formula for Grand Prix cars. Daimler-Benz had in effect won every race by proving its vast superiority in just one. It was in the end, however, something of a moot point. On September 1, 1939 Germany invaded Poland and World War II erupted, after which all racing activity was concluded.

Rudolf Caracciola

Rudolf Caracciola was born in the town of Remagen, Germany in 1901, the son of parents who originally came from Italy. He won his first race at age 22. While working as a salesman at the newly formed Daimler-Benz he was permitted to race on weekends if the race was within driving distance of the Dresden agency. After convincing the general manager at Daimler to lend him a factory race-car, he was required to enter the Grand Prix of Germany at Avus under his own name. The then 25-year-old weekend racer started the most important race of his young career and promptly stalled his car! His mechanic Otto Salzer was forced to jump out and push start the lonely Mercedes. At last the car sputtered to life, but starting the Avus from dead last in a 44-car field was not what the young Caracciola had had in mind.

Shortly it began to rain and cars were flying off the track. The 500,000 spectators were to get the shock of their afternoon when it was announced that a new driver, one completely unknown to them, had gone into the lead. But this lead was short lived as the Mercedes began to suffer from serious misfire. In those days the driver had to do any repairs required on the car, so Caracciola pulled into the pits and began pulling out each of the eight spark plugs one by one. It was not until the last plug that he discovered the culprit. By then enough time had elapsed that all seemed lost and he was urged to withdraw, but Caracciola would hear none of this and chose to continue, spurred on by a sense of duty to the factory. By the 13th lap the rain had stopped but Caracciola had no sense of his position and soldiered on, driving flat-out for nearly three hours and 243 miles. Exhausted, he finally crossed the finish line and only then did he learn that he had won the first Grand Prix of Germany.

Caracciola would gain fame throughout Germany racing the legendary white SSK for Mercedes. Renowned for his wet weather prowess, in 1929 he scored one of his greatest victories at the Tourist Trophy in Northern Ireland. Racing against the cream of Great Britain, including Bentley ace Tim Birkin, he came from a five-lap handicap to win the 30-lap race in a rain storm. His record victory for Mercedes in the 1931 Mille Miglia was not equaled by another non-Italian for 24 years, until Mercedes-Benz race driver Stirling Moss won it in 1955.

The starting positions were still selected by drawing lots in the 1935 Spanish Grand Prix and Caracciola found he would have to start from the last row. His style had always been to get to the front as quickly as possible, but this time things would be a little more

One of the greatest race drivers of all time, Rudolf Caracciola is seen here in a more relaxed state of mind with his 1930 Nüburg Cabriolet C.

In the early 1930s Rudolf Caracciola made his name driving the Model SSK and SSKL.

Caracciola and Mercedes-Benz racing team manager Alfred Neubauer in 1934.

Caracciola behind the wheel of a W 25 heading for victory in the 1934 Klausenrennen.

Caracciola in the lead at the 1934 race at Monza.

111

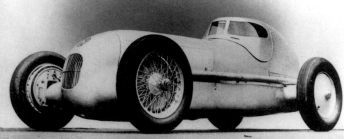

Above: At Monaco in August 1937 Mercedes-Benz team driver Manfred von Brauchitsch leads Caracciola in car No. 8. The team finished 1-2-3 with von Brauchitsch leading the W 125 pack.

April 2, 1939, it's Caracciola leading van Brauchitsch in the Grand Prix of Pau. (Tomasz Szczerbicki Archives)

Pictured right to left at the Grand Prix of Switzerland (August 20, 1939) are Alfred Neubauer, engineer and former race driver Max Sailer, and team drivers Hermann Lang, Rudolf Caracciola, and Manfred von Brauchitsch. (Tomasz Szczerbicki Archives)

Center: Caracciola during a pit stop in the Coppa Acerbo, August 14, 1938. (Tomasz Szczerbicki Archives)

Right: Caracciola drove the W 125 to victory in the 1938 Coppa Acerbo, winning not only the race but his third European driving championship title. (Tomasz Szczerbicki Archives)

difficult. The flag fell and he roared off down to the first corner. Mistaking the pedal arrangement in his Grand Prix car with his touring car, he stepped on the accelerator instead of the brake. The leaders, seeing this maniac charge from way behind could only give way, and in spite of almost crashing in the first corner he took the lead!

The year had been a special one for Caracciola as he returned to racing after suffering serious injuries to his body and his heart. His beloved wife, Charly, had died in an avalanche. Hobbled by injuries, his comeback victory at the Grand Prix of Tripoli had a legendary quality to it. That year he became European Champion. In 1936 he won the Grand Prix de Monaco but the year belonged to Bernd Rosemeyer and the Auto Union. Mercedes roared back in 1937 and Caracciola was again European Champion. In 1938 he won the Coppa Acerbo at Pescara and his third title.

In a career plagued by painful leg injuries and, later ill health, he continued to win many honors. His battles with Bernd Rosemeyer and Auto Union ended in the World Land Speed Record for Caracciola and the tragic death of Rosemeyer. During World War II he lived in exile at his home in Lugano, Switzerland. After the war, his love of racing unabated, he continued in the sport in spite of worsening health brought on by bone disease. He died in 1959 at age 58. According to the legendary Mercedes team manager Alfred Neubauer, with whom he had a long and close friendship, " ... of all the great drivers I have known, Nuvolari, Rosemeyer, Lang, Moss or Fangio, Caracciola was the greatest of them all."

Some 500Ks ordered late in 1935 were delivered with the new 5.4 liter engines thus becoming transitional 540s, such as this Cabriolet A which carries the earlier 500K-style coachwork from Sindelfingen. It was ordered as a 500K Cabriolet A on June 25, 1935 and delivered on July 15 to the Vogel Publishing House with one of the first 5.4 liter engines built. It is estimated to be one of only 13 documented 500K models fitted with the newer engines in 1935-36.

Below: The new 540K chassis was a work of machine art that provided an extraordinary platform upon which to build a custom body. It was comprised of two main frame rails, and was cross braced by one heavy front I-beam, which supported the radiator and independent front suspension mounting; a smaller bolted-in cross member, used to support the rear of the engine and transmission; a large box section cross brace located behind the transmission; and in the rear, two small cross members which served as front and rear supports for the differential. Output from the new 5.4 liter, supercharged straight eight was 115 horsepower, increased to a spirited 180 horsepower with the Roots compressor set in motion. The 540Ks were equipped with a four-speed manual transmission and were capable of better than 100 mph.

By the start of World War II Mercedes-Benz had produced tens of thousands of automobiles, but only 354 of the 500K chassis (from 1934 to 1936) and 406 of the more powerful 540K models – 97 in 1936; 145 in 1937; 95 in 1938; and 69 in 1939. In the overall scheme of things not a great number of automobiles, yet their influence on the automotive world were as though production had been ten times greater. Not surprisingly, the aforementioned production figures are "estimates" at best since it is known that some 380s ordered in 1934 were delivered as 500Ks while others ordered in 1936 as 500Ks, were fitted with the new 5.4-liter engines, thus becoming 540Ks. Further confusion comes from the fact that Mercedes-Benz cars were dated by the year in which the chassis was built. The completed chassis were produced in two wheelbase lengths, 2980mm (117-inch) and 3290mm (129-1/2-inch), and sometimes sat at Untertürkheim for up two years before being fitted with coachwork. A handful of 540K models, mostly sedans with special armor and bulletproof glass, were assembled during 1942 for the "Aktion P" series, built for military use, along with the 770 Grosser Mercedes staff cars and immense 770-based G4 half-tracks.

Aside from a handful of one-off customs, Sindelfingen designed and produced nearly all the coachwork for the 500K and 540K series. The factory created more than a dozen different body types including a Limousine, also called an Innenlenker or Saloon; a formal Pullman-Limousine; the Kombinations-Coupé (a convertible Coupe with optional removable hard top); the Autobahn-Kurier or Stromlinien-Limousine; a Normal-Roadster, sometimes referred to as Sport-Roadster; the Spezial-Roadster, distinguished by its concealed top, metal boot, and divided V

Although just 25 Type 540K Special Roadsters were produced, the influence of the Sindelfingen-designed body was acknowledged on two continents. Today, the 540K Special Roadsters are regarded as one of the 10 greatest automotive designs of all time.

The streamlined rear deck design of the 540K Special Roadster was offered in two versions, one with the spare concealed, and the other with an open recessed spare.

Far right: Seating in the Special Roadster was cozy, either up front or in the rumble seat.

114

Here & bottom left:
Rare among the rare, only three 540K Special Coupes were produced. One might think the styling of a roadster could not be successfully translated into a two-passenger coupe, but the artisans at Sindelfingen created one of, if not the most spectacular of all 540K models in 1937.

Below center & right:
With a sleek, streamlined exterior truly appreciated from the rear, the interior was very cramped for such a large automobile. There was also a small jump seat in the rear but no actual legroom.

Outside of the factory design studio, there were a handful of Karosserie designing coachwork for the 500K and 540K chassis. The most prolific was Erdmann & Rossi-Jos.Neuss in Berlin-Halensee. The Sport Cabriolet was one of their most popular models, a four-passenger car with the exterior styling of a two-seater.

The builder's plate of Erdmann & Rossi-Jos.Neuss of Berlin-Halensee was seen on more than 220 Mercedes models bodied between 1926 and 1939.

Left: Interior styling of the Erdmann & Rossi Sport Cabriolet was different that Sindelfingen styling, as was the seat design. The only styling element left unchanged was the beautiful 540K instrument cluster and mother of pearl fascia.

windshield; Spezial Coupé (hard top version of the Spezial Roadster); Offener Tourenwagen (open tourer or phaeton); and a series of Cabriolet models – A, B, C, D, and E, the latter two being exceptionally rare. The factory also produced one-off special orders. Adding to this little bit of confusing nomenclature, Mercedes-Benz itself often gave the same body style two or even three different names over the years.

A small number of 500K and 540K bare chassis were also delivered to outside coachbuilders, predominantly Erdmann & Rossi, which was responsible for producing several exceptional body designs including the 500K Stromlinien (streamlined) limousine and roadster, and the distinctively-styled Sport Cabriolet. The majority of coachwork produced at the Berlin-Halensee Karosserie was for Mercedes-Benz. More than 220 cars were bodied between 1926 and 1939, most of which were commissioned by the Daimler-Benz factory. A variety of roadster, cabriolet, phaeton, and limousine coachwork was provided for Daimler-Benz, with approximately 21 from the 500K series and from 8 to 12 of the 540K bodies bearing the Erdmann & Rossi-Jos.Neuss emblem on their bodies.

During the 1920s and 1930s Erdmann & Rossi designs lent a sporting air to the Mercedes-Benz chassis, as well as those of Maybach, Bentley, Rolls-Royce, and Horch. With only a few exceptions, such as the 540K Special Roadster, Special Coupe, extremely rare Kombinations-Coupé, and the Autobahn-Kurier, all of which were designed at Sindelfingen, Erdmann & Rossi body styles were vastly more progressive.

Of those produced at Sindelfingen, the Streamline Limousines, or Autobahn-Kurier (Courier) were the most advanced for the era. Daimler-Benz stylists were inspired by the theories of R. Buckminster Fuller and Norman Bel Geddes, visionaries of American streamline forms. In the early 1930s Bel Geddes hypothesized that, "To achieve greater speed, one needed to reduce or eliminate the resistance of the wind. Doing so meant subscribing to one or two schools of thought. You could cut through the air like a rapier with aerodynamics or bludgeon it with sheer horsepower." Until 1933 it had been mostly the latter.

Streamlining created a magical language transcending cultures and national borders. The design influences in Germany were mainly those theorized and put into practice by Professor Wunibald Kamm, director of the Research Institute for Motoring and Vehicle Engines (the F.K.F.S.). Kamm worked with Daimler-Benz on the Type 80 land speed record car, among others. More importantly, he sowed the seed of aerodynamic theory throughout Germany in the 1930s, especially in the mind of Daimler's new technical director in charge of racecar development and testing, Rudolf Uhlenhaut.

Outside of Sindelfingen, the most prominent new styling cues were being penned by Erdmann & Rossi, whose designs featured double frame V windshields, rear-mounted spares, and bold, horizontal hood vents, each accented with a raised chromed spear that served as a handle to open and close the louver. These specific features, either individually or in combination, appeared on Mercedes-Benz chassis

They say that traditions are made to be broken, but seldom does the one establishing the tradition break it. Of course, when the Vanderbilt name enters the picture, anything is possible. This stylish 540K Special Cabriolet C was custom built at Sindelfingen in 1936 for Mr. Wm. A.M. Burden, the great-great-grandson of Cornelius Vanderbilt.

Far right, top & middle: Among the many special-order features was a unique slanted grille with the Mercedes-Benz badge on the top edge and no exposed radiator cap or star emblem. Pontoon fenders were another request.

Here & right: One of the last 540K models built before production was ended by the war, the styling of this Cabriolet A is a bit more modern, and the dashboard is a new design which incorporated a built-in radio.

bodied throughout the 1930s. The most popular Erdmann & Rossi body style was the Sport Cabriolet, of which 18 were built between the 500K and 540K chassis, plus an additional 17 for the smaller, 2.9-liter Mercedes-Benz, and a single example on the original 3.8-liter 380 chassis.

Although it would be difficult to refer to any 540K as anything less than breathtaking in design, some were simply beyond mere words. The 540K Special Coupe and Special Roadster, rarity notwithstanding, were two of the striking, if not the most striking, of all the Sindelfingen designs. Introduced

at the 1936 Berlin Auto Show, which conveniently coincided with the 50th anniversary of the Benz Patent-Motorwagen, the 540K Special Roadster was the most expensive Mercedes-Benz model offered. In all, there were six variations dubbed Special Roadster by Daimler-Benz, beginning with the 1933 Type 380 and progressing through the 500K and 540K, each becoming gradually more sophisticated and streamlined in its styling.

Among the features that exemplified the 540K Special Roadster was the use of chromium embellishments along the length of the fenders, hood, doors, and rear deck. These, and the

Designed by Rudolf Uhlenhaut, Mercedes' new Chief Engineer, the W 125 was an evolution of the older and highly successful W 25, with the chassis modified more extensively than was the super-charged eight-cylinder engine. The engines now generated up to 646 horsepower from a displacement of almost 5.7 liters. With the W 125, Mercedes-Benz was again a big step ahead of all other manufacturers in 1937.

119

Driver Hermann Lang waits behind the wheel as the pit crew changes tires and refuels his W 125 in the 1937 Grand Prix of Germany.

Top right: Mercedes-Benz had a car for every race. Pictured is a 3-liter with supercharger (left) and smaller supercharged 1.5-liter racecar. (Tomasz Szczerbicki Archives)

Bottom right: Unloading cars for the 1938 Grand Prix of Tripoli.

chromed handles for doors, hood, and rumble seat, were all special castings. Another unique feature was the sharply angled vee-windscreen. Spotlights on either side of the frame were also specially made for the cars, each with a convex mirror attached to the back of its housing, serving as the only means for the driver to see alongside or to the rear. The 540K Special Roadster was also the first Mercedes-Benz to offer silver metallic paint, known at Daimler-Benz as "fisch-silver grau," and the first model to enjoy a completely disappearing convertible top, stowed beneath a metal lid. The interior was also atypical, highlighted by the all in the white steering wheel, gearshift knob, emergency brake handle, and reserve fuel knob. Instruments for the 540K had the appearance of a hand-made Swiss timepiece, and were usually surrounded by a mother-of-pearl fascia, adding a final touch of elegance to the car's luxurious interior.

At the other end of the spectrum, both in terms of price and performance, was another model introduced in 1936, the 260D, the world's first diesel production car. Benz had been the first to delve into diesel manufacturing before the merger, and at Daimler-Benz the efforts were redoubled. The 260D was the fruit of that labor. From 1936 to the present day, Mercedes has been the world leader in diesel design, engineering, and production, having built more than three and a half million of those automobiles.

Not every great car with the Mercedes name was expensive. The lower-priced series, such as the 290, was far more important to the company's continued existence than the 500K and 540K. Powered by an inline six-cylinder engine, the 290 was never intended to be as flamboyant as the eight-cylinder supercharged cars, yet they were often fitted with exceptional factory coach-

Von Brauchitsch had the look of a movie star and an incomparable sense of style in front of a camera or behind the wheel of a Mercedes-Benz race-car. He spent almost his entire career with Mercedes. On February 5, 2003 von Brauchitsch passed away at age 97. He was the oldest living race driver in Mercedes-Benz history.

One of Mercedes' greatest and longest-lived drivers was Manfred von Brauchitsch, who earned his stripes with the team in 1929 by winning his first race in a privately owned Mercedes-Benz SS in the international Gaisberg hillclimb race in Austria. He also established a new track record for touring cars at an average speed of 72.6km/h.

work. For the period, the 290 was an evolutionary model, incorporating advanced designs such as a dropped box section frame with four-wheel fully independent suspension, overdrive gearbox, divided track rod steering, hydraulic brakes, and one-shot lubrication.

Most 290 bodies were traditional and rather ordinary, distinguished mainly by the Mercedes-Benz grille and star. The few exceptions were the Streamlined Saloon, roadster, and cabriolets. One book on Mercedes-Benz catalogs 25 different body styles on the 290's 2880mm (113-inch) Kurz chassis and 3300mm (130-inch) long chassis. While nearly all of the 290s built were assembled at the Mannheim factory and bore the Mannheim emblem just forward of the driver's door, a handful of special orders were also bodied at Sindelfingen including a 1935 cabriolet A, 1936 roadster, and certain long wheelbase versions of the 1934-37 B and D cabriolets. Additionally, a short wheelbase 290 sport cabriolet was built in 1934 by Karosserie Papler, and cabriolet D and F long wheelbase models by Erdmann & Rossi, in 1935-

Rudolf Caracciola driving the W 125 in the August 1938 Coppa Acerbo in Pescara, Italy. (Tomasz Szczerbicki Archives)

121

Above: In 1932 von Brauchitsch won the laurels at the Avus race in Berlin.

Below: The author had the opportunity to meet von Brauchitsch in 2000. He was 94 years old at the time and walked into the meeting with the stride of a man half his age. During the brief time we had together he recounted in vivid detail his 1929 victory in the Gaisberg hillclimb that earned him an interview with Mercedes-Benz. He is pictured here in a 1999 photo from the Stars and Cars Show.

37. The average price of a luxury 290 model was exactly half that of a 540K in 1937.

The total of 290s built between 1933 and 1937 was 8,214, still hardly mass production. In comparison, Mercedes-Benz turned out more than 39,000 of the popular and affordable little 170 and 170V models during the same period.

If one were willing to overlook the fact that the car's best effort in top gear barely exceeded 100 km/h (60 mph), or that it took better than 30 seconds to get there, and if one had the marks equivalent to $1,250 U.S., a Mercedes-Benz could be purchased. At that price a much greater market existed for the cars bearing a silver star atop their grilles. These were Mercedes' bread-and-butter models. A total of 10 catalogued body styles for the 170 series were offered from 1931 through 1942, with production totaling nearly 100,000 units before the war ended all commercial automobile manufacturing.

The original series was introduced in 1931 in response to the stumbling European economy that had arrived on the threadbare coattails of the 1929 stock market crash, a financial calamity that had not only humbled the American economy and denied Europe one of its most lucrative export markets, but spread across the Continent like a bad cold.

Although designed to be a conservative car, the 170 nonetheless blazed some technological trails, offering features not available from any other European car company. The base price model came with a responsive 1.7-liter, six-cylinder engine, four-wheel fully independent suspension, central lubrication, four-wheel hydraulic brakes, pressed steel wheels, and an anti-theft steering wheel lock. While any one of these features might have been found on competitive makes, no other European car of the day offered all of them at anything like the price of a Mercedes-Benz 170.

Originally there were only three body styles available: a four-door sedan, cabriolet A, and the more spacious cabriolet B. A roadster was added in 1932 and a two-door phaeton in 1934. Although they sold well, the first 170 models were not regarded as having true Mercedes-Benz "style," so in 1936 the design department gave the cars a new, more daring look with the model 170V. Now even the most affordable Mercedes was a tony-looking automobile.

To improve structural design and ride quality, a new tubular backbone frame replaced the original box-section chassis. The 170V was also noticeably longer than its predecessor, riding on a 2,845mm (113.8 inch) wheelbase versus the original's 2,600mm (104 inch) platform. The greatest change, however, lay beneath the hood, where a more efficient four-cylinder engine replaced the original six-cylinder motor. While that might sound like a step

Racing was one thing, speed records were something else altogether and Mercedes-Benz wanted its place in the record books during the late 1930s. In 1936 Rudolf Caracciola drove the V12 GP chassis fitted with a full envelope body, recording the fastest speeds then known for an automobile, 226.4mph for the kilometer and 228.0 for the mile Class B record.

Professor Wunibald Kamm worked with Daimler-Benz and Ferdinand Porsche on the Type 80 land speed record car. The unusual design by Porsche, working as a consultant in 1938, resulted in this six-wheel, 44.7-liter, 12-cylinder streamliner that looked like a Manta Ray with wheels. The car was designed for a speed record attempt at the Bonneville Salt Flats in Utah but it never made the trip. Today the body hangs on the wall of the Mercedes-Benz Museum.

backwards, the 170V displaced 1,697cc, with a bore and stroke of 73.5 x 100mm and output of 38 horsepower at 3,400rpm, whereas the old six with a 1,692cc displacement and 65 x 85mm bore and stroke had produced only 32 horsepower. Top speed was improved as well, to a maximum of 108km/h (67mph). A new transmission completed the mechanical revisions, with a four-speed manual replacing the old three-gang gearing.

The most attractive new 170V bodies were the cabriolet A and roadster. Both were two-seat designs, although the roadster allowed a second couple to squeeze together in a narrow rumble seat. The cabriolet had the traditional fabric stack and folded landau irons when the top was lowered, whereas the new roadster featured a cleverly designed top that collapsed backward and then swiveled down behind the seats. The completely concealed top allowed the driver an unobstructed rear view and lent new sophistication to the affordable little two-seater's profile.

More than a high water mark for Mercedes-Benz, the 170V would also provide the foundation for Mercedes' revival after WWII. The 170V sedan was the first postwar Mercedes, basically a 1942 model reintroduced in 1947. Regrettably, nothing remotely

In 1938 this W 125, modified with a streamlined body, was driven by Caracciola along a closed stretch of the Autobahn between Halle and Dresden. He recorded a flying kilometer record speed of 432.692km/h (259.6mph) and flying mile speed of 432.360 (259.4mph). (Tomasz Szczerbicki Archives and Daimler-Benz Archives)

Introduced in 1936, the 260D was the world's first diesel production automobile. Benz had been the first to delve into diesel manufacturing before the 1926 merger, and at Daimler-Benz the efforts were redoubled. From 1936 to the present day, Mercedes has been the world leader in diesel design, engineering, and production.

like the sporty 170V rumble seat roadster would reappear until the 1950s.

At the same time traditional models like the 170V, 230, 260D, 290, and 370 Mannheim were being produced, Daimler-Benz turned its attention toward an even lower-priced line, with the innovative rear-engine Type 130, 150H and later 170H, a car which by no small coincidence would foreshadow another soon to be popularized German model, the Volkswagen.

Initially, the VW's designer, Ferdinand Porsche, had built two prototype versions of the car, a two-door coupe and a convertible coupe. In December 1934, Porsche was given approval to build a trio of test cars by the German Automobile Manufacturers' Association (RDA), which was to oversee the new car's development. The Porsche test cars had four-wheel independent suspensions with spring torsion bars in the front axle tubes and, at the rear, a floating axle with a longitudinal control arm on each side and transverse spring torsion bars in the axle tube. They utilized a central tubular frame, with the engine mounted behind, and the four-speed gearbox in front of the rear axle. These same features would become the underpinning of the Porsche 356 after World War II.

The project appeared to be going well but the Porsche prototypes were not roadworthy within the 10-month terms of the initial agreement. The RDA accused Porsche GmbH of breach of contract, declaring that the VW would be built as a common effort among its members, which included Daimler-Benz. In July 1935 D-B

Not every model with a silver star was expensive. The lower-priced series, such as this 290, was far more important to the company's continued existence than the 500K and 540K. Powered by an inline six-cylinder engine, the 290 was never intended to be as flamboyant as the eight-cylinder supercharged cars, yet they were often fitted with exceptional factory coachwork. A full line of body styles were available for the 290

The Type 230 was introduced in 1936 and produced through 1939. Powered by an inline six, output was a modest 55 horsepower. The Cabriolet A, pictured, was the sportiest model in the line, which included a Cabriolet D, open touring, and Pullman-Landaulet.

The Type 320 was another lower-priced model offered with stylish coachwork. This is a convertible coupe, which was also available, as shown, with a removable hardtop – an idea that would be reprised after the war on the 300 SL roadsters and on SL models for more than a quarter of a century.

If one were willing to overlook the fact that the car's best effort in top gear barely exceeded 60 mph or that it took better than 30 seconds to get there, for the German equivalent of $1,250 one could purchase a Mercedes-Benz 170 beginning in 1931. These were Mercedes' bread-and-butter models.

undertook the responsibility for designing an experimental body, while other automakers attended to engineering calculations. Porsche GmbH was still involved but the RDA had essentially put Porsche's work up for grabs. Daimler-Benz finally built 30 pre-production VW prototypes in the spring of 1937, one year after the debut of the Mercedes-Benz Type 170H, thus preempting the Porsche design. The unmistakable similarity between the last rear-engine model to be produced by Daimler-Benz and that of the Volkswagen left little doubt that Ferdinand Porsche was facing strong opposition not only from the RDA but his former employers as well.

As Europe began to spin irreversibly toward another war, the greatest era in Mercedes-Benz history was coming to a close. In the aftermath of six war-torn years it would take more than a decade for Mercedes-Benz to rebuild its factories and its image as a leader in automotive design and engineering. Many German automakers would not survive at all, becoming the economic casualties of a war that would very nearly claim Mercedes-Benz among them.

In 1934 Daimler-Benz introduced two new cars with their engines mounted in the rear. The Type 130 and Type 150 (pictured), a sports car version of the 130 with the engine actually mounted in front of the rear axle, rather than over it as on the 130. Unfortunately, the styling did not appeal to buyers and the car was discontinued in 1936.

In 1936 the design department gave the 170 a new, more daring look with the model 170V. Now even the most affordable Mercedes was a tony-looking automobile, especially the sporty Cabriolet A. Powered by a four-cylinder engine delivering 38 horsepower, the 170V could attain a top speed of 65 mph.

170 V Cabrio A

Too close for coincidence, the Mercedes-Benz 170H was built at the same time the company was assisting in the development of the Volkswagen. The 170H utilized Porsche-designed underpinnings and a rear-mounted four-cylinder engine, and was introduced by Mercedes in 1936, a year before the VW prototypes were completed.

The Pope's Mercedes

The First Daimler-Benz For Vatican City

In July 1930, a custom-made version of the Nürburg 460 was handed over to Pope Pius XI. It was the first "Popemobile" from Mercedes-Benz, thereby establishing a long-standing tradition of providing the Holy Father with cars. Pius XI, the Roman supreme pontiff from 1922 until 1939, personally took delivery of the Nürburg in the Vatican. Being one of just a few of its kind, this car has the Pullman bodywork of the 770 Grand Mercedes, with adequate power being generated by a 4.6-liter eight-cylinder engine. From the rear seat, wishes concerning destination or speed can be relayed to the chauffeur by means of a light signal system. The car was restored by Mercedes-Benz in the early 1980s and handed back in 1984 to the late Pope John Paul II who set out on a trial run straightaway.

The restored 1930 Mercedes as it appears today.

Below: In 1930, a single throne-chair in the rear of the Pullman limousine was created for the Holy Father.

Return to the Vatican: In 1984 Pope John Paul II received the lavishly restored Mercedes-Benz Nürburg.

Left: The 460 Nürburg in Rome, c.1930.

Above left: The Holy Father and his Mercedes: In 1930 Pope Pius XI took personal delivery his Mercedes-Benz Nürburg 460. This Nürburg 460 was the first "Popemobile" from Mercedes-Benz, thereby establishing a long-standing tradition of providing the Holy Father with cars.

The G4 shown is owned by the Spanish royal family and is one of just a few surviving units of this three-axle model produced by Daimler-Benz during World War II. Today just three of a total 57 G4s built in the 1930s are considered absolutely authentic. Additional units exist, but with ambiguous proof of their originality.

A Call To Arms

Daimler-Benz in Peace and War

War is an ugly word. Certainly no nation goes to war without conviction – that of being on the right side of an injustice and of winning at all costs. This belief is as old as the human race, but World War II somehow defied those ancient tenets. Outside of the inner circles of Hitler's Third Reich, many German citizens and even members of the military did not believe that der Füher was justified in his invasion of Poland in 1939, or the unspeakable atrocities that would transpire during the course of the war against dissidents, prisoners, and in particular those of the Jewish faith, which included many managers at Daimler-Benz, Porsche, Auto Union, BMW, and other German industrial firms.

In the book *Mercedes in Peace and War*, written by Bernard P. Bellon in 1990, it becomes all too painfully clear that the Nazis insinuated themselves throughout the highest levels of Daimler-Benz management, particularly through Jakob Werlin (the "house Nazi" as historian Beverly Rae Kimes dubbed him). As an advisor to Hitler his power at Daimler-Benz was irrefutable. Those managers who failed to comply, or had differing opinions with the Third Reich, such as Daimler-Benz supervisory board member and Deutsche Bank director Hermann Köhler, were arrested, tried, convicted, and executed. Others, who had Jewish relatives or wives, were forced out of the company, if they were lucky. Similar events were taking place at BMW, which was second only to Mercedes-Benz in the German war effort, and at the Porsche werke in Zuffenhausen.

On April 25, 1931 Ferdinand Porsche had opened the doors to his new firm on the outskirts of Stuttgart with Porsche, his son-in-law Dr. Anton Piëch, and former Mercedes-Benz race driver Adolf Rosenberger all equal partners. By the late 1930s, however, the sinister and immoral undertone to Hitler's plans for a new Germany had convinced Rosenberger to quit Porsche and leave the country. He was Jew-

The interior of the G4 resembled the 770 Grosser passenger cars.

Left: Before the G4 joined the royal fleet, it was used by General Franco who had been given this car as a present from the German government. During the past decades, the G4 was serviced and maintained by the Royal Guard in Madrid. The latter hold the classics in the royal fleet in high esteem. When it was decided to have the G4 restored by the Mercedes-Benz Classic Center, the car was given an almost ceremonial farewell in Madrid, and an armed escort accompanied the truck convoy to the French border. It arrived at the Center in Fellbach near Stuttgart in September 2001. The work on the G4 was completed in December 2004, as a present by Mercedes-Benz España to the Spanish royal family.

ish and quite understandably saw no future for himself in Germany under the new political system. But by the time Porsche and Piëch found an investor to buy out Rosenberger's interests so that he would have some money with which to leave Germany, it was too late – he had already been arrested and imprisoned by the Nazis. Feeling a deep responsibility to his friend and partner, Ferdinand Porsche used his influence to appeal for his release. Hitler complied. Once out of prison Rosenberger immigrated to America where he spent the rest of his life.

Franz Josef Popp, chairman of BMW, was forced to resign under threat of internment in a concentration camp. The Nazis put their own man in charge. In point of fact, neither Daimler-Benz, BMW, nor Porsche really had control over events, and this is something most people need to be reminded of more than half a century later. Many company officials and managers, knowing full well what had happened to Köhler, felt compelled to cooperate, as this was the only way to live through the nightmare that Hitler had created.

Wilhelm Kissel, who had led Mercedes-Benz since the 1926 merger, went so far as to join the National Socialist party in an effort to keep his company as free as possible from Nazi influence, but Werlin usurped his power at Daimler-Benz, and after the loss of his son in December 1941, a grieving and distraught Wilhelm Kissel died of a heart attack on July 18, 1942. The German war machine moved on and Kissel was replaced by his colleague Wilhelm Haspel, whose cooperation was ensured by Werlin's guarantee of protection for Haspel's wife, who was Jewish.

As Kimes pointed out in *The Star and the Laurel,* "What happened at Daimler-Benz was on one hand relatively simple and on the other unbelievably complicated and ironic. Daimler-Benz products were as much a part of the German war effort as GM, Ford and Chrysler products were of the American or Rolls-Royce aircraft engines were of the British."

The Mercedes-Benz 770 "Grand Mercedes" was built through 1942. When the imposing car pictured was introduced at the Berlin Motor Show in 1938, there was no need to worry about its image – this had already been established by its predecessor. The technical highlights of this car, newly developed from the ground up, included an oval tubular frame, independent wheel suspension with coil springs at the front, a De Dion axle at the rear, and a newly developed five-speed synchronized transmission. The car was powered by a supercharged eight-cylinder engine which now developed 230 horsepower. Many similar models were used as military staff cars during the war.

Above: A top-flight prestige passenger car powered by a 7.7-liter, eight-cylinder in-line engine, the Type 770 developed 200 horsepower with the compressor engaged and could attain a top speed of 160km/h (95mph). Measuring nearly 19 feet overall, and weighing up to 3-1/2 tons depending on the range of appointments installed, the 770 was the largest, heaviest, and most expensive vehicle from the Mercedes-Benz product range. As a touring car, Pullman sedan, and in several Cabriolet versions, such as the example shown, the 770 was destined to challenge Karl Maybach's V12 Zeppelin in the upper luxury car sector.

This striking 770 Pullman Saloon was built in 1935 for the Imperial Family of Japan.

Postwar Resurrection

Rising from the Ashes

When the menacing chorus of tanks, planes, and machine guns at last fell silent on May 8, 1945, the most powerful automotive manufacturer in Germany laid bare and broken. Later in the year when Daimler-Benz managers were permitted to return to the sites under authority of the Allied Occupation Forces, they found what was best described by one official as the total devastation of their company. Mercedes-Benz would have to be resurrected, quite literally from its own ashes – some still warm to the touch.

In 1946 the Americans Occupation Forces, which were responsible for Stuttgart-Untertürkheim and Zuffenhausen (the home of Porsche), permitted Mercedes-Benz employees to return to work at Untertürkheim and begin reconstruction of the automotive assembly lines. Initially work was confined to the repair of existing cars and limited manufacturing of the Type 170V, the only model for which tooling had remained mostly undamaged. Within a year more than 6,000 of the prewar 170V models had been assembled, and within five years from the day employees returned to the bombed out ruins of their company, Daimler-Benz had its assembly lines and factories rebuilt.

Having resurrected itself in 1952, Germany's premier automaker would again leave the automotive world utterly amazed, and at a time when something amazing was least expected.

The country had been divided into two, the new West German Federal Republic, and East Germany, which had been under the control of the Soviets since the end of the war. Fortunately for Daimler-Benz they were in the west. The same could not be said for BMW, which had lost all of its major East German manufacturing facilities in Eisenach. It would take years before BMW was able to rebuild itself.

The first models produced at Untertürkheim in 1947 had been, for all intents and purposes, 1942 models, but by 1948 the rebuilt assembly lines were producing cars equipped with either a four-cylinder gasoline engine or a new 1.7 liter, pushrod ohv diesel, developing 38 horsepower at 3200rpm. Since fuel was still in short supply, the tidy little 170 diesels were an immediate success. An improved 170Da was introduced in May 1950 with production running through April 1952. The 170Da was slightly more powerful, having a larger displacement of 1.77 liters and an output of 40 horsepower. The 170Da was followed by a further improved Db model with a wider track, hypoid rear axle, a slightly revised hoodline, and a larger windshield. This version was continued until October 1953. The final series, beginning with the 170DS, was built concurrently with the 170Da and 170Db, from January 1952 until August 1953. The very last version, the 170S-D, was produced from July 1953 until September 1955, when the entire 170 series was retired, as were the old prewar body styles.

If there was one feature distinguishing American cars built in the early 1950s from those produced in Germany during the same period, it was styling. Designers in America were experimenting with new ideas, trying to break away from the prewar look which had seemingly been held in a state

The most remarkable sports car of the early postwar era, the Mercedes-Benz 300 SL Gullwing Coupe, was produced from 1954 through 1957 and sold almost exclusively in the United States through New York importer Max Hoffman. Of the 1,400 coupes produced, Hoffman sold nearly 1,000.

The postwar reconstruction of Daimler-Benz was built, quite literally, on the back of the 170V, about the only car for which tooling remained intact. The first postwar production cars, such as the example pictured, were introduced in 1947. They were essentially carried-over 1942 models. However, within two years the rebuilt assembly lines were producing 170 models equipped with either a four-cylinder gasoline engine or a new 1.7-liter diesel.

of suspended animation until the early 1950s. Throughout much of Europe, and Germany in particular, the battlefield had extended right up to the front door of the world's oldest and most established automakers, leaving them little choice but to pick up the pieces of a broken industry and start from scratch; but unlike American stylists who tossed everything out the window and started over after the war, European designers began with a clean sheet of paper that still had tracing lines put down in the late 1930s. The result was a brief generation of cars whose styling aesthetically integrated the classic bodylines of the 1930s with the contemporary look of the 1950s. At Mercedes, these were to become some of the greatest automobiles of the postwar era, and among the most coveted by today's collectors.

Dr. Wilhelm Haspel, who had returned as company director in January 1948, had instructed body engineer Karl Wilfert and his staff to ensure that the traditional, upright Mercedes radiator motif remain an integral part of the all-new range of cars being planned for the early 1950s. In an era when traditions were being cast aside, that decision was crucial and has not since been violated. A Mercedes-Benz is still unmistakably a Mercedes-Benz more than half a century later.

In the early postwar years Daimler-Benz, like all German automakers, and Germany for that matter, was under the watchful eye of a mistrusting

New car design was impossible in the late 1940s, but there were a few improvements made in the early postwar 170V series including the 170Vb and 170Da, Db, 170DS, and 170S-D diesels. The 170V series remained in production until 1953. Pictured is a completely restored 1952 Model 170Da powered by the postwar 4-cylinder diesel engine which developed a modest 40 horsepower. It is rare to see a 170 diesel model so flawlessly returned to its postwar originality. (Walter and Theresa Worsch collection)

world. Mercedes-Benz still bore the stain of the Third Reich which was being perpetuated by war-time photographs of Hitler and his generals with Mercedes automobiles. It would have taken years for Mercedes-Benz to disassociate itself with those unpleasant images but then something miraculous happened. In 1952 Mercedes-Benz built a sports car that so totally captured the imagination of automotive enthusiasts the world over, that all Mercedes had come to stand for in the 1930s was reclaimed almost overnight. It was perhaps the most remarkable automobile ever built by Daimler-Benz. It was the 300 SL.

In 1952 Mercedes-Benz had decided to go racing again, and it needed a new car, not a Grand Prix car, at least not yet, but rather a sports car to run at Le Mans. Upon returning to work for Daimler-Benz after World War II, Rudolf Uhlenhaut was appointed chief of the experimental department. As the head of research and development, he was also responsible for the

factory's new postwar racing program along with his prewar colleague, Alfred Neubauer, who resumed direction of the works' race team in 1951.

Uhlenhaut was facing a difficult challenge in his new position, that of repeating what he had done for Daimler-Benz in the 1930s with the W 125, only this time he had little more than production car engines and spare parts at his disposal, and a budget allocated by management for competition cars well below Neubauer's vision of a factory racing effort.

Having watched Jaguars dominate the French 24-hour day-into-night marathon at Le Mans in 1951, Uhlenhaut and Daimler-Benz Technical Director Fritz Nallinger reasoned that they could do essentially the same with Mercedes-Benz 300s that William Lyons had done with the XK-120 Jaguars. Raid the parts bin! The championship Jaguar XK120C had been little more than an aerodynamic body covering a slightly mod-

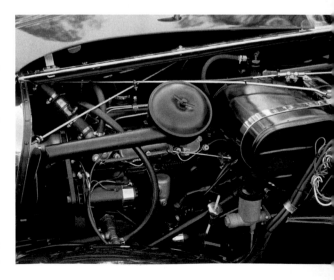

The Webasto top was designed to fold over itself allowing fresh air and sunshine to pour over both front and rear seat passengers. Similar sun-roof designs date back to the 1920s and 1930s, both in Europe and America. Mercedes-Benz offered it as well on the 170Sb, but few cars had a folding sunroof on as grand a scale as the 300c.

Below: In 1951 the 300 S models added an air of luxury and sporty style that hadn't been seen since the prewar 540K models. The sporti-est of the new postwar coupes and cabriolets, the model would be fur-ther improved with the fuel-injected 300Sc vari-ant. This is an early fac-tory photo of the 300 S Cabriolet, a model which became eminently popu-lar in the United States.

form to follow function. Entry would literally be "through the roof," using large panels hinged at the top, that could be lifted straight up allowing driver and co-driver to step into the car and over the wide sill. The raised doors would later be described by the automotive press as looking like the wings of a gull.

At Daimler-Benz men with vision had always been the company's greatest asset (and sometimes lia-bility), but with Alfred Neubauer, Fritz Nallinger, Karl Wilfert, and Rudolf Uhlenhaut, Mercedes had an unparalleled team who would bring the company into the postwar era and restore honor to the legend of the Silver Arrows.

The son of a German bank director and an English mother, Rudolf Uhlenhaut was born July 15, 1906. Edu-cated in Great Britain and Germany, he earned a degree in mechanical engineering in 1931 from the Munich Technical Institute and began his 41-year career with Daimler-Benz that same year, as a passenger car test engineer.

His easy-going manner and reputation for finding creative solutions to engineering problems helped him to advance within five years to the position of Technical Director in charge of race car construction and testing. At the time of his appointment in 1936, the once triumphant W 25 race cars were getting long in the tooth and being trounced so badly that the company actually withdrawn from several events toward the end of the season. He was only 30 years old when management gave him a daunting task: turn the situ-ation around. To everyone's amazement, he did it in less than a year. By 1937 Mercedes-Benz had returned

At the same time Mercedes was enticing buyers with sporty cabriolets and coupes, the luxurious 300 sedans were gaining a reputation as the car of choice for foreign embassy use as well as a place among the wealthy as the "high-status" German motorcar. Somewhere in between was the 300 b convertible, a well-styled blend of both extremes.

Below: In 1951, faced with the seemingly impossible task of returning Mercedes-Benz to racing prominence, Rudolph Uhlenhaut and his engineering and design staff created the 300 SL in just one year, and virtually dominated European sports car racing in 1952.

to the competition forefront with Uhlenhaut's redo of the W 25 – the W 125 Grand Prix car.

In 1937, the W 125s won the Tripoli, German, Monaco, Swiss, Italian, and Masaryk Grands Prix. Uhlenhaut and his team later guaranteed Daimler-Benz dominance of Grand Prix racing for the rest of the decade, with the W 154 and W 163 GP cars.

It was during this period that Uhlenhaut developed his driving skills to the extent that he could easily have become a champion race driver himself. By 1939 he was as fast as anyone on the team, if not faster, and would often investigate complaints about a race car being down on speed by taking it out and analyzing its performance from behind the wheel. He was often admonished by his superiors for these actions, not just for test-driving race cars, but for doing so at speeds that rivaled the factory's top drivers. Uhlenhaut was far too valuable to Daimler-Benz as an engineer and designer to be put at risk in competition, which makes one wonder exactly what they thought of their drivers. Nevertheless, Uhlenhaut's abilities behind the wheel allowed him to develop cars not only from an engineer's perspective but from that of a race driver's as well.

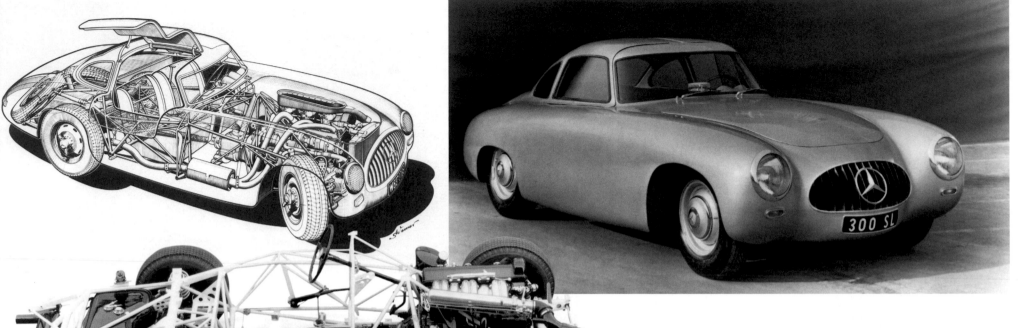

The 300 SL sprang almost full born in 1951 from the imaginations of Rudolph Uhlenhaut, Fritz Nallinger, and Karl Wifert. Using essentially off-the-shelf parts, they created a tubular space frame to support the engine and suspension, taken from the production 300 models. A year later the 300 SL racecars virtually dominated the European racing scene.

Above left & right: The tubular space frame for the 300 SL was designed to support the six-cylinder engine which had to be mounted at a 40 degree angle in order to clear the swept-back line of the hood. The SL body was a perfect match for the tubular spaceframe. Slipping through the air, the 300 SL carried no superfluous cargo, no chrome-plated bumpers, door handles, or outside rear-view mirrors, nothing that might increase wind resistance.

As a starting point, Uhlenhaut and his team started with the new 300 sedan, which compared to an XK-120 Jaguar was admittedly a big, cumbersome car, but it had the engine Mercedes needed, a 2996cc inline six with a compression ratio of 6.4:1 and an output of 115 horsepower at 4600rpm. Rugged and simple, the engine was built for sturdiness and long life, and reliability was the name of the game in endurance racing. Although Uhlenhaut would make extensive modifications, the final version used in the 300 SL closely relied on the original 300 Series passenger car engine. Not surprisingly, Neubauer objected to its use. He wanted more horsepower and less weight. He also objected to the standard transmission of the 300, complained about the quality of the brakes, and criticized the diameter of the tires. All of his arguments were just, and as the racecar progressed Uhlenhaut and Nallinger addressed each of them as Neubauer played Devil's advocate to their every decision.

In the end, they extracted 170 horsepower from the 300 series engine without increasing its displacement, but the 300 SL's real success would rely as much on engineering as horsepower. In addition to the engine, the racecar would require a lightweight frame and a streamlined body like the Jaguar's in order to become a winner. Uhlenhaut and Nallinger already had the weight problem solved with the birdcage-like spaceframe, and Wilfert was applying his experience in aerodynamics to a sleek, streamlined body. All that remained was to fit the pieces together like some elaborate erector set.

In building the 300 SL, numerous parts and components were taken directly from the 300 sedan's parts bin. For the front axle, the only modifications required were holes drilled in the upper spring and shock supports for weight reduction. The gearbox and long-arm shifter were taken from the sedan without significant modification. Another feature was the regular cast iron gearbox. Uhlenhaut simply added an oil pump and modified the gear profiles in order to cope with the higher torque.

One area where the sedan's design had little influence was the 300 SL's track. Uhlenhaut hypothesized that while a narrow track would help reduce frontal area, the rear axle would require a wide track to counter the significant weakness of the swing axle design and the propensity when cornered smartly to swap ends. Uhlenhaut and his drivers knew that a wider rear track was the only way to reduce the undesirable changes in rear wheel camber. The final result was a narrow front and wide rear track, 1340mm (52.76 inches) front, 1445mm (56.89 inches) rear. The first few cars built were fitted with five stud disc wheels, which were replaced as soon as possible by light alloy rims using a central locking knock-off hub and 6.70 x 15 tires. The choice of tire dimensions had also been a concession. While Neubauer

had insisted on 16-inch tires which offered the advantage of lower operating temperatures, the final decision was to stick with the 15-inch tires from the sedan. This offered twin advantages of lower unsprung weight and a tiny reduction of the swing axle's nasty habits.

The next hurdle was the engine. Uhlenhaut's revised inline six was too tall for the profile of the hood. The solution was to tilt the engine 40 degrees to the left thus moving the crankshaft to the right of the car's centerline. [1] As a result of this change the car became lower and its center of mass was now almost exactly in the center. Another advantage was that this gave the driver more legroom, albeit at the co-driver's expense. The final result ensured that the six-cylinder engine could devote more horsepower to speed and less to overcoming aerodynamic drag.

Wilfert's sleek, rounded contours for the SL body were a perfect match for the tubular spaceframe. Slipping through the air, the 300 SL carried no superfluous cargo, no chrome-plated bumpers, door handles, or outside rearview mirrors, nothing that might increase wind resistance. The wind tunnel revealed a drag coefficient of 0.25, a figure that auto manufacturers still find challenging in the 21st century.

[1] *As noted by Daimler-Benz archives on the specifications for the 1951 prototype coupe.*

Mercedes finished 1-2-3 at the Grand Prix of Berne, and at the Nürburgring, with the cars converted to roadsters, the team crossed the finish line in order, first through fourth.

Below left: Having been virtually unbeatable in Europe, Mercedes took on the Mexican desert in the 1952 Carrera Panamericana. The team finished 1-2.

Mercedes-Benz raced the 300 SL coupes (and later roadsters) for only one season, in which they finished first and second in all but their inaugural race, the Mille Miglia, where they finished second, just four minutes behind Giovani Bracco driving a new Ferrari. From then on, the Mercedes-Benz team never saw the exhaust of another car across the finish line. They finished 1-2-3 at the Grand Prix of Berne, 1-2 at Le Mans, and at the Nürburgring, the team crossed the finish line in order, first through fourth. Having been virtually unbeatable in Europe, the Mercedes team concluded the 1952 season on the other side of the Atlantic, competing in a grueling Mexican road race known as the Carrera Panamericana.

The cars were untried in the desert and the team was fraught with bizarre problems from the start. On the first leg from Tuxtla Gutiérrez to Oaxaca, a buzzard crashed through the windshield of Karl Kling's 300 SL and landed in his co-driver's lap, yet the Mercedes-Benz team (with one car disqualified) managed a remarkable 1-2 finish, moving through the desert at such a speed that racing manager Alfred Neubauer's chartered DC 3 spotter plane could barely keep up.

From the very beginning the subject of producing the 300 SL as a road car had been considered. With a little added persuasion from U.S. importer Max Hoffman, the board gave Uhlenhaut and his design staff approval to turn the championship racecar into a production sports car.

The change from race car to road car demanded numerous revisions to the engine and fragile lightweight body, yet the fraternal relationship between the 300 SLs which had swept the 1952 racing calendar and those that would dazzle sports car cognoscenti was unmistakable. The

On the first leg of the Carrera, from Tuxtla Gutiérrez to Oaxaca, a buzzard crashed through the windshield of Karl Kling's 300 SL and landed in co-driver Hans Klenk's lap!

production 300 SL was also suitable for competition and was accepted by the FIA in the Grand Turismo Class. Production cars were entered in almost every major sports car race on both sides of the Atlantic, scoring victories in the Mille Miglia, Liège-Rome-Liège, Alpine, and Tulip rallies in 1955. In 1956, Prince Metternich finished sixth in the rain-soaked Mille Miglia, the team of Shock and Moll won the Acropolis and Sestrière rallies, Stirling Moss finished second in the Tour de France, and Willy Mairesse won the '56 Liège-Rome-Liège contest.

Karl Wilfert and his colleague Paul Braiq had done a remarkable job of turning a racecar into a civilized, road-going sports car. Underneath, however, the road car was little changed from the racecar. Driver and passenger still had to clamber over the wide, elbow-high door sill (always a test of one's grace), baggage was restricted to what could be packed behind the seats or folded into the optional leather luggage, and in general, unless one had the skills of Stirling Moss, driving the 300 SL at high speed was a daunting task.

Hans Klenk (left) and driver Karl Kling wait to get underway after their car has been repaired and fitted with a "buzzard guard" over the windshield.

In these spectacular studio shots taken almost 50 years later, two of the 1952 Carrera Panamericana cars look like they are ready to take on the Mexican road race again. The Karl Kling car even had its "buzzard guard" restored.

The dashboards of 1952 racecars were nothing like the 1952 production cars. This was all business. Note the long neck gear shift taken directly from the 300 series passenger car parts bin.

What was more amazing than the fact Mercedes-Benz had actually put the 300 SL into production was its world introduction on February 6, 1954 at the International Motor Sports Show in New York City. This was an unprecedented break with tradition, the first time the company had ever introduced a new model in the United States before its debut in Germany. And while New York in the throes of winter might have seemed an unlikely venue to unveil a sports car, this was the home of Max Hoffman, the man who almost single-handedly established the German automotive market in the United States after World War II.

With an elegant Frank Lloyd Wright-designed showroom situated in the heart of New York City, the Austro-American entrepreneur had been responsible for bringing Porsche, Jaguar, and Alfa Romeo to the United States in the early 1950s. Having seen the 300 SL racecars in 1952, he was convinced that a road-going version would sell in the United States as quickly as Mercedes could build them. And he was correct. Of the 1,400 coupes produced through 1957, Hoffman sold 1,100.

In the late 1950s he queried Mercedes-Benz regarding the production of a second 300 SL model, a roadster similar to the smaller 190 SL that had been introduced alongside the coupe in 1954. Hoffman, who had convinced Mercedes-Benz to build the production versions in the first place, now believed a 300 SL roadster would be better suited to the tastes of American drivers. He noted that owners, particularly women, often found the cockpit of the Gullwing less than inviting with its high door sill. Then there was the lack of good ventilation, especially during the summer months when a roll-down window would have been a godsend. The production 300 SL coupe was a magnificent sports car but it wasn't necessarily a comfortable one.

Unbeknownst to Hoffman, or anyone outside Rudolf Uhlenhaut's design studio in Stuttgart, a roadster version of the 300 SL had been on the drawing boards since 1954, thus in 1957 the Gullwing was replaced by the new roadster.

While there has always been great speculation surrounding the Gullwing's demise, it was the opinion of Heinz Hoppe – the Daimler-Benz executive who established Mercedes-Benz of North America – that the decision was in part a reaction to comments made to Daimler-Benz management by Hoffman about the coupe.

Every victory in 1952 was cause for celebration at Mercedes. One of the ways of celebrating was with beautifully illustrated racing posters.

The 300 SL racecars were withdrawn from competition after the 1952 season. By 1953 work was under way for a production version. A prototype is shown here looking somewhere between racecar and road car.

"A vast majority of the cars went to the States, and Hoffman told us time and again that his pampered customers wanted a bit more comfort, a larger boot, and a bit more fresh air," recalled Hoppe. "In addition, we didn't know how long customers, who can be pretty choosy in this price range, would accept a car so similar to the racing version with all its compromises. That's why we started considering a roadster offering that extra creature comfort American customers like so much."

Whether or not Hoffman prompted the decision, in 1957 the last 70 Gullwings were delivered and by year's end 618 roadsters had already come off the assembly line. It was the first time that a convertible had taken the place of a coupe, rather than becoming a second model offering.

As a convertible, most of the problems associated with the Gullwing were assuaged – ventilation, headroom, and ease of entry being the most obvious – while an improved rear suspension for the roadsters made the car more manageable. The Gullwing had used a conventional swing-axle with two pivot-points outboard of the differential and as previously noted if driven on trailing throttle through a tight curve, the camber change tended to lift the inside rear wheel and induce sudden oversteer. To correct this, the roadsters were fitted with a new swing axle design utilizing a single low pivot point, thereby improving the car's cornering behavior and predictability. A horizontal compensating spring included with the new axle also gave them a somewhat gentler ride. Improvements in the engine compartment, including a standard-equipment sports camshaft, increasing output of the fuel-injected straight six to 235 horsepower, made the roadster not only a better-handling car than its gull-winged predecessor but a faster one, despite a 200-pound weight penalty.

Introduced in March 1957 at the Geneva Motor Show, Daimler-Benz proudly stated that the "...300 SL Roadster is our response to the demand in many countries for a particularly fast, comfortable, open sports car. This automobile offers a wide range of technical achievements for even greater driving safety and motoring comfort as well as a high standard of practical everyday value for touring in real style." Had the car been introduced in the United States one might have though Max Hoffman wrote the press release.

The story of the roadster's development is closely tied to that of the four 300 SL competition cars converted to roadsters for the 1952 Nürburgring. They led to the development of the SLS prototype, built from one of the four Nürburgring cars, chassis 00009/52. It was refitted with a 300 SL fuel-injected motor in 1953 as a test mule and in 1955 used again as the platform upon which the production 300

Above: From the very beginning the subject of producing the 300 SL as a road car had been considered. With a little added persuasion from U.S. importer Max Hoffman (pictured), the board gave Uhlenhaut and his design staff approval to turn the championship racecar into a production sports car.

With a maximum of 215 horsepower (240 horsepower with the sports camshaft) from an improved straight six equipped with direct fuel injection, the production 300 SL Gullwing coupes could easily top 150mph, making them the fastest production sports cars available at the time.

153

SL roadster was prototyped and tested. Thus both the production coupe and roadster models evolved from competition cars.

In August 1956, photojournalist David Douglas Duncan wrote an article for *Collier's* magazine about "The Secret SLS" which was published in the October 12, 1956 issue. Today, automotive journalists would call that a long-lead preview, an article timed to go into print just as the car is released for sale. In 1956 it had very much the same effect, and by the time the roadsters were ready to be introduced in 1957 there was already a demand for the new Mercedes model.

Converting the coupe into a roadster was a far more difficult task than simply cutting away the roof and adding conventional doors. Nothing about the 300 SL coupe or roadster was conventional. To ensure the integrity of the chassis after removing the roof and modifying the frame to accommodate the doors, Uhlenhaut and his engineering team used larger diameter and much heavier gauge tubing in order to provide the necessary strength. The SL frame remained virtually as it was on the coupe from the firewall forward, and the cross member above the rear axle also remained at the same height; however, from the firewall back the frame became much lower and more compact in order to provide space for the doors and the larger luggage compartment. This accounted for much of the roadster's 200 pound weight increase.

Inside, the instrument and dashboard design was all new and

Karl Wilfert and his colleague Paul Braiq did a remarkable job of turning a racecar into a civilized, road-going sports car. Underneath, however, the road car was little changed from the racecar. Driver and passenger still had to clamber over the wide, elbow-high door sill.

the handbrake was repositioned to the driver's right. The interior dimensions were otherwise quite similar to the coupe, but with a lot more headroom!

Though not seen as often in competition as the Gullwing, the roadster was the more comfortable and practical of the two 300 SL models. With the addition of Dunlop disc brakes in March 1961, and an optional removable hardtop, the roadster reached its pinnacle – the final evolution of the cars that had come from the parts bin, and the imaginations of Rudolf Uhlenhaut, Fritz Nallinger, and Karl Wilfert.

Produced through 1963, a total of 1,858 roadsters were built. And as predicted by Max Hoffman, most were sold in the United States.

The Gullwing evolved, at least mechanically, from the first all-new postwar passenger cars; the earliest to incorporate entirely new styling, with a more stream-lined, envelope-type body incorporating the head-lamps into the front fenders. The Type 300 was also the first Mercedes designed with the American market

in mind, a market 20 million deep, and clamoring for anything new.

Coachwork for the Type 300 series was produced at the rebuilt Daimler-Benz factory in Sindelfingen and was first available in two body styles, a slim-pillar four-door sedan and a pillarless four-door convertible. The 300 series looked modern, yet quintessentially Mercedes. In Europe the popularity of the 300 grew rapidly and in the new Germany it became the high-status motorcar of the 1950s, the choice of foreign embassies, dignitar-ies, and heads of state. In Germany it was often referred to as the "Adenaur-Wagen" after West German Chancel-lor Konrad Adenauer, one of many prominent political figures who chose the 300 for personal transportation.

Known in Germany as a Limousine 4 Türen, the 300's design concept was ultra-conservative, an attempt, and a quite successful one, to produce a prestige Ger-man motorcar that would garner the same esteem as a Rolls-Royce. Retired Daimler-Benz design direc-tor Bruno Sacco, who was responsible for many of the

Mercedes-Benz staged the world introduc-tion for the 300 SL on February 6, 1954 at the International Motor Sports Show in New York City. This was an unprece-dented break with tra-dition, the first time the company had ever introduced a new model in the United States before it debuted in Germany.

The 300 SL had been accepted by the FIA for international competition in the Grand Turismo Class. The presence of 300 SLs at motorsports events across the U.S. and throughout Europe in 1955 and '56 focused as much attention on Mercedes as had the factory's racing efforts in 1952. A total of 29 alloy-bodied cars were built for competition, like this example from Ralph Lauren's collection.

Below: The powerful M 198 fuel-injected, six-cylinder engine used in the 300 SL was as much a work of art as the body surrounding it. It delivered 240 horsepower at 5800rpm when equipped with the sports camshaft.

exemplary S-Class models of the 1980s and 1990s, noted that "When you consider that this car concept was continually being improved and rolled off the assembly lines in Sindelfingen until 1962, you will conclude that the clientele was happy with it."

In its overall design the Type 300 was a tremendously impressive car, particularly the four-door convertible sedan. In America the 300 Series was virtually in a class by itself, with the exception of the latest Rolls-Royce models. Even Cadillac, the unrivaled American standard of luxury, could not compare with the Mercedes 300.

One of the longest running models in the company's history, the 300 line had an 11-year production life. The first series sedan was built from late 1951 through March 1954, with regular production of the four-door convertible beginning in April 1952. The original 300s were succeeded

by the 300b, externally unchanged, but delivering 10 more horsepower and equipped with larger brakes. Although popular, production figures were never high, approximately 6,200 sedans and a negligible 591 convertibles in both series through the summer of 1955. The 300c was introduced in September 1955 and produced through June 1956, and here Daimler-Benz built 1,430 sedans and 51 convertibles. The last in the series, the 300d, were assembled on a longer 124-inch wheelbase, versus the original 120-inch span. The body was updated with a flatter, more squared-up roofline, longer rear fenders, and a slightly wider grille. And, in keeping with contemporary styling, the d-series sedan lost its fixed center pillars to become a true four-door hardtop. Mechanical fuel injection from the 300Sc was also adopted, along with a higher compression ratio, increasing output to 160 horsepower. Offered from late 1957 through

This is literally the very last 300 SL ever built. It was completed in 1996! The car was constructed from factory parts that had never been assembled. It sat, in pieces, from the time all of the components were shipped to original owner, Bob Doehler, a senior stylist at Studebaker-Packard, until being assembled by noted restorer Scott Grundfor in 1996.

The 300 SL Roadster was a long time coming but there was little doubt that a demand existed. This had first been proven in 1954 when the 190 SL Roadster (pictured) made its debut.

The sporty, four-cylinder 190 SL was a terrific little car that has, historically, lived in the shadow of the 300 SL. Even so, Mercedes-Benz delivered more than 25,000 between 1954 and the early 1960s, a significantly greater number than achieved by either the 300 SL coupe or roadster.

early 1962, nearly 3,100 hardtops and 65 convertibles were produced.

The 300's success in the home market was matched by its popularity and celebrity in America and throughout Europe. Owners included legendary American architect Frank Lloyd Wright, and film stars Gary Cooper, Bing Crosby, and Yul Brynner. The 300 also became the state car for Ethiopian ruler Haile Selassie, India's Jawaharlal Nehru, the Shah of Iran, and King Gustav of Sweden. Even British military hero Field Marshal Montgomery, who had seen more than his fair share of Mercedes-Benz vehicles during World War II, was taken in by the 300. You might call that the ultimate example of a conquest sale.

Although total production figures may not have been remarkable, 11,430 examples built over an 11-year span, the real value was in reestablishing the luxury image Mercedes-Benz had created in the 1930s. The 300 Series accomplished this feat in a manner unparalleled by any automobile produced in the last half century.

With the sportier Type 300S and Sc models Mercedes reawakened emotions in automotive enthusiasts that had lied dormant since the 540K first stirred their souls. The new cars were a perfect marriage of hand crafted old world coachwork, classically inspired styling, and an impressively contemporary chassis, suspension and driveline. While the rest

Available with a removable hardtop, the 190 SL established a styling cue that would be picked up by the 300 SL Roadster mid-way through its production run.

Left: Small in size, but big enough to make the 190 SL an honest sports car in the minds of American buyers who were making comparisons with the 1954 Corvette and XK120 Jaguar. The four-cylinder engine used in the 190 SL delivered a robust 105 horsepower at 5700prm.

The 300 SL Roadster began life in 1956 as an experimental factory test mule known as the SLS, a racing version of the 300 SL produced for competition in SCCA. The car shown was then used as the basis for the production SL Roadster introduced in 1957.

of the automotive world was rushing as quickly into the future as possible, Mercedes-Benz had paused just long enough in the 1950s to give prewar classic elegance one last hurrah.

After two years, the 300S was updated to the 300Sb with the addition of finned brake drums, vent windows, improved heating, and a Becker Mexico in place of a Becker Nürburg radio. The 300Sc, which was introduced late in 1955 as a 1956 model, brought about sweeping changes, proof that Daimler-Benz was continually improving its cars, even if they were only going to build 200 of them. The 3.0-liter, six-cylinder ohc engine was now fuel-injected like the 300 SL and displayed the boldly lettered Einspritzmotor legend impressed across the rear bumper. The new Sc engine used a Bosch injection pump in place of the three Solex 40 PBIC downdraft carburetors in the 300S. With a compression ratio increased from 7.8:1 to 8.55:1, the Sc developed 175 horsepower at 5400rpm, bettering the S by 25 horsepower from the same 182.7 cubic inch displacement. Power was dispensed via a fully synchronized four-speed manual transmission, with either a standard column or sportier floor-mounted shifter available. Rear axle ratios

A page from the 1957 300 SL Roadster sales brochure proclaimed the heritage and success of the 300 SL series.

Top left: To ensure chassis integrity after removing the roof and modifying the frame to accommodate doors, larger diameter and heavier gauge tubing was used to provide the necessary strength. The SL frame otherwise remained as it was on the coupe from the firewall forward. From the firewall back it became much lower and more compact in order to provide space for the doors and the larger luggage compartment.

Here & bottom left: The production 300 SL Roadster was an immediate success, not so much because of its predecessor but because it was a better, more practical, and more appealing sports car. The cars were now being sold in the United States by Studebaker-Packard.

159

Top left & right: Inside, the instrument cluster and dashboard design was all new with vertical gauges, and the handbrake was repositioned to the driver's right. The interior dimensions were otherwise quite similar to the coupe, but with a lot more headroom!

Luggage was again offered for the 300 SL; however, for the roadster it was designed to fit the contours of the trunk. It was elegant, functional, and with enough capacity to really get away for a vacation, not just a weekend.

changed with the introduction of the Sc to a lower 4.44:1 from the previous 4.125:1, and the addition of fuel-injection also increased torque from 170 ft.-lb. to 188 ft.-lb. Mercedes-Benz sales literature for the 1956 models later claimed 200 horsepower for the Sc engine and a top speed of 112mph. Despite a curb weight of nearly 2-1/2 tons (4,450 pounds) a 300Sc could still clock 0 to 60 in 14 seconds.

Comfort and performance were also given greater consideration in the Sc, which introduced a new and more responsive independent rear suspension design, utilizing the same single, low-pivot point rear swing axle with coil springs that would be adopted the following year for the 300 SL roadsters.

Aside from the engine changes and the use of larger brake drums to scrub off speed, the 300S and Sc shared the same specifications of design and were available in similar models: cabriolet, coupe, and roadster. All three had a wheelbase of 114.2 inches, an overall length of 185 inches, and a front and rear track measuring 58.2 and 60.0 inches, respectively.

Interior appointments were done in a fashion commensurate with the luxurious prewar cars, with plush, roll-and-pleat leather upholstery and fine wood veneers in a choice of burlwood or straight-grain walnut lacquered to a glass-like finish. And there was never a problem fitting your suitcases into the car's steeply angled trunk. Every 300S and Sc came with its own custom leather luggage set designed to stack in the trunk.

For the 1950s, the 300Sc offered features precious few automakers even had on their drawing boards: four wheel fully independent suspension and ventilated bi-metal vacuum-assisted brakes along with a number of safety and convenience features such as backup lights, turn signals, non-glare mirrors, and windshield washers. Inside, there were reclining seats, a signal-seeking radio, and appointments that today are seen on only the most expensive, handcrafted automobiles like Jaguar, Maybach, and Rolls-Royce.

Virtually hand built to order, the S and Sc were more expensive than other Mercedes-Benz models, the Sc demanding over $12,500 – nearly twice that of the sporty

The removable hardtop gave the 300 SL Roadster all-season practicality. The design was first seen on the 190 SL.

300 SL and more than almost any automobile sold in America. Among the rarest of Stuttgart's early postwar cars, only 760 were built between 1952 and 1958. Of the limited production 300Sc, produced from September 1955 to April 1958, there were 98 coupes, 53 roadsters, and 49 cabriolets.

While the 300S and Sc might have been the Mercedes flagship and the 300 SL the sports car icon of the era, at the forefront of Daimler-Benz models was the lower-priced, though no less distinguished, 220 S and 220 SE. The 220 S (S for Super) came along in 1956 as the third of three new models making their debut at the Frankfurt Auto Show. Along with the new 190 and 219, the 220 S, the most powerful and expensive of the trio, represented Mercedes' new contemporary look, and bid farewell to the vestigial fender lines of the classic 1930s and 1940s. The new styling was integrated, fenders and body sides forming one surface, seasoned perhaps with just a hint of classic lineage in the rear quarter panel treatment.

The new 220 S four-door sedans, compared to most other prewar and mid 1950s American cars, were quite subdued in appearance. Similar to the lower-priced 190 and 219 models, they formed the center of a model line topped by the 300 SL and the last of the luxurious 300Sc series. For the first time in nearly two decades Daimler-Benz was able to offer a full range of models.

The 220 S had forsaken the old concept of a separate body and frame, using the body as an integral part of the chassis, popularly known today as unit-body or uni-

With the addition of Dunlop disc brakes in March 1961, and an optional removable hardtop, the 300 SL Roadster reached its pinnacle. The example pictured was one of last cars built, and is fitted with the optional luggage rack and extra third luggage case. Aspen anyone?

The 300 Sc appeared late in 1955 as a '56 model. Equipped with the fuel-injected 3.0-liter, six-cylinder ohc engine, the Sc delivered 175 horsepower at 5400rpm, bettering the S by 25 horsepower from the same 182.7 cubic inch displacement. The Sc model's lower-priced companion was the 220 SE (left). Among the first of Mercedes' contemporarily styled postwar models, it was equipped with a fuel-injected 2.2 liter six delivering 130 horsepower.

The 300 Sc was the last classically inspired design to come from Sindelfingen. The interior was plush and covered in fine hand-sewn leather, Wilton wool carpeting, and hand polished burlwood veneers. The trunk was fitted with leather luggage and dual spares. (Jerry J. Moore collection; photos by Dennis Adler)

The design of the new 220 S and SE clearly departed from all past styling cues traditional to Daimler-Benz, save for the upright grille and three-pointed star hood ornament. The interior was just as sumptuous as its predecessor, but all new in every detail.

Models like this 1959 220 SE led the way into the 1960s with two-tone color combinations, luxurious interior, and a potent fuel-injected six-cylinder engine. (Dave Stitzer collection; photos by Dennis Adler)

of manifold injection, rather than port injection, allowed high-pressure fuel to be infused through a calibrated jet placed upstream of the manifold and cylinder head junction. The new fuel-injected six produced 130 horsepower, increased torque by five percent over the S, and fuel efficiency by eight percent.

With the introduction of the new 220 Sb, known today as the "Finback" sedans, Mercedes discontinued the round-body 220 SE sedans, but the sportier and more luxurious 220 SE coupe and convertible remained in production, overlapping that of the 220 SE b through November 1960. Production of the 220 SE b coupes began in February 1961, and 220 SE b convertible production commenced seven months later.

The first full decade of the postwar era had seen Mercedes-Benz return to prominence in the design and manufacturing of luxury cars, diesel cars and trucks, and the production of sports and racing cars, a feat hardly anyone but Mercedes-Benz would have thought possible. This was proof beyond doubt that the Silver Star was back.

The 220 S sedan was the successor to the 220 a, from which it was distinctively differentiated by trim and greater performance from the 2195 cc, six-cylinder engine. The cars originally developed 100 horsepower, which was increased to 106 horsepower in August 1957. (Color from Frank Barrett collection; photo by Dennis Adler)

Here & left: One step down in price and performance was the entry-level Mercedes-Benz 190 with an 84-horsepower engine. In 1959 Mercedes race drivers Karl Kling and Rainer Günzler piloted a 190 D to victory in the Africa Rally from Algiers to Cape Town, thus proving to buyers that even the lower-priced Mercedes could win a race.

Bread and butter and oil. The fuel-efficient Mercedes-Benz 180 D diesel was described by the factory as "thrifty." This sedate-looking sedan was offered from 1959 to 1961 and replaced by the 180 c and then 180 Dc from 1961-1962.

Only the names remain the same. In 1959 Mercedes-Benz closed out the first full decade of the postwar era with the introduction of the Type 220 S b, more popularly known today as the "Finback" Mercedes. The new design was built from 1959 through 1965 and powered by a fuel-injected six delivering 110 horsepower.

Predicting a look
that would appear
on Mercedes-Benz
models in the 1960s,
Italian designer Sergio
Pininfarina, known
for his historic work
with Ferrari, bodied a
pair of Mercedes, one
in 1955 and a second
1956, a 300 B Coupé
and 300 Sc Coupé,
respectively.

Triumph and Tragedy

By the time Daimler-Benz withdrew the 300 SLs from racing at the end of their victorious 1952 season, the factory had already set its sights on a new series of racecars for 1954. It was a forgone conclusion that the new models could not be developed in time for the 1953 season, and since Daimler-Benz had nothing more to prove with the 300 SL, a one season hiatus from racing seemed an appropriate course. In the wake of the groundbreaking 300 SL Gullwing coupes and roadsters came the 1954 W 196 Formula 1 monoposto (with exposed front wheels) and its derivatives, the W 196 streamliners and 300 SLR roadsters.

The new 2.5 liter Formula 1 cars raced for the first time at Reims-Gueux in the 1954 French Grand Prix. Considerably different from the straight six that had powered the 300 SL, the M196 engine used in the monoposto was a 2496cc straight eight with Bosch direct fuel injection. The M196 was designed with a central crankshaft drive providing a power takeoff from the center of the engine (four cylinders in front, four behind). This design significantly reduced torsional vibration and

A world championship racecar needs a world-class car hauler, and in 1954 the Mercedes-Benz team had a doozie!

In the wake of the groundbreaking 1952 300 SL coupes and roadsters came the 1954 W 196 Formula 1 monoposto (with exposed front wheels) and its derivatives, the W 196 streamliners and 300 SLR roadsters. A monoposto is pictured on the starting grid of the 1954 GP at Bern. The legendary Juan Manuel Fangio is pictured behind the wheel of a monoposto on the way to clinching his first of two back-to-back world championship titles with Mercedes.

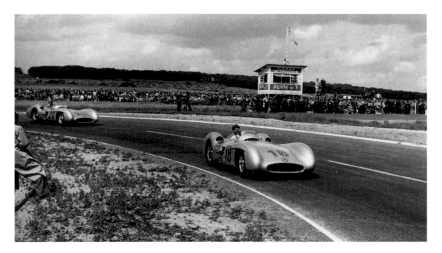

placed the strain of only four cylinders upon the crankshaft. The output was originally 257 brake horsepower at 8250rpm, later increased to 280 brake horsepower at 8700rpm with a maximum torque of 182 lb-ft at 6300 revs.

In all, 10 of the W 196 Grand Prix cars were built, divided between the 1,433 pound monoposto and the 1,544 pound Reims-type streamliners with sleek, aerodynamic bodies. Five of these cars are in the Daimler-Benz Museum today, and one each in the Turin Car Museum in Italy, the Beaulieu Car Museum in England, the Indianapolis Motor Speedway Museum in Indiana, and the Technical Museum in Vienna. The 10th car was destroyed in an accident on the factory test track in 1959.

In the 1954 and 1955 seasons, the W 196 models won a total of 11 out of 14 races, with Juan Manuel Fangio collecting two world championships along the way.

The 300 SLR sport version arrived in the spring of 1955 and utilized the same platform as the W 196, but with the engine enlarged in displacement to 3.0 liters. The SLR roadsters were built specifically to compete in the 1955 World Championship of Makes, and in order to conform to Fédération Internationale de l'Automobile (FIA) specifications for sports cars, the W 196 chassis was fitted with a body similar in design to the 300 SL roadsters first seen in 1952 competition.

The 300 SLR's technical features remained virtually unchanged from the monoposto and streamliner; however, since engine size in the World Championship of Makes was limited to 3.0 liters, the capacity of each cylinder was increased from 312 to 374cc, changing the overall swept volume from 2496cc to 2992cc. The engine block was also modified for the SLR. The W 196 power unit had been welded together out of steel plate, while the SLR engine used two "silumin" aluminum-alloy and magnesium blocks of four cylinders each, and a desmodromic valvetrain (valves both opened and closed by camshafts). Maximum engine speed was reduced to 7600 rpm and the compression was 12.0:1. The power takeoff was again from the center of the engine, rather than having an output shaft exiting at the rear. The idea as before was to trim length from what would otherwise be a very long engine configuration. Power went

It was one of Mercedes' greatest triumphs, the 1955 victory by Sterling Moss and Denis Jenkinson in the Mille Miglia. Here they are seen at the start in car 722, which was their exact starting time, 7:22 AM.

through the front-mounted clutch to a rear-mounted five-speed transmission. To keep the hood as low as possible, the straight-eight engine was mounted at a 33-degree angle. However, in so doing the driveshaft had to run from the clutch at an angle under the driver's seat. As a result, the driver had to straddle the driveshaft tunnel, operating the clutch pedal on the left, the accelerator and brakes on the right! Output was 310 horsepower at 7,500rpm, with 230 lb.-ft. of peak torque at 5,950rpm. This remarkable powerplant weighed only 520 pounds.

Depending upon the race, engine output was varied from 276 brake horsepower at Le Mans, to 302 brake horsepower in the Swedish Grand Prix and was reported to be as high as 345 brake horsepower, an almost unbelievable rating of nearly 2-horsepower per cubic inch. (Cubic inch displacement for the W 196 S engine was 181.9).

The 300 SLR's space frame chassis, derived from the 300 SL, was light yet strong. Suspension was independent all around, using torsion bar springs, and the car rode on 16-inch wire-spoke wheels.

In 1955 Mercedes-Benz engineers considered disc brakes an unproven technology and so they equipped the 300 SLRs with hydraulic-assisted drum brakes. These proved effective in the Mille Miglia but by race's end, the pads and much of the aluminum brake shoes had worn away!

The original plan for the SLR had been to build Gullwing-door bodies (like the 300 SL) for the W 196 S chassis ("S" denoting sport version), but the drivers who were selected by racing manager Alfred Neubauer for the team showed a preference for open cockpit cars, this according to journalist Denis Jenkinson, who co-drove the 1955 Mille Miglia with Stirling Moss. Wrote Jenkinson: "It would have been difficult to find a more successful sports/racing car and certainly one so advanced technically." And he should have known. Born in rural England, "Jenks" was actually an engineer by trade, but he started writing for British motorsports magazines such as *Motor Sport* and *Autosport* in 1946. His greatest claim to fame, however, would be his partnering with Moss in the 1955 Mille Miglia. The 300 SLR driven to victory by Moss and Jenkinson in the classic Italian road race set a course record that would never be broken. As Moss's navigator, Jenkinson had mapped the entire Brescia-Rome-Brescia circuit, recording the details on an 18-foot roll of paper secured in a roller device similar to a scroll. The duo had rated all of the difficult corners, grading them as "saucy," "dodgy" and "very dangerous," each type denoted by a distinct hand signal from Jenkinson. Moss's car carried number 722, for 7:22 A.M., the time it launched from Brescia on May 2, 1955. That Moss could attain speeds in excess of 170 mph in his 300 SLR spoke to the trust he had placed in his naviga-

tor. The team won this challenging and dangerous race in just 10 hours, 7 minutes, and 48 seconds for an average speed of 97.96 mph – nearly 10 mph faster than the previous course record.

The Mille Miglia was run from 1926 through 1957. The 1954-1957 races followed a route over public roads through the center of Italy, from Brescia in the north to Rome in the south and back along a different route. The 300 SLR was both brutally fast and astonishingly tough on the 1,000 mile course. The Mercedes-Benz team of three cars took first, second, and fourth places in 1955 and each at some point had gone off the road and been damaged during the race – a tribute to the car's toughness. The no-holds-barred event was discontinued after some horrific accidents, but the Mille Miglia lives on today – in slow motion – as an annual road rally for classic cars produced from 1926 through 1957. In order to qualify at least one model of a particular car must have participated in one of the 24 original road races. Mercedes-Benz is one of the event's current sponsors.

The 300 SLR body was made from a tough yet malleable form of sheet magnesium – which was lighter than aluminum. Race weight, including the driver and navigator, two spare wheels, and fuel, was 3,067 pounds. In conjunction with the aerodynamic bodywork, the 3.0 liter engine was capable of propelling the SLR to a top speed in excess of 185mph, superbly countered when necessary by the car's massive inboard brakes and innovative hydraulic airbrake, a refinement of the experimental design tested at Le Mans in 1952.

The airbrake was one of the SLR's most remarkable features. With a surface area of 7.5 square feet, the light-alloy wing had a significant braking effect as well as enhancing the car's cornering ability. The idea for this "wind brake" came from Neubauer, who was looking to develop a system to reduce the wear on conventional brakes and tires during long-distance races such as Le Mans and Reims. He wanted to use wind resistance to slow the car, in particular at Le Mans, as the French track forced drivers to use the brakes hard and often to bring the car down from its maximum speed to as little as 25mph. The SLR's airbrake measured the width of the rear cowl and also contained the driver's head fairing. When deployed, the downward load it imposed was arranged to pass through the center of gravity of the car and provide additional braking.

The two hydraulic arms that raised the airbrake were energized by a pump driven off the gearbox. A lever operated by the driver opened a valve elevating the flap. The original idea was to assist the wheel brakes at the end of the long Mulsanne Straight at Le Mans, where hard braking from 180mph was needed. At the end of the straight the Mulsanne cor-

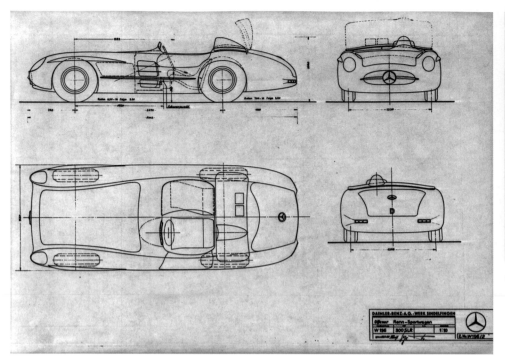

The eight-cylinder engine in the 300 SLR developed 300 horsepower.

ner was taken in second gear and a linkage was fitted to the gear lever mechanism so that when second was selected by the driver the airbrake was automatically lowered. However, driver Stirling Moss discovered he could use the airbrake for most corners and further reduce wear on the wheel brakes. He also became aware that he cornered better at some points by putting the airbrake only half way up, thus increasing the load on the tires! As a result, the SLRs were modified so that the airbrake could be operated completely by the driver. Moss, who had one of the best seasons ever behind the wheel of an SLR, said of the airbrake, "It feels as if a giant hand had reached down and grabbed the car by the rear end."

In something of a reverse-engineered concept, after the initial 300 SLR roadster were started, Uhlenhaut decided to build a pair of 300 SLR Gullwing Coupes. Better known to car enthusiasts as the Uhlenhaut Coupes, they first appeared on the road in 1955. Incorporating the design of the 300 SL Gullwing with the technology of the 300 SLR, the coupe's long hood was complemented by side-mounted exhaust pipes, dramatic air vents, and wire-spoke wheels. The cockpit, with its wraparound windshield, was elegantly sculptured and Uhlenhaut referred to his latest automotive work of art as a "hot-heeled touring car." The 300 SLR coupes lived up to their billing.

Uhlenhaut first appeared in his "company car" at the Swedish Formula 1 circuit, providing a fascinating side-show to the race itself. As much of a racecar as the SLR roadsters, Uhlenhaut's coupe recorded a speed of 180mph during a test conducted by *Automobil Revue* magazine at four o'clock in the morning on a closed section of motorway outside Munich. "We are driving a car which barely takes a second to overtake the rest of the traffic and for which 120mph on a quiet motorway is little more than walking pace. With its unflappable handling through corners, it treats the laws of centrifugal force with apparent disdain," scribbled the lucky test reporter after a total of more than 2,000 miles. His only regret was that this was a sports car "which we will never be able to buy and which the average driver would never buy anyway."

Like the 300 SL racecars in 1952, the 300 SLRs were virtually unbeatable in 1955. Entering seven races in the '55 season, they crossed the finish line victorious in all but one. The single loss came at Le Mans in what is still regarded as the most tragic racing accident in motorsports history.

In 1955 Mercedes-Benz and Jaguar were considered the two top competitors at Le Mans and both were counting on their latest cars to win the race. In terms of power and speed, the improved D-Type Jaguar and new 300 SLR Mercedes were equally matched. It was the skill of the drivers and that intangible element of luck that would determine the

The distinctive Mercedes-Benz car haulers arrived at the racetracks with their charges in full display – almost as intimidating as chief engineer Rudolph Uhlenhaut's arrival in his 300 SLR Coupé. In 1959 he took over as the head of passenger-car development at Mercedes-Benz and continued to define the technology and character of the brand's cars until his retirement in 1972. He died on May 8, 1989, just short of his 83rd birthday.

outcome. Mercedes had pinned its hopes on Juan Manuel Fangio, while Jaguar had Mike Hawthorne. In 1955, however, there was a change in the rules and for the first time different classes of cars were competing together. Fangio and Hawthorne were in the fastest group, and as they battled it out, they had to pass less powerful cars, which laid the foundation for a disaster. At 6:30 in the evening, as the light was just beginning to fade, Hawthorne was approaching the pits when he overtook one of the slower cars, an Austin-Healey driven by Lance Macklin. As Hawthorne passed, Pierre Levegh, driving another 300 SLR, came up right behind him. Macklin later recalled, "Hawthorne passed and then pulled across in front of me. To my amazement, his brake lights came on and I swerved to avoid him." This all took place in an instant. Macklin had unknowingly cut Levegh off just as he was accelerating and the Mercedes slammed into the rear of the Austin-Healey. Macklin said he could feel the heat of the SLR's exhaust as the car spun around, careening off the rear of the small roadster and into the barrier wall. The car burst into flames on impact and Levegh was killed instantly, but that wasn't the worst of it; burning parts of the 300 SLR were flung into the crowd, taking the lives of 82 spectators. It was the worst accident in the

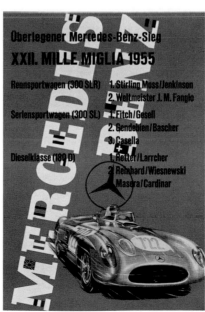

Posters were quickly designed to celebrate the 300 SLR's victories in 1955.

The Stirling Moss 300 SLR as it is today, fully restored and part of the Mercedes-Benz Classic Center collection. Sir Stirling is seen driving the car during an exhibition in the late 1990s.

history of motor racing.

When word of the tragedy reached Fritz Nallinger in Untertürkheim he wired back to Neubauer at Le Mans, "The pride of designers and drivers must now bow to the grief suffered by countless French families in this appalling disaster." Although they were leading, Neubauer called in the remaining two cars and retired them from the race, Hawthorne going on to win a sad and hollow victory for Jaguar.

In October 1955, shortly after Stirling

Car No. 722 and one of the two Uhlenhaut 300 SLR Coupés now fully restored and on exhibit at the Mercedes-Benz Museum.

The interior of one 300 SLR Coupé is red gabardine and leather, the other is done in blue. Uhlenhaut drove both.

The airbrake was one of the 300 SLR's most fascinating features. It is shown in use here at the 1955 Swedish Grand Prix by Fangio and fully extended in a static display. The full width of the body, the air brake also included the driver's head fairing.

Sir Stirling Moss today, photographed by the author in 2005, and as he appeared prior to his record-setting dash around Italy in 1955. It seems half a century has done nothing to dim that beaming Moss smile.

Moss/Peter Collins and Juan Manuel Fangio/Karl Kling had completed a one-two victory in the season-ending Targa Florio, the Daimler-Benz board of management stunned the racing world when it announced Mercedes-Benz would withdraw from motor racing. Word had also come that the Mexican government had cancelled the 1956 Carrera Panamericana for safety reasons, and the shock of the Le Mans tragedy of June 11, 1955 was still very keenly felt in Germany and France. A period of reflection away from motorsports appeared to be the best move at the time. Had Mercedes-Benz not chosen to withdraw its cars at Le Mans they would have won, and 1955 would have been a perfect season. No season marked by such sadness, however, could ever have been perfect. In 1955, nobody could have imagined that it would be decades before Mercedes would make a return to the track.

The lightning-fast SLR coupe never made it into series production. Mercedes felt that the mid-1950s was not the right time to bring out such a powerful sports car and the SLR coupe project was put on ice, but not forever. The all-new Mercedes McLaren SLR supercar is nothing short of a modern realization of Rudolf Uhlenhaut's legendary 300 SLR coupes. He would have liked that.

Mercedes-Benz in America

America in the postwar era was an incredible place to be. Soldiers were returning home, industry was booming, and Americans were car starved. To quell those pangs of automotive hunger, beginning in 1947 Max Hoffman dished up some of the finest imported cars built in Europe. Initially he sold French Delahayes, Italian Lancias, and a handful of British makes, including the stunning new Jaguar XK120, one of his personal favorites. By the early 1950s he had become the sole United States importer and distributor for both Mercedes-Benz and BMW, and was soon to become the principal dealer for the Volkswagen, which made its U.S. debut on July 17, 1950 at Hoffman Motors.

As an automaker, Daimler-Benz had set its sights on the American market around the same time the 300 SL was introduced in New York with the intent of establishing its own marketing network and eliminating Hoffman and his New York and Los Angeles dealerships, which sold competitive models from Daimler's old partner BMW.

The plan was set into motion after the 300 SL's debut, and in the fall of 1954 Daimler-Benz hired an English-speaking Austrian businessman named Heinz Hoppe, who was sent to the United States to lay the groundwork. By 1957 Hoffman was out, but his replacement was perhaps even more problematic.

Mercedes-Benz began its American venture with an unlikely alliance between Daimler-Benz and a struggling automaker in need of a way to boost its declining image –Studebaker-Packard. What made Studebaker-Packard attractive was its acquisition by aviation giant Curtiss-Wright in 1956. This appealed to Daimler-Benz management, since they had wished to find an aircraft engine builder as a U.S. partner. The agreement, drawn up between the two companies in 1957 by Hoppe's superior in Stuttgart, Carl Giese, instantly gave Mercedes-Benz a distribution network of 2,500 dealers. Unfortunately, as Hoppe had feared, Studebaker-Packard salesmen hadn't a clue how to sell foreign cars, or how to handle the temperamental nature of customers interested in such unusual automobiles. Giese's "marriage made in heaven" was slowly heading the other way but Hoppe managed to keep it working for nearly a decade, establishing Mercedes-Benz Sales Inc. in August 1958, as a subsidiary of Studebaker-Packard.

"I am looking for 1,000 Americans who are willing to invest in something different. I will give them free fuel, motor oil, oil filters and lubrication for the first 15,000 miles"

After an unsuccessful sales relationship with Studebaker-Packard, Heinz Hoppe established Mercedes-Benz of North America in April 1965. He may well have been the very first automotive executive to appear in an advertisement pitching his company's products.

To say the relationship between Daimler-Benz and Studebaker-Packard was rocky would be a kind assessment. Curtiss-Wright had hoped the alliance with Daimler-Benz would prop up faltering Studebaker and Packard sales. It did not. To make matters worse, the marketing people in Germany had expected Studebaker-Packard to establish Mercedes-Benz as an import flagship model line. That too, failed to materialize and Daimler-Benz further complicated the situation by wanting Studebaker-Packard dealers to sell the little two-stroke Auto Union cars. Even one that looked like a 1957 Thunderbird failed to impress American buyers. [2]

When the South Bend automaker finally folded its tents in 1964 and moved what remained of its operations to Canada, Hoppe convinced the Daimler-Benz board to act quickly and separate itself from the ill-fated company through a $3.75 million buyout of the contract binding Mercedes to Studebaker-Packard. Hoppe orchestrated the deal and then established Mercedes-Benz of North America as a separate company in April 1965, selecting the best of the former Studebaker-Packard dealers to be the first Mercedes-Benz dealerships in the United States. By this time Giese had been replaced by Günther Wiesenthan, who was appointed president of MBNA. However, Wiesenthan remained in Germany, with Hoppe, as executive vice president, running the company from the U.S.

The first home office for MBNA was in Fort Lee, New Jersey, just across the Hudson River from Manhattan, where it had all begun with Max Hoffman almost 20 years earlier. Under Hoppe's management MBNA established a dealer network, vehicle preparation centers, parts depots, and training schools, making the American sales and marketing division almost totally self sufficient.

In 1970 Hoppe returned to Germany and took a seat on the management board, helping guide the expansion of Daimler-Benz across Europe in the same way he had established Mercedes-Benz in America. Hoppe was ultimately responsible for Daimler-Benz subsidiaries in Great Britain, France, Belgium, the Netherlands, Switzerland, Italy, and Austria. But it had all begun in America.

---

[2] After the war Daimler-Benz had purchased what remained of the Auto Union, one of its biggest motorsports competitors back in the 1930s. Auto Union was manufacturing small cars with 2-stroke motors. Selling a car to Americans that required mixing oil with gasoline was truly the definition of foreign.

1960s

Establishing New Standards

From a purely historical perspective, the Sixties changed the world. And that's not an exaggeration, not if one considers the sweeping sociopolitical revolution that came about during that remarkable decade. Music changed. Television changed. Movies changed. World governments changed. America nearly went to war with the Soviets over the Cuban missile crisis, and shortly thereafter had to deal with the first Presidential assassination since William McKinley in 1901. Americans set foot on the Moon, but couldn't set foot in East Berlin. In 1966, the National Traffic and Motor Vehicle Safety Act and the Highway Safety Act were passed, and the Department of Transportation was established.

For Mercedes-Benz this would be a decade underscored by improvements in design and engineering that would bring to market some of the finest motorcars to come from the world's oldest automaker.

Progress in the design and development of the automobile had never been a problem for Mercedes...after all, they'd invented the thing! It might have appeared as though there was little need for change around Daimler-Benz in 1960, but change was indeed on the horizon.

In February 1961, some 35 years after the two oldest automobile companies in Germany merged to form Daimler-Benz AG, the 75th Anniversary of the Benz Patent Motorwagen was celebrated with the opening of the new Daimler-Benz Automotive Museum in Stuttgart. In 2006, to commemorate the 80th anniversary of the merger of Daimler and Benz, a brand new state-of-the art museum is set to open in Untertürkheim. Back in 1961, the festivities also included the public introduction of a new model, the Mercedes-Benz 220 SE Coupe.

The all-new 220 SE b, also referred to as the "Jubilee Year Mercedes," differed greatly from the 220 SE it replaced. It was a handsome, prestige version of the 220 SE sedan, with two doors, four seats, and a sleek new body – a perfect synthesis of sports car and touring car. A fuel-injected, 134-horsepower 2.2-liter overhead cam, six-cylinder engine and floor-mounted four-speed shifter provided sports car-like performance, in vivid contrast to the luxuriously appointed interior, finished with leather upholstery and fine burlwood trim.

Although built in the same fashion as the previous 220 models, with unitized body construction, single joint, low pivot swing axle independent rear, and traditional Mercedes independent front suspension, the new SE b coupe and cabriolet rode on a 2.5 inch longer wheelbase (108.5 inches). They were eight inches greater in overall length at 192.5 inches, some three inches wider at 72.7 inches, and three inches lower, measuring just 56.1 inches at the roof. It was the design ideology that GM's legendary Harley Earl had preached throughout his career: "longer, lower, wider." Someone at Daimler-Benz had listened.

Mechanically, the new SEb was the first Mercedes model to offer front disc brakes. In most other respects, it was unchanged from its predecessor, pow-

---

If there was one Daimler-Benz model that defined the 1960s, it was the 600, the largest and most luxurious Mercedes since the 1930s.

Much of what Mercedes had to offer in the very early 1960s was rooted in its late 1950s designs, such as this attractive 1960 Type 220 SE Coupe.

Bottom left:
Interior appointments were lavish with even the smallest of details attended to in the Mercedes tradition with leather, fine carpeting, and hand-crafted wood.

Bottom right:
Mercedes was continually entering cars in the most trying of races. In 1960 this lower-priced Mercedes-Benz sedan took on the East Africa Safari rally with drivers W.A. Fritschy and J.L. Ellis.

ered by a 2.2-liter six with Bosch intermittent induction-manifold injection, and an output of 134 horsepower at 5000rpm, providing both coupe and cabriolet with honest sports car acceleration right up to their maximum speed of 105mph.

Recalled Bruno Sacco, who had joined the Sindelfingen design staff in 1958, "[The '61 Coupe] was one of the most beautiful Mercedes ever designed, but not only that: it was one of the most beautiful cars ever designed anywhere. The proportions were just right, and there were no transient styling elements except for the buffers attached to the four corners of the vehicle."

In his 1988 book, *Mercedes-Benz Design*, Sacco wrote, "The vertically arranged headlight unit, introduced with the 300 SL Roadster reached its height with the 220 SEb. Also of particular interest, was the horizontal arrangement of the very large rear light unit," a styling cue that Sacco would revisit many times during his years as director of design.

While the merits of any automotive design are purely conjecture – what plays well in Stuttgart might be received less charitably in Des Moines – few will argue that the 220 SEb coupe was as near perfect a blend of form and function as any automaker in the early 1960s achieved.

The new "Finback" sedans were proving their mettle in competition as well. Shown here are cars running in the 1960 Acropolis rally and the 1962 Argentine road race. Note the chase plane in the upper right.

Below: With that background there's no doubt Mercedes-Benz drivers Walter Schock and Rolf Moll have won the 1960 Acropolis rally driving a Type 220 SE "Finback."

The greater challenge Mercedes had to face was creating a suitable successor to one of the greatest sports cars ever conceived, the 300 SL. Management had taken note of the disparity in sales between the 300 SL coupe and roadster (with combined sales of 3,258) and the smaller, more affordable 190 SL. Priced exactly half that of the 300 SL, 190 SL deliveries had reached 25,881 cars in nine years. Now both were due to be replaced in the 1960s, and Rudolf Uhlenhaut, promoted in 1959 from chief engineer to head of passenger-car development, managed to replace both with a single car.

His plan had been to combine the performance of the 300 SL with the high production capability and affordability of the sporty little 190 SL. These characteristics, together with all new styling and improved handling, brought to the highways the next generation Mercedes sports car, the 230 SL. On its own, the 230 SL and later 250 (2.5 liter) and 280 (2.8 liter) variants were consummate examples of Mercedes-Benz design and engineering.

Although this had worked on paper, and in production cost analysis, when the 230 SL appeared in 1963, many of the sports car cognoscenti still smitten with the 300 SL found the 230 SL was not an altogether suitable heir. The new model not only had to live up to the 300 SL's image, but had the misfortune of arriving at the same time as Jaguar's new XK-E, and Chevrolet's Corvette Stingray, two sports cars of decidedly different character than the Mercedes, but nonetheless competitors in the lucrative American market. The 230 SL

had a difficult mission to fill the brake shoes of a legend and bridge the gap between one that had been more racecar than boulevardier with another that by its very design would be regarded as a contemporary sports car.

Introduced at the Geneva Auto Show in March 1963, the 230 SL was more than it appeared to be, but less than the motor press had expected. Where once had been a sleek, curvaceous, race-bred roadster now stood a squared off two-seater powered by a sohc 2.3-liter, six cylinder engine developing only 150 horsepower. Despite the fact that the car had better handling, vastly improved comfort, and a higher level of options, most found the 230 SL wanting.

Perhaps knowing this beforehand, Mercedes-Benz wasted little time in proving the car's mettle, entering a virtually stock 230 SL in the grueling Spa-Sofia-Liège Rally, Europe's equivalent of the Carrera Panamericana for its sheer abuse to car and driver. Just as the 300 SL coupes had been victorious in 1952, speeding to victory through the Mexican desert, the 230 SL, with driver Eugen Böhringer, claimed a decisive win in this important European endurance race, leaving little doubt that the new car was cut from the same cloth as its predecessors. It was, however, sewn in a very different fashion.

Built on a comparatively short 94.5-inch wheelbase, the 230 SL had a very wide track, 58.3 inches front and 58.5 inches rear. The stance was some eight inches wider than that of the new E-Type Jaguar. The result was an exceptionally well-mannered two-seater with very predictable handling, a better transmission and better brakes than either the Gullwings or Roadsters. The 230 SL also featured an advanced low pivot swing-axle rear suspension with semi-trailing arms, coil springs, and telescopic deCarbon shock absorbers. The front suspension consisted of wishbones, coil springs, telescopic deCarbon shock absorbers, and an anti-sway bar. The deCarbon shocks were replaced with Bil-

---

Retired Daimler-Benz director of design Bruno Sacco wrote of the all-new 1961 Type 220 SE, "(it) was one of the most beautiful Mercedes ever designed, but not only that: it was one of the most beautiful cars ever designed anywhere."

The 220 SE introduced new body styling that broke away from the classically inspired lines of the late 1950s 220 SE coupe and cabriolet models. The new design had a lower, wider, and sportier stance than its predecessors. In 1961 Daimler-Benz delivered 2,537 cars. By the end of production in 1965 the sales total would reach 16,902 cars.

To give the 220 SE a sportier look and add a touch of sports car styling, the models were offered with a floor-mounted, 4-speed stick shift.

Far right: The 1961 SE was the first Mercedes production car to come standard with front disc brakes. The new binders had the same responsibility as their drum predecessors, bringing to a stop the 134 horsepower from the fuel-injected 2.2-liter six.

Mercedes-Benz was never shy about touting the all-season drivability of their cars. Here the drivers of a 200 SE sedan and 220 S "Finback" sedan head out for a skier's weekend.

stein shock absorbers on the 250 SL and 280 SL models.

As good as they were the 230 SL, 250 SL, and 280 SL never achieved the cult status of the 300 SL. In the end it was no great loss to Mercedes because the cars appealed to a greater number of people, and outsold the 300 SL Coupe and Roadster by better than 15 to 1.

Whereas the 300 SL had essentially been regarded as a man's car, and a man with exceptional driving skills at that, the 230 SL cleared the way for an entirely different market. They were immediately more popular with women drivers and among those who wanted a sports car but not the sports car compromises. From 1963 to 1971 Mercedes-Benz sold 48,912 of the sporty 230, 250, and 280 SL models. Even factoring in 190 SL sales with the 300 SL, the figures were still nearly twice that of the earlier models, thus if success were measured in units sold, in this race the new Mercedes sports cars had handily defeated their predecessors.

What primarily differentiated the 230, 250, and 280 SL was power. When the marketplace demanded more from the 230 SL, Mercedes responded with increased displacement, with the 2.3 becoming a 2.5 in 1966 and a 2.8 in 1968 (thus the 250 and 280 designations). Oddly enough, none of the later versions ever surpassed the first 230 SL in performance, even though the 280 SL had 170 horsepower. In the June 1963 issue of Road & Track, a 230 SL equipped with the 4-speed manual transmission and 3.75:1 ratio established a 0 to 60 time of 9.7 seconds and a top speed of 124mph. When the R&T staff tested a 280 SL in August 1968, best 0 to 60 was 9.9 seconds and top speed was down to 114mph. What happened? It seems that somewhere along the way the 280 SL had gained 65 kilograms in unsprung weight, or about 140 pounds, just enough to offset the additional 20 horsepower provided by the 2.8-liter engine. In the sales brochures 170 horsepower looked better than 150, and most customers were buying the 280 SL for image.

Was the new SL a true sports car? If you judge by the automotive magazines of the time, you come to only one conclusion – a resounding "yes." In August 1967 *Sports Car Graphic* suggested that the car could be competitive in SCCA competition, in F Production, where the 230 SL was classified. "To return to the everyday aspects of the car," said SCG, "it'd be easy to sum up as 'faultless.'" *Car and Driver* wrote, "Every driver who has more than a purely utilitarian interest in automobiles should drive a Mercedes-Benz 250 SL at least once in his life. The car is an almost perfect yardstick against which to measure any other car." And *Road & Track* delivered the consummate summation of the 280 SL by writing, "For those who value engineering finesse and high-quality construction, it's alone in the field."

Throughout the first half of the 20th century Mercedes-Benz had taken on many different roles – builder of world-beating racing and sports cars; manufacturer of the finest touring cars; and among heads of state, capitalists, and captains of industry, builder of the world's most prestigious automobiles. In the

1960s Mercedes-Benz would earn this accolade once more with a new statement in luxury, performance, and style to rival its prewar triumphs with the 770 Grosser Mercedes. This new 20th century icon would be known as the 600.

Without question the 600 was one of greatest achievements in the history of Mercedes-Benz. Like its acclaimed predecessor, it was built for an exclusive clientele of European and Middle Eastern royalty, government leaders, and those of immense wealth. It was also built in limited numbers. In its 18-year life span, from August 1963 to June 1981, the longest for a single Mercedes-Benz model, only 2,677 were built. Production of the 600 ran highest in 1965, when 345 Limousines and 63 Pullmans were delivered. The last 600 built, a short-wheelbase sedan, went straight into the Mercedes-Benz Museum.

Throughout its history, government leaders, industrialists and the like have shared, at one time or another, ownership or at least the use of these incomparable automobiles. Among prominent names associated with the 600 were Queen Elizabeth II, King Hussein, Mao Tse-tung, the Shah of Iran, Marshal Tito, Prince Rainier, and the president of Rumania. They were frequently used by foreign embassies as official state cars,

Top left: The Type 240 D diesel was introduced in 1968 as the latest in a line of economical diesel-fueled passenger cars dating back to the 1930s. Diesel engine options are still a staple of 21st century Mercedes.

Top right: Replacing both the 300 SL Roadster and 190 SL Roadster with a single car was not easy, but Rudolf Uhlenhaut managed to do just that with the 1963 Mercedes-Benz 230 SL.

Right: The 230 SL was smaller on the outside but roomier on the inside than the 300 SL, and it was also a better handling car.

A striking departure from the smooth, rounded contours of its predecessors, the squared-off 230 SL with its removable "pagoda" roof didn't initially impress the automotive press, so Mercedes-Benz decided to put on a little demonstration. The factory took a virtually stock 230 SL and entered it the Spa-Sofia-Liège, Europe's equivalent of the Carrera Panamericana. When the race was over, drivers Eugen Böhringer and Klaus Kaiser had claimed a decisive win, thus dismissing any doubts about the car's capabilities.

and in 1966 the Vatican commissioned a special 600 Pullman Landaulet for the use of Pope Paul VI. The 600 remained the official car of the Vatican for 20 years, after which it was donated to the Mercedes-Benz museum, where it is prominently displayed today.

The new 600 was powered by a mechanically fuel-injected, overhead cam V8 with a swept volume of 6,330cc, or 386 cubic inches. The 90-degree V8 design, designated M100, had a compression ratio of 9.0:1, bore and stroke of 103mm x 95mm and a peak output of 300 horsepower at 4,000rpm. Peak torque was a colossal 434 lb.-ft. delivered at 3,000rpm. This was the first production V8 engine Mercedes-Benz had ever built. It was used exclusively in the 600 series until 1968, after which it appeared in what can only be described as the first high-performance sports sedan ever built, the 300 SEL 6.3.

The author photographed the restored 230 SL, now part of the Mercedes-Benz Museum collection, in September 2000. The 43-year-old racecar does get out occasionally, and early that September the author rode in the Spa-Sofia-Liège winning car with its original driver, Eugen Böhringer, at the Salzburgring race track in Austria.

Below left & right: The 230 SL had a much broader appeal than its predecessors, making it one of most popular sports cars of the 1960s among both men and women.

The suspension for the 600 utilized compressor-fed air units. Brakes were discs all around with twin calipers at each front wheel, and tires were 9.00 x 15 radials on 6-1/2 x 15 wheels. The enormous sedans and Pullmans consumed fuel at an average of 10mpg from an oversize tank accommodating just under 30 gallons. To help provide power for the many auxiliary systems, the engine drove two alternators, one on the left, the other on the right, with a total of five vee belts to manage the alternators, air-conditioning compressor, hydraulic pump, cooling fan, and air compressor.

Rudolf Uhlenhaut once said that the cost of building the 600 was of secondary importance. Virtually every part used in the cars was designed and built especially for that model. According to Uhlenhaut, the 600's design demanded "sufficient room for tall people; the best possible suspension; low body roll while cornering; a wide range of adjustability for all seats; well functioning ventilation, heating and air conditioning; silent operation of the whole car; and power assistance for all manual operations."

In terms of performance, the criterion was no less demanding. The 600 would require good road holding, precise power-assisted steering and supe-

The 250 SL came on the heels of the 230 SL, offering a larger 2.5 liter displacement.

Bottom left: When the cry arose for an even larger displacement engine under the hood, Mercedes answered with the 280 SL in 1968. Ironically, the car was the heaviest of the three models and, despite having a larger engine and more horsepower, it wasn't any faster than the original 230 SL.

Bottom center & right: One of the 230, 250, and 280 SLs most endearing design characteristics was the removable pagoda-style roof. This gave the sporty two-seater all-season flexibility.

Elegance had a new name in 1963. It was called the Mercedes-Benz 600.

When President John F. Kennedy traveled to Germany in June 1963, to give his historic speech at the Berlin Wall, he was a little too early to get a ride in a new 600 Pullman Cabriolet. The President was paraded through Berlin in a luxurious Type 300 Cabriolet, often used as an official car for foreign dignitaries.

The 600 was the most lavishly appointed production automobile ever manufactured by Mercedes. These two views show the immense size of the rare six-door Pullman Landaulet, the most elaborate of the three 600 versions produced.

What can only be described as the "first high-performance sports sedan," the 300 SEL 6.3 used the same V8 engine that powered the mighty 600 Series. The 6.3 was Mercedes' answer to the American muscle car craze, but this was a real wolf in sheep's clothing, and elegant clothing at that. The 6.3 could easily surpass most so-called performance coupes built in the U.S. in a 0 to 60 run, and reach triple digits well ahead of the competition. A few years later the 450 SEL 6.9 would appear, and most other cars would disappear in the rear view mirror.

Bottom right:
The 600 model most often seen on American roads in the 1960s was the short wheelbase sedan.

This special car for Pope Paul VI was based on the Mercedes-Benz 600 with long wheelbase. Compared to the production version, the car had been modified extensively. The rear doors were 10 inches wider and directly adjoined the front doors. They were also given new controls so as to be easier to reach from the Pope's centrally arranged individual seat, and the roof of the Pullman Landaulet was raised by almost three inches to provide adequate headroom. Today, the 600 Pullman Landaulet with the legendary registration SCV 1 is displayed in the Mercedes-Benz Museum in Untertürkheim. The registration stands for "Stato Città del Vaticano" and the number one identifies the Pope's official car at any particular time.

194

for the Pullman, the 6.3-liter powerplant and its accompanying 4-speed automatic transmission could propel the cars to speeds well over 120mph. European versions accelerated from 0 to 60 in anywhere from 9.7 to 12 seconds and covered the standing start quarter mile in 17 seconds flat. European road tests recorded top speeds of 129mph for the Limousine and 124mph for the Pullman.

Revered around the world for its features, quality, and performance, throughout its 18-year production run the Mercedes-Benz 600 was the finest automobile that money could buy, or build.

As the 1960s came to an end Mercedes-Benz had finally succeeded in establishing itself in North America. The 280 S, 280 SE, and 300 SEL were its most popular models, followed by the high-performance 300 SEL 6.3, sporty 280 SL, 280 SE coupe and convertible, and the luxurious 600. Heinz Hoppe's work here was done. In 1970 he would return to Germany and lead the company's expansion throughout Europe. But for Mercedes-Benz and the rest of the world, what the coming decade had in store was something that no one could have anticipated. By 1973 the U.S. would be mired in a recession, Nixon in Watergate and Agnew in tax evasion, leading to both their resignations (Agnew in '73, Nixon in '74). Just when things couldn't get much worse, the Arab oil-producing nations embargoed shipments to the U.S., Western Europe, and Japan in retaliation for their support of Israel, precipitating a worldwide energy crisis, and virtually crippling U.S. auto sales.

And that was the good news.

When introduced, the 300 SE came with an impressive list of standard features headed by a new 4-speed automatic transmission, power steering, limited slip differential, and power-assisted four-wheel Dunlop disc brakes. In the 1960s, the 300 SE was regarded as one of the best cars built in the world. It was also one of the most expensive. The 1966 model pictured listed for $11,511. The Cabriolet version sold for $12,295. Over a six-year period a combined total of only 3,127 were built.

Introduced in March 1962 at the Geneva auto show, the 300 SE was virtually identical to the new 220 SE b coupe (the official nomenclature used the lower case b, but the cars are referred to as 220 SE, just as were their predecessors), but in place of the 2.2-liter engine was a new, more powerful 3.0-liter inline six-cylinder engine.

1970s
A Changing World

The world is always changing, from decade to decade and one generation to the next, but no matter how many things change there are constants that seem to remain a part of our humanity. And not all of them are good.

Today we have a war in the Middle East, rising gasoline and heating oil prices, economic instability, a fear of terrorism, recession, a loss of jobs and industry – yet these situations can be paralleled by events from every decade and every generation. And we have a fairly diverse palette from which to choose: the Revolutionary War, the Civil War, the Spanish American War, World War I, World War II, Korea, Vietnam, and both Gulf Wars. Suicide bombers were once known as Kamikaze pilots. Postwar recessions, inflation, deflation, bank failures, banking scandals, even the Great Depression – which covers just about all of the aforementioned financial issues – are a part of our history. If one looks back at the 20th century, or any century for that matter, the world has always been unstable. In the 1970s, however, it seemed to be worse than usual.

The escalating war in Vietnam was testing our nation's, and the free world's, conviction to fight Communism at every step, but moreover it had emphatically divided America to the point where on May 4, 1970 the National Guard was summoned to Kent State University in Ohio to deal with student protests against the war. This wasn't the first time there had been protests against America's involvement in Vietnam, but it was the first time that shots were fired into a crowd of protesters, and in the aftermath of an incident that would galvanize American opinion, the rallying cry of the antiwar movement changed from "Hell no I won't go" to "Four dead in Ohio." Whether or not that was a major turning point in our history is likely to be debated ad infinitum, but after Kent State things began to change.

Under the direction of Béla Barényi, Mercedes' "Father of Passive Safety," Daimler-Benz began crash testing cars back in 1951. Barényi was the first to propose the development of crumple zones and rigid passenger cell structures for passenger safety. He received patents for both concepts in 1951. Shortly thereafter, this Model 170 S hit the wall and crash testing was born.

Left: In 1991 the author produced this striking image for an advertising campaign entitled "Your Car is a Reflection of You." The setting shows the side of a 300 SEL 6.3 with the reflections of a 300 SL and SSK Mercedes. All of the cars were from the Don Ricardo collection.

The 280 SE remained in production from 1968 to 1972 but the six-cylinder models, like this 1970 Cabriolet, became something of an orphan when the V8-powered 280 SE 3.5 debuted in 1970. Mercedes literature described the six-cylinder 280 SE as, "(a) proud descendant of a long line of distinguished Mercedes-Benz cars. Magnificent machines like the supercharged 540K of the 1930s, and the classically simple 300 S Cabriolet of the '50s."

You might wonder what all of this has to do with Daimler-Benz; actually, quite a lot, because the events of the early 1970s set the stage for one of the most difficult periods in the company's history. How Mercedes dealt with the 1970s truly defined the character of the company, especially in the United States, which had become the single most important market outside of Germany.

By 1973 the war in Vietnam was "officially" over, though it really didn't end until the evacuation of U.S. forces, civilians, and refugees in 1975, the year that South Vietnam was overrun by the Communist North Vietnamese. Of course, so much had happened between 1973 and 1975 that we had more to be concerned with than the fall of Saigon.

In October 1973 the Organization of Petroleum Exporting Countries (OPEC) had instituted an oil embargo, which led to severe fuel shortages, long lines, short tempers, and big price hikes at the pump. Overnight people became less concerned with how fast their cars could go, and more interested in how far. The American market

for large, high-performance cars began to evaporate as did interest in one of the most uniquely American automotive concepts of the 20th century, the muscle car. By the early 1970s the Muscle Car Era was over. More and more consumers were turning toward Japanese imports, feeling that they offered better value, gas mileage, and quality for the dollar than American cars (which for the most part was true at the time), and compared to European makes like Mercedes-Benz, were far less expensive than even the lowest-priced Mercedes diesel models. And the problem wasn't just in the United States. The auto industry was in serious trouble on a global scale due to the oil embargo's devastating impact on foreign economies. Inflation was rampant and economic growth was at a virtual standstill. The Dow Jones Industrial Average fell to 663 – a number that seems unfathomable today, but helps put the 1970s into perspective. It was not a good time to be an automaker.

With the fuel crisis strangling the auto industry, the federal gov-

Here & top left: An early 1970 model 280 SE 3.5, this 1970 Coupe looks almost identical to the 280 SE, however, one glance at the numbers on the back of the trunk, or watching it disappear in traffic, confirmed that this was not a regular 280 SE.

ernment instituted a national 55mph speed limit in 1974. There would even be a brief period in the '70s when speedometers on American cars, as well as all import cars, were limited to a maximum readout of 85mph. This was an idea that flew in the face of performance, especially for a company like Mercedes-Benz, which had built its reputation on performance. Tightening federal emission standards exacerbated the domestic manufacturing problem as automakers scrambled to build cars that could comply. And just when it seemed that smaller, more fuel-efficient models were going to be the salvation, the oil crisis ended. Gas was freely available again and prices declined, although they would never return to pre-embargo levels. Overall, though, little had changed. The 55mph speed limit remained, as did new government standards, which forever changed the way automakers design cars. Most of their R&D money was now being allocated to engineering, in order to meet government safety and fuel consumption regulations, regulations which were applied with equal prejudice to imported models.

In 1977 the U.S. Department of Transportation ordered that air bags should be installed in all new cars beginning with the 1982 model year, thus presenting automakers with yet another predicament (they were just finally figuring out how to incorporate low-impact bumpers into

Bottom left:
Equipped with Bosch fuel injection, the 280 SE six delivered 180 horsepower at 5750rpm. This was the same engine used in the new 280 SL.

under the trunk. On rough roads, body shudder and cowl shimmy were virtually non-existent. Of all Mercedes-Benz models, this was perhaps the quintessential German-engineered luxury touring car. It was also, by nature of its advanced design, capable of meeting U.S. safety standards. In fact, Mercedes exceeded most of the new U.S. regulations before they were even established! This was the legacy of Béla Barényi, Mercedes' "Father of Passive Safety."

The key principles of passive safety were conceived under Barényi's direction beginning in 1948. Barényi joined Daimler-Benz in 1939 after having worked at Styer in Austria, alongside Erwin Komenda (later to become Ferdinand Porsche's chief designer) and Karl Wilfert, who left Styer for Mercedes in 1929, and had since become director of the experimental design department at Sindelfingen. It was Wilfert who brought Barényi into the company just before World War II.

His solitary desire since the early days at Styer had been to build safer cars, and it was Barényi who advanced the theory of "crumple zones." He began research in 1951 by doing crash tests at Daimler-Benz, which, at the time, caused quite a sensation. Barényi was putting ideas to the test that he believed were essential to passenger safety since receiving a patent in 1951 for what was then described as a "rigid passenger cell structure surrounded by front and rear crumple zones." This was followed in 1953 by the self-supporting chassis-body structure with protective side moldings, and a three-part steering column, which first appeared in the Mercedes-Benz 180. The overall concept of the passenger cell was finally put into practice with the 1959 Type 220 "Finback" Mercedes. It was to become the forerunner for an entire generation of improved models led by the six-cylinder 220, 220 S and 220 SE sedans, coupes, and convertibles.

One look at the 280 SE 3.5's interior and words simply failed. This was luxury at a new level for the 1970s.

Left: Daimler-Benz was passing the torch to itself with the 280 SE 3.5 Cabriolet and Coupe. Both were tagged a collector's car by German motoring enthusiasts. *Road & Track* called them "fabulously handsome" and further opined that it was "one of the best-looking body designs to come from any German concern."

By the 1960s Barényi's safety program had led to significant progress in passenger protection. Among his designs were the "pagoda" roof used on the 230 SL, which was engineered to provide improved all around visibility and greater structural integrity in the event of a rollover. Head restraints, safety steering column with impact absorber, and padded or rounded-off interior appointments designed to reduce the injury hazard in an accident were all visible results of Barényi's influence at Mercedes. The restraint systems were redesigned, too, and a three-point seatbelt became standard on Mercedes-Benz models by the early 1970s. Passive safety and engineering were to become another hallmark of Mercedes-Benz. And the timing couldn't have been better for the U.S. market.

Throughout the troubled decade of the 1970s Daimler-Benz stressed safety in its advertising, as author, editor, and automotive authority David E. Davis, Jr., wrote in the January 2001 issue of *Car Collector* magazine, "One of the greatest advertising campaigns in Mercedes history was titled: There Are Times When Mercedes-Benz Almost Wishes It Didn't Have To Be Mercedes-Benz." Bruce McCall, who has written for the leading automotive magazines, and has now become famous both as a comic writer and artist, wrote Mercedes-Benz advertising for the Ogilvy and Mather ad agency from 1965 to 1979. In that capacity," contended Davis, "he was the clos-

Styling for the 280 SE bore just a hint of tailfins, not so much a continued acknowledgement of American styling, but rather a refinement of the American-influenced "Finback," which had not been an overly popular design.

est thing we had to the great Ted McManus. The mission of those ads was to sell small diesel sedans and fast, luxurious S-Class dreadnoughts, of course, but the leitmotif of every ad and commercial was the glory of Mercedes-Benz engineering, or 'over-engineering.' McCall worked within the framework of the long-standing David Ogilvy tradition of erudite copy filled with facts large and small. The net effect was months and years of advertising that added up to a veritable encyclopedia of the tremendous trifles that made Mercedes-Benz what it was – the imported luxury car that simply stole the business out from under Cadillac and Lincoln."

By the time Barényi retired from Daimler-Benz in 1972, the designed-in safety measures that might have seemed extravagant to some automakers had become de rigueur at Mercedes. Cars were built with crumple zones to absorb impact and isolate the passenger compartment in a collision, and the fuel tank, all too vulnerable on many automobiles, was surrounded by a metal bulkhead and positioned deep within the body in a protected area over the rear axle. Mercedes doors used tapered cone latches, built to withstand impact and still work. The steering wheel, often criticized for being too large, was designed with a telescoping column and a large padded hub to protect the driver. And the steel passenger shell was developed to protect occupants from side impacts and in the event of a rollover. Thus Mercedes-Benz, along with Volvo and Saab, who followed along similar lines, came to be regarded by consumers as the safest cars one could purchase. In such company the Mercedes were also the most stylish.

Styling in the 1970s was commensurate with Mercedes' new safety features, and what rolled out of Sindelfingen was a fresh, exciting generation of cars, including the third series of SL Roadsters.

The 1970 Type 350 SL offered 3.5 liters of V8 power surrounded by an entirely new and even more luxurious body that would become the darling of café society from Beverly Hills to the Côte d'Azure.

The 350 SL was quickly followed by the even more powerful 4.5-liter 450 SL, truly the first Mercedes-Benz sports car to break traditional lines. The 450 SL had the same appeal to gray-haired executives on Madison Avenue as it did to long-haired Levi-clad rock stars on the Sunset Strip, and to both men and to women. As a two-seat sports car, this was the Mercedes for all seasons.

This was the look that would become one of the most popular on boulevards from Rodeo Drive to Madison Avenue, throughout North America and across Europe from 1971 until 1989. This was the new, and soon to be most successful, SL ever designed.

The new 350 SL (and 450 SL) chassis measured 96.9 inches, and was greater both in wheelbase and overall length, at 172.4 inches, than the 280 SL. This provided additional interior room to accommodate the installation of air conditioning up front and occasional seating in the rear.

In 1972 when the new SL models first arrived in the U.S. they were equipped with the larger 4.5 liter engine and badged 350 SL 4.5. The following year they were officially badged 450 SL. Most early cars were retrofitted with the new emblem by dealers in 1973.

The 450 SL, which replaced the 350 SL in 1972, combined for the first time sports car performance and handling with a measure of luxury that had previously been reserved for Mercedes touring cars. Author and historian Richard Langworth described the 450 SL as a sports car "the like of which had rarely been seen by any manufacturer, including D-B itself." In the U.S. the bible of American motoring, *Road & Track*, named the 350 SL among the "Ten Best Cars in the World" along with the 300 SEL 6.3 and 280 SE. This dazzling affirmation of the latest Mercedes-Benz models came at a time when it was most needed. If one had the money and desire for an imported luxury or sports car in the 1970s, Mercedes-Benz had a car to fulfill every desire.

However different from their predecessors, the 450 SL models continued traditions established in the 1950s by the 190 SL and 300 SL roadsters: the choice of either a fabric convertible top or a removable hardtop; a sweeping open grille with the Mercedes-Benz star and barrel; and luxurious seating just for two.

Also known as the Type W 107, the new 350 SL (and 450 SL) chassis measured 96.9 inches, and was greater both in wheelbase and overall length, at 172.4 inches, than the 280 SL. This provided additional interior room to accommodate the installation of air conditioning up front and occasional seating in the rear – the occasion however was limited to small children, pets, an extra suitcase, or some grocery bags. Adults need not apply.

The cars were not only larger in exterior and interior dimensions, but in their structural design and overall weight. The bodies were wider (70.5 inches) to accommodate door guard beams federally mandated for the American market and to cover wider section tires on a front/rear track of 57.2 and 56.7 inches, respectively. Bodied in steel, rather

Mercedes-Benz made history with the 300 SL's double victory in the Carrera Panamericana in Mexico in 1952. The 450 SLC then added a new chapter in 1978 with another double victory in the grueling 40-day, 30,000 kilometer (18,000 mile) South American Rally, which was run through ten countries! Regulations did not allow tuned engines, so the four works-supported Mercedes-Benz 450 SLCs had standard 4.5-liter V8 engines, albeit they were top-of-the-range with 227-234 horsepower.

Next time you see a "luxurious" 450 SLC on the street, think about this: In 1980 an AMG-Mercedes 450 SLC won the Grand Prix race at the Nürburgring counting towards the European Touring Car Championship Title.

The oil crisis in the early 1970s had deeply shocked the western world, causing, among other things, the launch of a unique model from Mercedes-Benz – the 450 SEL 6.9 (W 116 series) – to be postponed. An engine with a displacement of 6.9 liters was, after all, difficult to sell, to put it mildly. Mercedes finally took the risk and in May 1975, one-and-a-half years later than planned, presented a car that instantly intrigued buyers.

450 SL was the European-only version, which had a robust 220-horserpower output compared to the emissions-choked 190-horsepower U.S. model.

The 450 SL Roadsters also had a companion model, the 450SLC Coupe. The two models shared the basic body lines and essentially the same parts, but were intended to appeal to different buyers, and were by design two very different automobiles.

While the image of the new 450 SL was that of a sports car, the SLC version was intended as a gran turismo. Daimler-Benz had taken a similar approach in the late 1920s with the Type SS and SSK touring models. The distinction in the 1970s was between that of a two-seat sports model, the SL, versus a four-passenger grand touring car designated as a 2+2, the SLC. For the additional +2 the wheelbase of the SLC was extended by 14.2 inches and the roofline was higher by 1.2 inches to allow more rear seat headroom.

Although the 1970 SLC was introduced with a 3.5 liter V8 in Europe (it was also later available with a smaller 2.8 liter dohc six and a larger 5.0 liter V8), the 350 SLC versions that came to the U.S. in 1972 were again powered by the 4.5 liter engine in order to meet Federal emission requirements and still maintain the performance standards Mercedes-Benz had set down for the

The 450 SEL 6.9 was luxury refinement at the highest level. The car was, after all, the noblest representative of the Mercedes-Benz S-Class in the 1970s, and noblesse oblige. The interior was fitted with the discreet luxury of the automotive top league. Leather-covered seats were an optional extra, for instance – the standard seat covers were made of quality velour. The car was popular among customers employing a chauffeur; hence a great deal of attention was paid to the rear seating, which could be special-ordered with electrically adjustable heated cushions.

A brand-new premium-class vehicle generation was presented to the public in September 1972. The first officially designated "Mercedes-Benz S-Class" – internal designation W 116 – replaced the W 108/ W 109 series and was initially comprised of three models: the 280 S, 280 SE, and 350 SE. Six months later the S-Class sedan was also offered with the larger 4.5-liter V8 engine in parallel to the 450 SL and 450 SLC.

Powered by a 417 cubic inch V8, numbers more commonly associated with Detroit muscle cars than luxurious four-door sedans, the 450 SEL 6.9 proved to be the ultimate high-performance luxury car long before other automakers even considered the idea of combing these two antithetical features.

From 1978, the 6.9 was also available with the anti-lock braking system (ABS) – a safety system that made its debut in the Mercedes-Benz S-Class and once again moved the series into the top league of innovative engineering.

car. Like the Roadsters, models that arrived at the end of 1972, and all those following throughout the car's history, were 450 SLCs and the subsequent replacement of badges took place at dealerships. With a price of more than $16,000 (roughly the equivalent of two Cadillacs in 1972) the 450 SLC was regarded as the ultimate in automotive high fashion. In addition to rousing performance and handling, the SLC offered an unparalleled level of luxury and comfort. Air conditioning, automatic transmission, power steering, four-wheel power disc brakes, Michelin radial tires, Becker Europa AM/FM stereo, electric antenna, electric windows, central locking system, and a sumptuous leather interior were all standard. With a fully independent suspension, anti-sway bars front and rear, and virtually neutral steering, the 450 SLCs were quick, comfortable, luxurious cars, what every manufacturer of 2+2 sports coupes would have loved to build, the perfect gran turismo.

The 450 SL and SLC were among the last designs to come from Karl Wilfert and Mercedes' legendary Technical Director, Rudolf Uhlenhaut, who retired in 1972. Arguably the most civilized sports car ever built, the 450 SL became the most successful SL ever, with total production of the 4.5 liter series reaching 66,298 by 1980. The sleek, horizontal

styling created by Wilfert remained in production for another nine years, powered by eight different engines under the designations 280 SL, 300 SL, 350 SL, 380 SL, 420 SL, 450 SL, 500 SL, and 560 SL, leading to an astounding total of 237,287 vehicles sold worldwide between 1970 and 1989, more than all other Daimler, Benz, and Daimler-Benz sports models combined since the company's inception! The 450 SL and its variations remain an enduring tribute to Wilfert and Uhlenhaut's legacy of SL models dating from their first collaboration on the 300 SL in 1952.

There was one way to get an even more powerful Mercedes in the 1970s, if one were willing to forego the sports car image in favor of what can best be defined as the hottest German car of the era, the 450 SEL 6.9. This was a car that totally flew in the face of logic considering the times, but it was without doubt the last word in Mercedes-Benz design, engineering, and performance, if one were willing to part with a great deal of money. Born of the same philosophy as the earlier 300 SEL 6.3, the 450 SEL 6.9 was a no holds barred touring car with one of the largest engines available anywhere. It delivered a massive swept volume of 6,834cc, 417 cubic inches, and a bore x stroke of 107mm x 95mm (4.21 inches x 3.74 inches) combined with an 8.0:1

Although almost indistinguishable from the standard 450 SEL, the 6.9 models were fitted with slightly larger bumpers than those of other U.S. equipped Mercedes. Apart from that and the modest 6.9 badge on the trunk lid, all that differed went unseen and unheard. But it was definitely felt when you applied pressure to the accelerator.

compression ratio. Even in U.S. trim, the 6.9 developed 280 horsepower and 360 lb.-ft. of torque.

Derived from the mighty M100 series that powered the 600 Limousines and 6.3 models, the 6.9's fuel injection system was updated from the Bosch pressure-measuring D-Jetronic to the third generation, mechanically controlled, continuous-injection K-Jetronic, drawing fuel from a truck-sized 25-gallon fuel tank. Dry sump lubrication, rarely offered on anything but racecars, was another standard feature of this uncompromising high-performance engine.

Because of its enormous low-rpm strength, the 6.9 was able to get by with a three-speed, torque converter automatic transmission, 2.65:1 rear axle ratio, and limited-slip differential, making the car smoother and quieter but no less powerful. The suspension was similar to that of the W116 series, but it eschewed coil springs and shock absorbers in favor of an elaborate hydropneumatic springing system. Similar to the 600, an automatic self-leveling feature compensated for passenger and cargo weight, keeping headlight aim and bumper height on an even keel. While the system gave a smooth compliant ride, it also took a firm set when driven hard.

Capable of rapid throttle response, a car of the SEL's 116.5 inch wheelbase would normally have been subject to considerable suspension squat under full acceleration and front end dive under braking, but not the 6.9. Two special torque linkages were incorporated into the semi-trailing arm rear suspension, assisted by a Watts linkage and larger diameter front and rear sway bars to reduce the 4,400-pound car's body roll in corners. These handling advantages were not wasted on standard passenger car tires, either; the 6.9 rode on Michelin XWX 215/70VR14 steel-belted radials mounted on 6.5x14 forged light alloy wheels. Although owners seldom became aware of these features, they formed as much a part of the 6.9's substance as its finely tailored leather upholstery and burlwood trim.

Ideal for touring the German autobahn at triple digits, on U.S. highways where the maximum was still 55mph, the 6.9 was perfectly suited to cruising along with the capability of passing anything on the road as the situation demanded, and virtually blowing the doors off Detroit's fastest cars at any speed. The author was witness to one such example when a friend who had just purchased a 6.9 was "challenged" by a Pontiac GTO. Somewhere east of 125mph the GTO became a pair of headlights growing smaller in the rear view mirror. Such was the 6.9. It had been engineered to be a driver's car capable of 0 to 60 in 8.2 seconds and a top speed of 137mph. Apart from the more formal 600, the 6.9 was the best of the best, offered to those who could pay more than $50,000 in 1975 to purchase one of only 1,816 such cars produced for the U.S. market. In all, Daimler-Benz built 7,380 examples of the 6.9 from September 1975 to May 1980, although sales in this country were limited to the 1977 through 1979 model years. Ringing down the curtain on the 1970s, the 450 SEL 6.9 proved to be an automobile worthy of many superlatives, but needing none.

As the 1970s became the 1980s little changed in the automotive world. These were still troubled times, and though the gas crisis had passed once again and prices had settled to new norms, consumers were still uncertain about the future and about what kind of automobile belonged in the driveway. Mercedes-Benz would give them a choice unlike any foreign automaker in history.

1980s

A New Generation of Mercedes

In the 1980s, the United States remained the most important market for Mercedes-Benz outside of Germany, but meeting new federal emissions regulations was becoming increasingly more difficult as each new standard lowered the performance of Mercedes' 4.5-liter engine, the bedrock of its most popular models. By 1980 output had been reduced to a meager 160 horsepower and Mercedes-Benz engineers came to a decision, that in order to comply with new federal regulations the 4.5-liter engine could no longer be sold in the United States. Thus, in 1981 the 450 SL models were withdrawn from the American market. In its place was a new SL engine signaling the first "technical" step backward in the company's history since the end of World War II. The 4.5 was replaced with a 3.8-liter V8 delivering a maximum of 155 horsepower. Adding to the frustration of American buyers who could afford the best, was the knowledge that in Europe there was a 450 SLC 5.0 pouring out 240 horsepower!

The resulting disparity between U.S. specification engines and those available for sale in Europe gave birth to one of the worst ideas in American automotive history, the "gray market" import. Worthy of its own book, the gray market was comprised of European spec cars brought into the U.S. through private importers, i.e., without factory approval or warranties, and modified to meet federal standards by independent certification facilities approved by the federal government. These facilities, however, were usually owned by the retailers who sold the cars, at a very high premium to their wealthy clientele. This import, certification, and marketing strategy became very lucrative in the 1980s with numerous, high-performance European-only models finding their way onto American roads through the gray market. Unfortunately, there were some unscrupulous certification facilities approving cars that did not actually meet federal safety and emissions standards, and when the government caught on, well, let's say things came to a rather abrupt and unpleasant end, which at times included the impounding of cars that had cost their owners an arm and a leg to purchase.

In the face of this problem, the 1980s was to be another decade of change for Daimler-Benz, one that would see the full implementation of pas-

---

Unlike Europeans, who were familiar with the sight of small commercial Mercedes used for taxis, Americans had never seen an "entry-level" Mercedes. In 1984 they would get their first look at what would come to be known as the190E, more popularly referred to by owners as the "Baby Benz." A smaller, more affordable Mercedes, the car quickly became a best seller in the U.S.

The "Baby Benz" was initially powered by either a 2.3-liter engine developing 113 horsepower (increased to 121 horsepower in 1985), or the less popular, but more fuel-efficient, 190D diesel version. The 190 series was available only as a sedan, offering many of the amenities found on the larger Mercedes, including a power sunroof, leather upholstery, and automatic transmission.

The evolution of the 190 as a mainstream car was swift, and with models such as the limited edition 190E sports sedan, everyone got a taste of AMG with ground effects, a rear wing, and a high-performance engine that allowed the cars to, as this full AMG version's nickname implied, drop the "Hammer" on the competition. The standard 190E 2.3-16 versions delivered 167 horsepower in U.S. trim, 185 horsepower in European spec. Also known as the W201, the cars did quite well in competition.

sive safety in every Mercedes model as a new and quite successful marketing strategy. Cars now offered ABS (anti-lock brakes), SRS (supplemental restraint system air bags), traction control, and 4-Matic, the latter being the first Mercedes passenger car to come with all-wheel-drive. The new AWD system was introduced at the Frankfurt Auto Show in 1985.

The image Mercedes-Benz had previously created for itself in the United States was that of a racecar, sports car, and luxury touring car maker. Americans had little knowledge that, in reality, Daimler-Benz was the German equivalent of General Motors (which at the time was a good thing) with a product line that ranged from luxury and sports cars to off-road vehicles, dump trucks, buses, and taxi cabs. To this day the rows of tan-colored, utilitarian-looking Mercedes sedans and wagons outside airports in Frankfurt

The automotive lines at Mercedes were divided between (left to right) the C-Class, E-Class, and S-Class, from the lowest-priced to the most luxurious models in the 1980s.

216

The E-Class was divided into three models by the late 1980s: sedan, coupe, and wagon, the latter introduced to the U.S. market in 1988 as the 300 TE. Although family wagons had been Mercedes fare for years, the 300 TE marked the first time Daimler-Benz offered a gasoline-powered model in the North American market. Replacing the venerable 300TD turbo diesel, the 300 TE was powered by a 3.0 liter, 177-horsepower straight six. The same engine used in the 300 E, 300 CE, and 300 SEL models of that period.

1990s

On the Threshold of a New Century

As the last decade of the 20th century began to unfold, Mercedes would offer cars and sport utility vehicles suitable to almost every pocketbook, and thanks to the factory-supported Starmark Program established in 1998, for refurbishing and warranting "pre-owned" Mercedes, owning a used car was far less risky. This was to become the most ambitious decade in the history of Daimler-Benz, and the last decade the company would use that name in public.

In 1990 came the long-awaited successor to the 450 SL series, which had been in continuous production (in various models) for 18 years. Drawing on the historic 300 SL name, Mercedes launched a new generation of sports cars powered by a six-cylinder engine, and in 1991 added an eight-cylinder 500 SL model. The two new cars introduced a litany of improvements over their long-in-the-tooth predecessors, including an automatic convertible top that disappeared beneath a solid boot. Once again the stylists at Daimler-Benz had created a seemingly timeless design, but it was the engineering department that would have the most to offer throughout the decade.

In 1995 the SL Series signaled the beginning of a new era in Mercedes-Benz marketing, and though the cars were little changed in appearance, their names and the clientele to whom they were being marketed were. For the first time in the history of the SL there would be as an obvious separation among models by features and price ranges. There were to be three distinctively different SLs, designated as SL 320, SL 500, and SL 600. Placing the alpha designation ahead of the numerical conspicuously divided the cars into three categories: six-cylinder, eight-cylinder, and twelve-cylinder, respectively, with styling similar to the 1990 AMG versions of the SL, which featured a more pronounced front end, deck lid spoilers, side skirts, and a rear valance.

Mechanically, AMG tuning for the SL in 1990 had offered a number of options, including a new rear differential gear set, which changed ratios from 2.65 to 3.27 and cut better than half a second from 0-60 acceleration. AMG sport exhaust systems added seven to eight horsepower, and the ultimate option, a 6-liter "exchange" motor, delivered 381 horsepower, compared to

---

By the mid 1990s, the S-Class flagship models had become the most luxurious Mercedes-Benz touring cars of the 20th century. Models like this 1995 S420 were among the world's most desirable high-status luxury cars. Combining exclusive S-Class features with a powerful V8 engine, the price was just under $80,000. (photo by Dennis Adler)

In 1991, after a 20 year absence from this segment of the market, Mercedes-Benz finally provided their customers with a four-seat convertible. Thanks to newly defined design principles involving diagonal braces and vibration dampers, the convertible was just as rigid, tremor-free, and crash-safe as the sedans, and came complete with electrically operated folding soft-top, heated rear window, and a roll-over bar integrated in the rear head restraints. The 1991 model is shown with its two famous predecessors. (Photo by Dennis Adler for Mercedes-Benz North America)

Right: The 1990's version of the SL was the most aggressively styled car since the original 300 SL. Features developed by AMG became standard styling cues on the 500 SL as the decade advanced. (Photo by Dennis Adler)

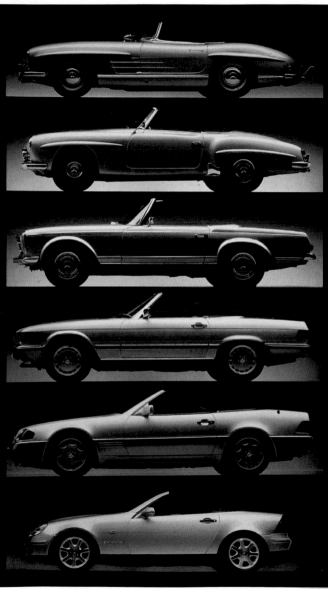

The SL lineage was depicted in this 1997 image showing all of the two-seat convertible models to bear the famed "SL" letters. Pictured from top to bottom, the 300 SL Roadster, 190 SL Roadster, 230-280 SL, 450 SL, SL 500, and SLK.

It was the beginning of a new era for Mercedes-Benz sports models when the 1997 SLK was introduced. Small, sporty, and equipped with a supercharged four-cylinder engine, the SLK opened the door for Mercedes enthusiasts who had been priced out of the market for more than 30 years. (Photos by Dennis Adler)

the stock 5-liter's 322 horsepower. An AMG-powered SL 500 could clock 0 to 60 in five seconds flat. It could also break the bank. The new 6-liter engine, including the trade-in allowance of the stock 5-liter, was an estimated $25,000! The body treatment, rear differential, and wheels and tires added another $18,000. For the privilege of making Porsches and Ferraris eat Daimler dust, SL owners paid up to $45,000 above the 500 SL's $91,000 base price in 1990. Five years later, buyers would be paying over $100,000 for the factory's ultimate SL, the high-performance V12 SL 600.

Daimler-Benz had, in a way, undone what the 450 SL had achieved with its universal appeal and price. The new SL Series established an economical and performance caste that separated owners of the $78,300 six-cylinder Mercedes SL 320 from those who purchased the V8 SL 500 at $89,000, and the ultimate Mercedes, the V12 powered SL 600, which listed for $120,100.

The greatest change at Daimler-Benz, however, had begun in 1993 when Mercedes introduced the all-new E-Class as a mid-range sedan. Developed in response to the Lexus and Infiniti luxury lines from Toyota and Nissan, and mid-range BMWs, all of which were beginning to eat into Mercedes' market share, the E-Class not only leveled the playing field but created an entirely new segment of Mercedes-Benz ownership.

After only three years in production the E-Class was completely revised for 1996. Filling the shoes

The heritage of the SLK comes from another legendary Mercedes, the 190 SL, which was the last Mercedes sports two-seater to be powered by a four-cylinder engine. However, the innovative SLK featured a convertible hardtop, making it the first such car to come from Daimler-Benz. (Photos by Dennis Adler)

of what had suddenly become the best-selling Mercedes-Benz model ever was an even better E-Class that finally accomplished what no previous model had been able to do: combine the luxury and style of the top-of-the-line S-Class with the size and practicality of a mid-sized model. Not since the great 220 SE of the late 1950s and legendary 300 SE of the 1960s had Mercedes-Benz offered so much automobile for the price. The E320, priced at $43,500, was more car than anyone should have reasonably expected for the money in 1996, a price that was some five percent less than the E-Class model it replaced!

The sweeping bodylines of the E320 gave it a powerful stance reminiscent of a sports coupe, despite having four doors. Unique in appearance from the laid-back headlight design to the wraparound rear lighting array, the car introduced a new style that set it apart from other Mer-cedes-Benz models. It was a design guaranteed to evoke a reaction. And it did. Gone from the E-Class were the last vestiges of that old Teutonic frost of flat textures and sterile surfaces. The E320 offered the warmth and character of a Jaguar saloon (a sedan to those of us in the Colonies) with stylishly contoured surfaces and contrasting color schemes. The car's innovative side impact supplemental restraint system also added to the interior design by necessitating a textured door panel that resembled the gathered leather seen in British and Italian luxury cars. Achieving impeccable levels of luxury, performance, and safety, the E320 established a new standard for mid-class luxury cars – a Mercedes-Benz that doesn't cost a fortune – but looked, and drove, like it did.

The next big change was the introduction of a second series of sports cars, the SLK, which took both its engine

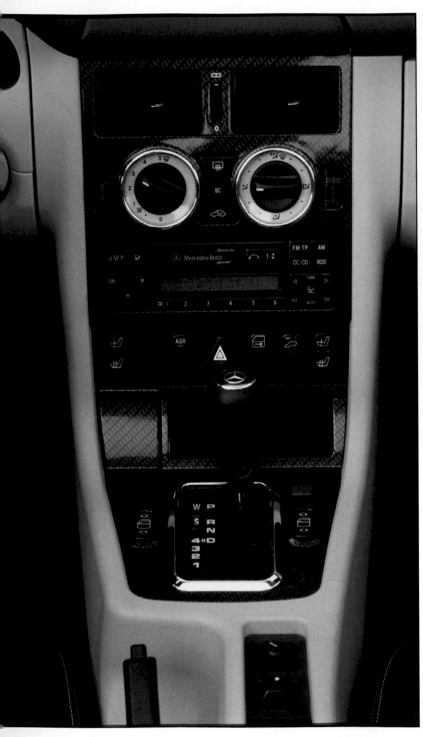

The SLK interior was a mixture of retro and modern with bold instrumentation and a comfortable center console that became second nature almost from the first time you sat behind the wheel. (Photos by Dennis Adler)

size and status in the Mercedes model line from the historic 1954 Type 190 SL. This had been a long time coming, more than 35 years. That was the last time Mercedes-Benz offered a low-price sports car powered by a four-cylinder engine. When the 190 SL retired from the road in 1963, so too did the concept of a small, sporty two-seater from Stuttgart.

In 1997 Mercedes reignited those old flames but with a car that burned so much brighter. Powered by a dohc, four-valve-per-cylinder engine, paired with a Roots-type supercharger, the SLK was the first supercharged Mercedes-Benz production car since 1939! The SLK played upon the same themes as the 190 SL – an ideal combination of compact size, modest but pleasing performance, all-weather practicality, and an affordable price. The engineers at Mercedes accomplished all of that with the SLK and at the same time raised their own bar by introducing a feature on the SLK that no sports car in its class had ever offered: an automatic folding hardtop. The 190 SL and all Mercedes-Benz roadsters since the first 300 SL roadsters had offered a removable hard top, but there was always one problem – where to put it. Most sat on furniture pads or hung from the garage ceiling when not in use. And it was never convenient to remove or attach the hardtop. The SLK solution, though hardly unprecedented (the concept dates back to the late 1930s) offered the best alternative in Mercedes-Benz history. The hard top would simply fold up automatically at the touch of a button and store away in the trunk. Perhaps it was ingenious, because this feature made the SLK the most innovative sports car Mercedes-Benz had ever built.

The 2.3 liter, super-charged SLK engine in standard tune developed 191 horsepower delivered through an electronically controlled 5-speed automatic equipped with driver-adaptive shift logic, which delayed up-shifts and quickly downshifted when the car was driven aggressively. The engine pictured is the AMG six-cylinder version which was added to the line in 1999 along with an optional 5-speed manual. A second six-cylinder model, the SLK320, with 215 horsepower, was also added in 1999.

The SLK roof was and still is, in the latest version introduced in 2005, absolutely fascinating from the moment the rear decklid lifts and the top rises up and away from the windshield until it settles quietly into the trunk. It only takes about 20 seconds. You can do it at a stop light and stop traffic. With the top raised, the SLK is a solid, secure coupe, fully protected from the elements. There isn't the faintest trace of wind noise, and no compromise in the car's aerodynamics. There is no hint from inside that this is a convertible.

Substantially shorter than the senior SL models, the SLK Series is a true two-seater – there is nothing behind driver and passenger but bulkhead. While there is more than ample leg, shoulder, and head room in the cockpit, the Mercedes-Benz designers didn't plan on SLK owners taking any long trips. Trunk space with the top lowered is at a premium. There is a pull-out divider in the trunk (like a window shade) that clips into a sensor lockout. This not only defines the usable cargo area in the trunk (whatever you can get below the divider) if you are going to lower the top, but acts as an inter-

lock to prevent the hardtop from coming down if it is not in place, and say a suitcase or set of golf clubs is there instead.

The first SLK Series has a sense of proportion that stands alone, top up or down. While creating a completely new design, Mercedes stylists were careful to retain traditional, if not historic characteristics – the grille opening that has represented the SL lineage since 1954, and on the hood a classic reprise of the twin power domes of the 300 SL. But what they did on the inside was even more impressive.

We spend our time behind the wheel, not on the outside admiring the fenderlines. When you slip into the driver's seat of the SLK, it is wide, with better sidelong support than big SL's offer. All of the controls fall at hand, almost in a second nature fashion; they seem to be where you would expect them – nothing clever or innovative, just a straightforward driver's cockpit. The design in the first Series is 1950's retro combined with 1990's carbon fiber; a curving dashboard binnacle and instruments that are a stand-out

design rimmed in chrome with attractively back lighted ivory faces and black numerals. Everything else is grouped in the center console, with the hand brake recessed alongside the driver's seat. It is a dynamic juxtaposition of timeless design and modern technology.

The car handles easily, and unless you really push the envelope, it is difficult to get this car out of shape. With ABS braking and ASR traction control, the SLK provides superb handling. It is suitably balanced for the power available, and the engine provides just enough agility to make driving fun. The original AMG SLK provides a little extra pizzazz and more power. Also more than up to the task is the braking system, adapted from the larger E-Class. Although most of the original and current SLK model's underpin-

nings are C-Class derived, the engineers reasoned, and rightly so, that putting the E-Class binders on a lighter-weight car like the SLK would deliver exceptional braking capability.

The SLK is a true sports car, cut from the same legendary cloth as the 190 SL, the MGA, Jaguar XK-120, and Porsche 356, a fabric that has not been so finely woven in decades. This car is fun to drive and it is in the real world of day-to-day life where the SLK proves itself. Pull into a parking lot, push a button, and less than 30 seconds later you're locking the door on a hardtop coupe. Such virtues, original or not, can't be denied.

The SLK models had plenty of company in 1998, giving Daimler-Benz the most diversified product line since the 1930s, when there were Mercedes

The 1998 M-Class "All-Activity vehicle" broke the sport-utility model with a design that was sleek and functional. (Just prior to their launch they were featured in the second Jurassic Park movie.) The first models were powered by a 3.2-liter V6 developing 215 horsepower.

The S-Class had become larger and more powerful by 1999, but an all-new, and even more powerful, generation of S-Class models were just around the corner with the coming turn of the century.

Top: The 1999 CL Class coupes provided Mercedes owners with a perfect blend of sports car performance and luxury car comfort.

As the 20th century was nearing its end, Daimler-Benz resurrected a name from its historic past: Maybach. By the dawn of the 21st century Mercedes would have not only a new luxury standard for the world, but a new brand name.

a stunning, historic move both for Daimler-Benz and Chrysler, two companies that appeared to be doing well enough on their own. Underlying the merger, however, was the deep-seated desire each company had for change. Chrysler had the most forward thinking design studio in the U.S. in the late 1990s, and Mercedes had brought engineering and technology to new heights. Daimler-Benz needed more dealers in the U.S., Chrysler more in Europe. It was a marriage not of necessity, as had been the merger of Daimler and Benz in 1926, but one of mutual benefit. Both Chrysler and Daimler-Benz stood to gain in countless ways. With DaimlerChrysler AG came an exchange of information, technology, and design that has led to a significant number of Dodge and Chrysler hybrid designs employing Mercedes engineering. Conversely, Mercedes-Benz gained new product platforms, one of which made it debut in 2005.

As the last decade of the 20th century came to an end and a new millennium dawned, so too did a new Mercedes-Benz.

Here & left: Mercedes' racing heritage was also intact in the 1990s with cars claiming checkered flags in Formula 1 with Mika Häkkinen's World Championship titles in 1998 and 1999 driving a McLaren Mercedes. The Silver Arrows also won the World Sports Car Championship series title with the CLK-GTR. A street version of the car was also available at a cool $1.5 million a copy!

The 21ˢᵗ Century
A New Era Begins

Mercedes-Benz entered what was technically its third century as an automaker with the most expensive cars in its history. Since these are contemporary models, one might say that this is "history in the making." Thus an overview of each model year through 2006 is provided, along with a preview of the all-new 2007 S-Class.

For the 2000 model year Mercedes-Benz launched, in spring 1999 the all-new S430 and S500 sedans, the all-new CL500 Coupe, the 340-horsepower ML55 "Super SUV" (joining the ML320 and ML430), a four seat CLK430 Coupe to (accompany the CLK320 Cabriolet), and the "Designo" Edition Series, which offered the sporty SLK Roadsters, luxury S-Class Sedans, CLK Coupes and Cabriolets, SL Roadsters, and the E-Class Sedans and Wagons in a limited series of exclusive color schemes.

Enhancing the company's reputation for excellence in passenger safety, new curtain-type airbags were introduced in 2000 to provide extra protection for head and upper body in the event of a side impact. Rear door-mounted side airbags were also introduced on the M-Class, S-Class, E-Class, and CL Coupe, once again making Mercedes a leader in airbag technology.

The Mercedes' Electronic Stability Program (ESP), designed to detect and prevent oversteer or understeer, was also made a standard feature on all Mercedes models with the exception of the SLK.

What was once thought of as "the far distant future" in science fiction movies became realized in 2001, as the company brought about even more dramatic changes in the cars from Stuttgart, including the debut of nine new models: the new generation C-Class C240 and C320, the S-Class S600 (V12) and S55 AMG, the CL-Class CL600 (V12) and CL55 AMG, the CLK55 AMG Coupe, and the SLK320.

Perhaps the most significant new models were the re-designed C-Class, which now looked like a scaled down S-Class Mercedes, giving the entry-level cars a sense of style that had always been reserved for the senior models. Among the new C-Class offerings were the 168-horsepower C240 with V6 power, and 215-horsepower C320 with a 5-speed Touch Shift automatic as standard equipment.

Among the top-of-the-line V12 models and AMG editions, the CL600 came equipped with a new-generation, 362-horsepower V12, while the

The star (so far) of Mercedes' 21st century is a $452,000 Super Sports Car, the SLR McLaren. The new limited production two-seater recalls the glory days of the 1955 300 SLR and Mercedes-Benz Gullwing, combining their classic styling with state-of-the-art Formula 1 racing technology to create the greatest sports car ever built by Mercedes.

From left to right: For the 2000 model year Mercedes launched the all-new S430 and S500 sedans, CL500 Coupe, and the ML55 AMG, joining the ML320 and ML430 (not shown). The E-Class continued to offer exceptional value and freshened styling, and the SL class remained the company's sports car flagship.

Exceptional sedans for 2001, the economical C320 and luxury S600.

CLK55 AMG came with a 342-horsepower, hand-assembled AMG 5.5-liter V8, AMG tuned suspension, racing-derived brakes, AMG Monoblock 17-inch aluminum alloy wheels and tires, AMG aerodynamic package, and AMG-exclusive interior package.

In production since 1998, the SLK was given its first styling update with redesigned bumpers, fog lights, rocker panels, taillights, and redesigned seats; revised rear suspension; newly standard six-speed manual transmission; Touch Shift manual control for automatic transmission models; standard ESP stability control; and a power increase from 185 to 190 horsepower. The new SLK320 version, with a V6 engine, delivered a rousing 215 horsepower, and was distinguished by a unique front air dam and five-spoke wheels.

The 2002 lineup was further expanded with the addition of three new C-Class models, the C230 Sports Coupe, C320 Wagon, and C32 AMG Sedan. These were not to be your typical family cars. The C230 Sports Coupe brought high performance down in price with a 192-horsepower, supercharged engine, coupled to either a standard 6-speed transmission or an optional 5-speed automatic. The C320 Wagon was ready to haul more than kids and groceries with a 215-horsepower V6 under the hood, and the top-of-the-line C32 AMG Sedan delivered family car practicality tempered with a hand-built, 349-horsepower, supercharged V6, AMG speed-shift transmission, AMG tuned suspension, racing-derived brakes, and twin-spoke alloy wheels.

The CLK Class was revisited in 2002 with the addition of a CLK55 AMG Cabriolet, expanding the line to three Coupes and three Cabriolets. The new AMG model came loaded with a hand-built, intercooled 349-horsepower V8 engine.

The AMG moniker appears on more and more models including the sporty 2003 C32 AMG Sedan.

It was cute but Americans were still slow to warm up to the idea of a Mercedes hatchback. The sporty little C320 was nevertheless bringing new owners into the Silver Star family.

Below: The all-season family car was both a styling and engineering triumph for Mercedes with the 2003 C320 4Matic station wagon. Providing upscale styling and all-wheel-drive, the 4Matic drive system was available on all Mercedes sedans.

The SLK finally received the AMG treatment in 2002 with the high-performance SLK32 AMG added to the line. Under the hood, the V6 was breathed upon by AMG to deliver a rousing 349-horsepower.

In 2002 the M-Class got its first facelift with new bodywork and interior design, and the high-performance ML430 was replaced by the new ML500, equipped with a 5.0-liter V8.

The long-awaited G-Class also bowed in North America (officially) with the G500, a rugged, no-compromise off-road vehicle handcrafted in Graz, Austria by Styer. Powered by a 5.0-liter V8, the G500 set the benchmark for Mercedes SUVs with a sophisticated four-wheel-drive system employing three locking differentials and four-wheel traction control. It also came standard with a GPS navigation system, ABS, and Brake Assist. What finally convinced DaimlerChrysler to bring its big European 4 x 4 to the North American market? General Motors and the Hummer H1 and H2. Point, set, match.

E-Class luxury had performance to burn in 2003 with the E500 Sedan.

Left: The European Mercedes SUV G-Class "Geländewagen" was running the back roads of America in 2003 badged as the G500.

Below left: At long last a new SL Series made its debut in 2003. This is the SL55 AMG model.

In 2003 the Silver Star once again came to mean ever-improving design and technology. While Mercedes certainly could have ridden on the laurels of its 2002 models, in '03 there were improvements across the board.

The C-Class introduced a new 4Matic all-wheel-drive variant of the C240 and C320 sedans and wagons. The new C240 wagon (2.6-liter V6) joined the C320 wagon, with a 6-speed manual transmission standard on both models. Definitely not your typical grocery getters!

For the already popular, mid-priced E-Class, there were two new-generation sedans: the E320 (3.2-liter, 221-horsepower V6) and E500 (5.0-liter, 302-horsepower V8). Both models featured Mercedes' award-winning electronic braking system (first introduced on the 2003 SL500) and smart front airbags.

The S-Class was now equipped with the award-winning PreSafe concept, which is still in use on the latest Mercedes models. This innovative system really is a life-saver. In an unavoidable impact, additional electric seat belt tensioners are activated, adjusting seats to an optimum safety position: backrest raised, seat bottom lowered and moved rearwards. If skidding occurs, the sunroof automatically

The C-Class Sports Sedan for 2004 had the look of a baby S-Class.

Below: A fresh look for the 2003 SLK320.

closes. All models, (S430, S500, S55 AMG, and S600) received a bold, new front fascia, headlight and taillight glass, and interior updates. New 4Matic all-wheel-drive S430 and S500 models (40/60 torque split front/rear) also debuted. The S600 model was now equipped with the new bi-turbo V12 engine delivering 493 horsepower and 590 lb.-ft. of torque. A new supercharged 493-horsepower V8 was made available for the S55 AMG, which came equipped with redundant SpeedShift buttons on the steering wheel, a new racing-derived braking system, and redesigned AMG interior. This was an unprecedented marriage of performance and luxury, even by Mercedes-Benz standards. The new bi-turbo V12 engine was also made available in the CL600 model and the new supercharged V8 for the CL55 AMG.

The CLK-Class added two new-generation coupes with dynamic pillarless design: the CLK320 (3.2-liter, 215-horse-power V6) and CLK500 (5.0-liter, 302-horspower V8).

The really big news was the much anticipated next generation SL-Class. For 2003 the all-new SL500 two-seater was unveiled, with an award-winning, industry-first electronic braking system, ABC active suspension, automatic retractable hardtop, and on-board navigation. The striking new body design was only outdone by the promise of the ultimate SL, the SLR McLaren, still in the prototype stage but turning heads at auto shows and in magazines the world over. Also new was the SL55 AMG model with a supercharged, 493 horsepower V8 capable of delivering the car from 0 to 60 in

The best in class for the CLK-Class was the sleek, sporty 2004 CLK320 Cabriolet.

Bottom left: The 2004 E500 Sedan, powered by a 5.0-liter 302-horsepower V8, carried the weight, performance, and styling to make it one of the best-selling models in the Mercedes-Benz line.

Below: The 2004 S400 and S500 luxury sedans delivered exceptional performance and comfort. All models (S430, S500, S55 AMG, and S600) received a bold new front fascia, headlight and tail light glass, and interior updates. New 4Matic all-wheel-drive S430 and S500 models (40/60 torque split front/rear) also debuted.

With its 2003 restyle, the SL was now one of the hottest looking sports cars on the road inside and out, and the SL600 (pictured) with a V12 under the hood was also one of the fastest.

just 4.5 seconds! Handling dynamics to match were provided by a reprogrammed active suspension and racing-derived brakes.

When the 2004 model year rolled around, no one expected to see much change in Mercedes-Benz models, except DaimlerChrysler engineers, who grabbed the '04 spotlight with new technology. The S-Class was the first recipient with a new 7-speed automatic transmission system for the S430 and S500. The same transmission was also offered for the CL500 and SL500. In addition, three new-generation CLK Cabriolets were introduced: the CLK320, CLK500, and CLK55 AMG.

In 2005, half way through the first decade of the 21st century, Mercedes-Benz left the automotive and sports car world breathless with the production SLR McLaren, the most expensive and most powerful two-seater in the com-

pany's 119-year history. This was, and remains, the closest Mercedes-Benz, or any automaker for that matter, has ever come to creating an incontestable heir to the fêted 540K Special Roadster.

The new SLR Super Sports Car, to quote DaimlerChrysler, "...marks a new era of Mercedes-Benz passion for high-performance sports cars and at the same time celebrates the formidable SLR race cars of the 1950s. The SLR McLaren combines unmatched power and performance with classic Mercedes-Benz design cues unlike any other. The SLR features a full carbon fiber monocoque, crash structures, and body panels. It is powered by a 617-horsepower supercharged 5.5-liter V8 that rockets the new SLR from zero to 60 miles per hour in under 3.8 seconds on its way to a top speed exceeding 200 mph."

Each supercharged, intercooled V8 engine in the SLR is

For 2005 the M-Class was offered in a Special Edition.

Left: The 2005 CL65 AMG was equipped with a 6.0-liter V12 capable of launching the sporty two-door from 0 to 60 in just 4.2 seconds!

Below: Top up and dressed to thrill, the 2005 SL65 AMG was powered by a 6.0-liter twin-turbo V12 producing a staggering 604 horsepower and 738 lb.-ft. of torque.

hand-built at AMG's manufacturing facility in Affalterbach, Germany. The engine is mounted behind the front wheels in a front mid-engine position, contributing to the car's long profile. Dry-sump lubrication eliminates the need for an oil pan, allowing the engine to be mounted as low as possible in the frame for better aerodynamics and a lower center of gravity, which benefits handling. Dry-sump lubrication also prevents oil starvation under the hard cornering the SLR is capable of.

Not only does the new SLR boast a rich heritage, but it is also the new flagship of the multi-dimensional Mercedes-Benz brand. With by far the broadest product portfolio of any luxury automaker, Mercedes-Benz now offers an array of models ranging from mid-size coupes to large premium sedans as well as luxury roadsters, the SLR Super Sports Car, and the Maybach Series.

If the introduction of the SLR weren't enough to earn DaimlerChrysler the full attention of the automotive world in 2005, there were further improvements in several of the traditional models as well, particularly the newly redesigned C-Class with the Sport Sedan, Sport Coupe, Luxury Sedan, and Luxury Wagon. All received new exterior and interior updates, including body styling, headlamps and tail lamps, radiator grilles, wheels, dashboard, instrument cluster, steering wheel, and seats.

Replacing the C32 AMG, a new C55 AMG was added with a hand-built, normally aspirated AMG V8 engine producing 362 horsepower and 376 lb.-ft. of torque. For the E-Class, a new E320 CDI (highly fuel efficient) diesel version of the E-Class was added, utilizing innovative fully electronic fuel injection for better performance and mileage. This is the right engineering at a time when such

Maybach
The Other Side of the Star

In the golden era of the motorcar, Mercedes were regarded as very stylish automobiles; the majority of Maybach's motorcars, however, were conservative in nature. Introduced after World War I and selling for an average of 31,500 to 35,000 reichmarks, Maybach automobiles were competitive with those built by Mercedes-Benz and, one might say, built "in revenge" for the shoddy treatment the Maybach father and son had received from the D-M-G board in the early 1900s. Then too, there must have been some satisfaction in seeing Daimler forced into the 1926 merger with competitor Benz & Cie., although it guaranteed the company's survival in the recession-torn post-World War I years. Of course, this merger only served to strengthen both Daimler and Benz, forcing Maybach to build an even better car. That model arrived in 1929, the same year that the Graf Zeppelin, powered by five 550 horsepower Maybach V12 engines, circled the world in 448 hours. Following the August flight, Maybach introduced the company's first V12 automobile, a car intended to outclass the finest Mercedes-Benz and compete in the luxury market against such lofty marques as Rolls-Royce and Hispano-Suiza.

The 1929 twelve-cylinder DS marked the high point of the elder Maybach's career. Wilhelm Maybach passed away on December 29, at age 83. His son Karl developed the 150-horsepower, 7-liter, 60-degree V12 DS 7 (Double Six Cylinders, Seven Liters) Zeppelin model which debuted in 1930. The high torque twelve had a bore of 86mm and a stroke of 100mm, delivering peak horsepower at just 2800rpm. In 1931 an even more powerful 8-liter version was introduced, with a bore x stroke of 92mm x 100mm delivering a robust 200-horsepower at 3200rpm.

Facing new competition from Daimler-Benz in the 1930s, in 1937 Maybach introduced the

The sportier Maybach 57 is built on a shorter wheelbase and is intended to be either chauffeur- or owner-driven.

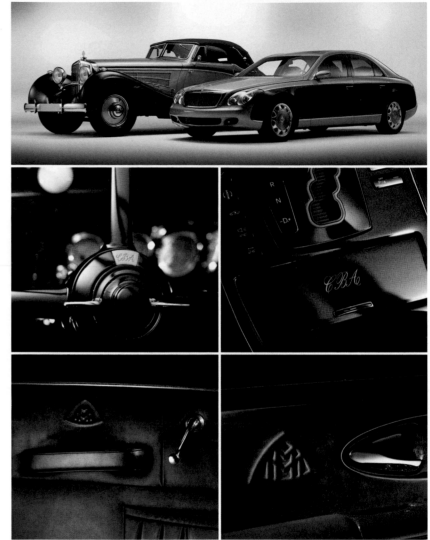

The Maybach heritage dates back to the post-World War I era, but it was the cars built in the 1930s which truly defined Maybach as a luxury car maker. Pictured is a new Maybach 57 compared to its historic namesake.

Zeppelin DS 8, a far more elegant looking automobile than the militaristic Grosser Mercedes-Benz 770 and also substantially larger. In Germany, general driver's licenses only permitted curb weights of up to two and a half tons, and because of its weight, more than three tons, a Maybach DS 8 owner had to pass the test for a truck driver's license! Despite

An impressive automobile for the 21st century, the design of the Maybach 57, like its 1930s ancestors, is unmistakable for any other automobile.

Bottom: The long wheelbase, ultra-luxury Maybach 62 is intended to be a chauffeur-driven car. Like Maybachs from the 1930s, these opulent motorcars are designed to wrest the luxury crown from Rolls-Royce, one of the few surviving competitors from the prewar era. In the 1930s the Maybach was marketed against R-R, Hispano-Suiza, and Isotta Fraschini, in Europe. And of course, Mercedes-Benz!

its massive size, the Maybach V12 was capable of attaining 100mph.

The bare chassis in U.S. dollars commanded a price in 1934 of $8,000—roughly the same as a Model J Duesenberg chassis cost in the United States. Maybach chassis were available in two wheelbase lengths, 144-inches and 147-inches, the former being discontinued in 1937.

The DS 8 line was produced though 1940, endowing Maybach with a reputation that ultimately came closer to that of Rolls-Royce than Mercedes-Benz. The Maybach Zeppelins came to be regarded as one of Germany's leading high-status luxury cars.

Always of conservative design, Maybach Twelve Limousines and Cabriolets appealed to the very wealthy, the German aristocracy who sometimes found Sindelfingen's styling for the Mercedes-Benz too flamboyant and the Auto Union's luxurious Horch line too middle class. Maybach also produced a companion line of six-cylinder models that culminated in the 1935 SW. In all, the company produced around 2,200 examples of 13 different models between 1921 and 1941, two decades of remarkable cars created by the Maybach father and son – cars that, had things gone differently, could have been Mercedes.

With the outbreak of World War II in 1939, Maybach began production of 12-cylinder diesel engines for use in tanks and half-track vehicles. This sustained the Maybach werke throughout the conflict, and after the war the company continued to manufacture diesels. As an automaker,

and hand-built by AMG, the 57S powerplant displaces six liters, a half liter more than the standard engine. With higher turbo boost pressure and other modifications, the engine produces a stout 604 horsepower as well as 738 pound-feet of torque from as low as 2,000 rpm. Revised ESP stability control and traction control programming help make the most of the additional power. In keeping with the car's high-performance character, the Maybach 57S rides about a half inch lower, with firmer air suspension and stiffer shock absorbers, as well as thicker stabilizer bars. The new sport chassis provides even more impressive handling without unduly compromising the car's whisper-smooth ride.

Maybach was finished, even though the factory briefly entertained the idea in the early 1950s. In 1960 Maybach Motorenbau GmbH and Daimler-Benz AG entered into an agreement whereby Maybach would produce Daimler diesel engines. Today, the company is part of DaimlerChrysler, producing Mercedes-Benz heavy diesel engines at Friedrichshafen, and of course, the Maybach automobile has at last become the top-of-the-line Daimler-Benz luxury model it should have been more than half a century ago.

The new Maybach models have been in production for several years, although their numbers are quite limited due to the time it takes to build cars to the customer's preference, and of course, the price. The latest model, the 2005 Type 57S Sedan delivers exotic sports car performance.

The 57S was developed in response to customers who expressed interest in a Maybach with even higher performance than the standard 57 model. The 57S is also expected to attract an eclectic mix of affluent buyers, many of whom currently own exotic sports cars. Building on the successful Maybach platform, the 57S offers more sportscar-like performance and handling. In addition to flatter cornering and crisper steering response, the 57S can rush from 0 to 60 in less than 5 seconds and is capable of reaching a top speed of 172mph.

The 57S model features a higher-performance version of the Maybach twin-turbo, intercooled V12 engine. Designed

Approximately 300 Maybach Zeppelins were produced between 1930 and 1939. This example from the Nethercutt Collection was built in 1932 and bodied by Karosserie Spohn in Ravensburg, as a four-door cabriolet (convertible sedan). It originally sold for $12,000; thus the coachwork would have comprised around $4000 of that price.

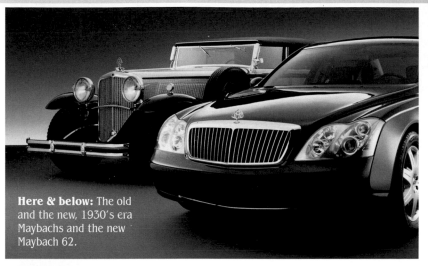

Here & below: The old and the new, 1930's era Maybachs and the new Maybach 62.

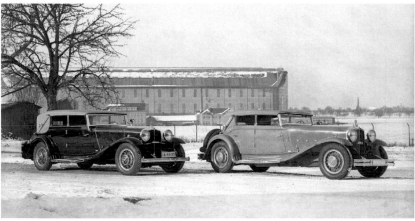

The sportiest Maybach model is the 2006 limited-edition 57S. Available in a choice of a unique black or silver paint scheme, and new 11-spoke, 20-inch alloy wheels with 275/45 R 20 Michelin Pilot Sport tires, the price is an equally impressive $360,000.

The limited-edition Maybach 57S comes in a choice of a unique black or silver paint and can be identified by new 11-spoke, 20-inch alloy wheels with 275/45 R 20 Michelin Pilot Sport tires, as well as a more aggressive grill, body-color headlight surrounds, chrome-trimmed fog lights, rectangular dual exhausts, and 57S badging on the trunk lid and front fenders. Inside, the 57S makes a bolder design statement with a choice of Black or Ivory White Grand Napa Leather seats, both embellished with dynamic black piping. Equally distinctive is true carbon fiber trim complemented by piano lacquer, which replaces the fine woods that usually set the tone for Maybach interiors. As an alternative to the carbon fiber trim, Maybach customers can also choose a black poplar wood trim which will debut on the 57S in 2006, and will only be offered on this special model. The Maybach 57S is priced around $360,000.

For 2005 Mercedes-Benz delivered the ultimate small sports car in the re-designed and re-engineered SLK. With a big, 266-horsepower, 4-valve-per-cylinder V6 engine and front end styling like the $452,000 SLR McLaren (bottom right), the SLK can turn heads and fast laps. An AMG version offers a first-ever V8 for the sporty 2-seater along with 355 horsepower.

things matter, with diesel fuel costing more than gasoline.

This was truly the year for AMG, as another new model was added to the SL Series, the SL65 AMG, powered by a 6.0-liter twin-turbo V12 producing a staggering 604 horsepower and 738 lb.-ft. of torque. Within the CL-Class a new AMG model debuted as well, the CL65 AMG with the same 6.0-liter twin-turbo V12.

Aside from the SLR, Mercedes saved the best for last and waited for the SLR McLaren's debut before unveiling an all-new 2005 SLK with front-end styling nearly identical to the $452,000 Super Sports Car. The SLK had already become a benchmark design with the first folding hardtop, AMG power, and SL lineage, but the restyle simply left everyone astounded. Here was a Mercedes sports car priced under $50,000 that looked like it should cost twice as much. In addition, an AMG version was available right out of the chute, providing not one, but two new models.

Utilizing an all-new platform, the 2005 SLK was powered by a new-generation engine with four-valve technology and variable valve timing, a more precise six-speed manual transmission, and came standard with 17-inch, 10-spoke alloy wheels, and an available sport suspension. In addition, the new V8-powered SLK55 AMG replaced the older SLK32 AMG, giving the sports model a high-performance V8 for the first time.

To quote DaimlerChrysler, "(The SLR Mclaren) marks a new era of Mercedes-Benz passion for high-performance sports cars and at the same time celebrates the formidable SLR race cars of the 1950s. The SLR McLaren combines unmatched power and performance with classic Mercedes-Benz design cues unlike any other. The SLR features a full carbon fiber monocoque, crash structures, and body panels. It is powered by a 617-horsepower supercharged 5.5-liter V8 that rockets the new SLR from zero to 60 miles per hour in under 3.8 seconds on its way to a top speed exceeding 200 mph."

The author had the opportunity to test both versions on a racetrack late in 2005 and from every conceivable aspect this is the best sports car in its price class, in the world, period. The SLK has everything – style, performance, comfort, and the cachet that only comes from a car with a Silver Star.

For the 2006 model year Mercedes-Benz celebrates two historic milestones, the 120th anniversary of the first Benz motorwagen, patented in January 1886, and the 80th anniversary of the merger of Daimler and Benz in June 1926, officially creating the Mercedes-Benz brand.

Aside from new models, DaimlerChrysler had something a bit more ambitious in mind for the dual anniversaries: the opening of a brand new Mercedes-Benz Museum in Untertürkheim, Germany. The magnificent new facility, not only a visual landmark from the exterior, but an equally dynamic museum from the inside, provides the greatest history of the automobile under one roof anywhere in the world and should quickly become a "must see" attraction for any European vacation.

To kick off the 2006 anniversary year, the first product combining Chrysler and Mercedes technology and engineering with the Mercedes-Benz name was introduced. In recent years the flow of technology has been to Chrysler in platform design for the Crossfire and Chrysler 300, among others, but with the R-Class, Chrysler's long history with the design and development of minivans has come to the fore, and it is the luxurious Chrysler Pacifica that has inspired this all-new class of Mercedes.

The R-Class combines the distinct advantages of several disparate vehicles – the sure-footedness of a four-wheel-drive sport utility vehicle, the performance and comfort of a fine sports sedan, and the versatility of a luxury wagon.

With its own unique styling and exceptional performance, the 2006 CLS500 is the sleekest sedan ever produced by Mercedes. With an unmistakable look that appears more like a coupe than a sedan, and a low, wide stance, the aggressive CLS500 (also offered in an AMG version) raises the bar for high-performance luxury cars. The CLS500 is powered by a 302-horsepower V8. The AMG upgrades boost output by nearly 170 horsepower.

The new platform makes use of power-assisted rack-and-pinion steering and four-wheel independent suspension with double control arms in the front and a new four-link suspension at the rear. Ample braking is provided by large four-wheel disc brakes with vented discs and double-piston calipers up front. The R350 has 17-inch seven-spoke light-alloy wheels shod with 235 / 65 R 17 tires, and the R500 comes with 18-inch wheels fitted with 255 / 55 R 18 tires. Either model can be ordered with an AMG sport package that includes 19-inch wheels and tires. The R350 and R500 models are powered by a 268-horsepower, 3.5-liter V6 and 302-horsepower, 5.0-liter V8, respectively.

The all-new and strikingly modern CLS-Class (which made its debut in 2005) offers a four-door coupe in two models, the 302-horsepower CLS500 and 469-horsepower CLS55 AMG. Both CLS models feature sleek, eye-catching exterior lines that continue through the interior, where leather and wood cover most surfaces. Large rear doors are by far the most striking feature of the coupe-like model. The CLS models have a look that is unlike any other Mercedes. The 302-horsepower CLS500 provides sparkling performance while the formidable CLS55 AMG adds nearly 170 horsepower through sophisticated supercharger technology that's similar to the E55 AMG and SL55 AMG.

The 2006 SLR McLaren, like its 2005 predecessor, is the first series production vehicle to utilize a front crash structure made exclusively of carbon fiber. Derived from Formula 1 racing, the carbon fiber crash structure absorbs four to fives times more energy in a severe frontal collision than similar structures made of conventional steel.

An all-new, second-generation M-Class for 2006 re-establishes the benchmark among luxury SUVs with two new models, the 268-horsepower, 3.5-liter V6 ML350, and 302-horsepower, 5.0-liter V8 ML500. Both offer a new seven-speed automatic transmission with the Direct Select column-mounted shifter introduced on the R-Class.

The SLK-Class adds a third model, the SLK280 with a 3.0-liter, 228-horsepower version of the new twin-cam V6.

For the CL-Class, the AMG Sport package becomes standard on CL500 and CL600, and in the S-Class, a new S65 AMG model with a 604-horsepower V12 joins the line to become the world's quickest four-door luxury car, with a 0 to 60 record of just 4.2 seconds!

While it is hard to believe that an automaker can make so many changes on an almost yearly basis today, Mercedes-Benz continues to surprise its loyal clientele as well as the automotive world. A look at model year 2007 proves this point.

Mercedes-Benz is already working on the launch of the next-generation S-Class – the company's new flagship sedan unveiled at the Frankfurt auto show in September 2005. The successor to a long line of premium luxury vehicles, the 2007 S-Class sedan will debut with a significantly evolved design and a stronger presence in 2006.

Sharper angles and cleaner lines frame a sedan that gains about 1.7 inches of length, almost an inch in width, and more than three inches in wheelbase over its predecessor. The "S" designation had long been used to identify top-of-the-line Mercedes-Benz sedans and coupes, and the S-Class has embodied the brand's flagship role for more than five decades.

In the U.S. market, the new S-Class line will be launched with an all-new 5.5-liter V8 engine delivering 382 horsepower and 391 lb.-ft. of torque, the first of a new-generation V8 engine family featuring four-valve-per-cylinder technology and variable valve timing. Later in 2007, an S600 model will be powered by a 5.5-liter twin-turbo V12 with 510hp and 612 lb.-ft. of torque.

The new S-Class comes with the world's first seven-speed automatic, a smooth-shifting, driver-adaptive transmission that maximizes both performance and fuel economy. An electronic parking brake is engaged at the push of a button on the dash.

The revolutionary S-Class Pre Safe system that made its debut in 2002 on the S-Class is further developed for the 2007 model and now automatically closes the side windows to provide better support for the window curtain air bags, and special seat cushions can inflate to provide greater lateral support for occupants and to help the side air bags provide even better collision protection.

The well-known Distronic cruise control feature that maintains a pre-

For the 2006 model year the American-made M-Class gets a total makeover with sportier, more aggressive styling inside and out. The M-Class is manufactured in Tuscaloosa, Alabama.

All-new for 2006, the R-Class is a sporty minivan with Mercedes luxury and performance. The new platform makes use of power-assisted rack-and-pinion steering, four-wheel independent suspension, and large, four-wheel disc brakes with vented discs and double-piston calipers up front. Either the R350 or R500 models can be ordered with an AMG sport package that includes 19-inch wheels and tires. The R350 and R500 models are powered by a 268-horsepower 3.5-liter V6 and 302-horsepower 5.0-liter V8, respectively.

set following distance behind the vehicle ahead is replaced by an optional "Distronic Plus" system. Integrated with the latest Pre Safe, the radar-based system operates at nearly all speeds up to 125mph and can be especially helpful in stop-and-go traffic.

Newly developed short-range radar with a frequency of 24 gigahertz sweeps the immediate 33 yards in front in a fan-shaped, 80-degree pattern, working in tandem with a narrower nine-degree beam of longer-range 77-gigahertz radar. The two radar frequencies complement each other to cover a full range of more than 160 yards – more than 1 1/2 football fields.

Making its debut on the 2007 S-Class, an enhanced version of the Mercedes-Benz Brake Assist system not only supplies full-power braking assist in emergencies as soon as the driver applies the brake pedal, but also monitors the distance to the vehicle ahead and adjusts brake pressure if the driver doesn't brake hard enough. While conventional Brake Assist is only triggered by the driver's reflex reaction on the brake pedal, Brake Assist

Plus also considers the closing speed of the vehicle ahead based on radar signals from the Distronic Plus system. It also incorporates 24 GHz radar-based Park Assist. This new option utilizes six radar sensors mounted behind the front and rear bumpers – eliminating the need for the visible "portholes" of the previous ultrasonic-based system. The result is clean, integrated, and invisible, with greater range and sensitivity.

Another innovative technology making its debut on the 2007 S-Class is infra-red night vision, a new option that can extend the driver's "visibility" to nearly 500 feet. An industry first, and in contrast to passive systems offered by other auto companies, this active system bathes the road ahead with infra-red light from two projectors mounted in the headlight assemblies. An infra-red camera discreetly mounted in the windshield receives the reflected images, which are viewed in a high-resolution display in the instrument cluster. The result is akin to a highly detailed black & white video image.

The 2006 S600 packs performance and power with a 60-degree V12 delivering 493 horsepower.

Among the advanced features of the new car is a slot in the dash that accepts a PCMCIA card. Such cards never need to be charged, and some versions can hold up to 1500 digital songs. Its data is to be displayed on the screen of the command system, and titles can be selected through the multifunction steering wheel controls.

High quality materials used throughout the cabin of the new S-Class are punctuated by sweeping lines of exotic wood accented with chrome trim, forming a practical yet luxurious environment that emphasizes easy access to vehicle features.

With the 2007 models on the horizon, DaimlerChrysler has realized the evolution of the Mercedes from the first motorcars to bear the name in 1901 to the latest luxury cars to proudly wear the three-pointed star. With the super-luxury Maybach line yet another prophecy has been

fulfilled, the joining once again of the two names that were responsible for the very first Mercedes. History has come full circle, and for Mercedes-Benz owners and enthusiasts alike, the future has arrived.

In today's very crowded automotive world, we often overlook or forget the significance of these two great German marques. Throughout the last 120 years, Benz, Daimler, and Mercedes-Benz have been responsible for either inventing or perfecting the greatest advancements in vehicle design, performance, and safety. Since the first motorcar to bear the Mercedes name, the very nature of the automobile – in both appearance and engineering – has evolved from that concept introduced by Wilhelm Maybach and Paul Daimler in 1901.

The catalog of achievements under the Daimler and Benz names, not the least of which is the patent for the very

A first look at the all-new 2007 S-Class reveals a fresh sense of style evolved from the rakish lines of the CLS500, but with an even more aggressive stance improved upon by bold fender bulges and a "Coke bottle" tapered rocker panel treatment.

Below: Celebrating the 120th anniversary of the Benz Patent Motorwagen and 80th anniversary of the Daimler and Benz merger in 1926, DaimlerChrysler christened an all-new museum in the historic city of Untertürkheim, Germany.

first automobile by Carl Benz in 1886, is filled with firsts, such as the vee-twin engine, the four-cylinder engine, 4-speed gearbox with gated linkage, jet-type carburetor, fuel-injection, supercharging, four-wheel independent suspension, crumple zones, side impact protection, anti-lock brakes, and air bags – all among the most noteworthy advancements in automotive design and engineering. But there are hundreds of smaller, unseen improvements to Mercedes' credit in areas of electrical systems, door locks, and even the materials that are used to build automobiles.

There is also more than a century of motorsports history surrounding the Silver Star and victories by the score in every decade of the 20th century. Today Mercedes-Benz continues to win its share of sports car and Formula 1 races by using the latest technology, technology that has for more than 100 years found its way into the cars we drive every day.

More than a celebration of the 120th anniversary of Daimler and Benz and the 80th anniversary of their merger, 2006 is a celebration of the automobile, and the company that invented and perfected it, a claim that no other automaker in the world can ever make.

The Mercedes-Benz Classic Center
Where the 20th and 21st Centuries Meet

The new Mercedes-Benz Classic Center in Irvine, California, offers the same unique restoration services as the German Classic Center in Fellbach, which had been responsible for some of the finest classic Mercedes restorations in the world.

What if you owned a rare, 120-year-old Swiss watch, and it broke? You would take it to a local watch repairman and hope he had the skills to fix it. But what if you could take that watch back to the company that made it more than a century ago, and you didn't even have to leave the country to do it? You could return it to the original manufacturer, to be repaired with original parts by skilled laborers with more than a century of knowledge behind them. How good would that be?

That was the question DaimlerChrysler was asking when they decided to build a second Classic Center. The original is in Fellbach, Germany, where vintage Mercedes go to get rebuilt by factory technicians using OEM parts. Now, a second facility, with the same capability, is open in Irvine, California. Irvine was chosen for the location because "California is the heart of car culture in America," according to DaimlerChrysler, "and has always been one of the most popular and best markets for Mercedes-Benz worldwide."

The Mercedes-Benz Classic Center, the first and only manufacturer-backed classic center of its kind in America, opened its doors for business in February 2006 and offers a full complement of services including retail sales, restoration, appraisal, and vehicle-search assistance for Mercedes-Benz models aged 20 years and older.

"Imagine the chance to step back in time and purchase the Mercedes-Benz of your dreams right off the showroom floor, and that is the magic of the Mercedes-Benz Classic Center," said manager Mike Kunz. "For those who longed for these cars when they were younger, or for customers who are new to the brand and value, the nostalgia and timeless style that comes with a vintage Mercedes, the Classic Center provides a unique opportunity unmatched by any other marque in the world to relive automotive history."

Vehicles are offered at a wide range of prices beginning at approximately $25,000 and reaching upwards into the millions. The Classic Center operates a full service department. All technicians employed at the Mercedes-Benz Classic Center are qualified to work on all Mercedes-Benz vehicles classified by the company as "classic" – currently up to and including the 126 series (280-560 models) built from 1979 to 1992.

Of course, you don't have to own a classic Mercedes-Benz to enjoy a visit to the Classic Center. The Center will offer something for all enthusiasts, from those who enjoy admiring expertly restored classic Mercedes-Benz cars to those shopping in the boutique for a full line of automotive and lifestyle accessories.

The Classic Center in Irvine maintains a direct link to the factory and Classic Center in Fellbach, with unequalled access to the parts, tools, service manuals, and production records needed to work on these great automobiles, especially in the case of vehicles long out of production, such as the spectacular 540 K of the 1930s. Owners who enjoy maintaining and repairing their classic Mercedes-Benz cars will find a wide selection of parts available through the Classic Center. And what is not in stock can be ordered. The Classic Center has access to 42,000 different parts for every regular production Mercedes-Benz from 1945 through the 126 series models. Should an original part not be available, the Classic Center can turn to the Mercedes-Benz Prototype Department and the Research and Development Department for assistance in remanufacturing the parts!

For Silver Star enthusiasts in America, this is a dream come true.

Mercedes-Benz
Poster Art

Automobiles and art have gone hand-in-hand for more than a century. First depicted in late 1890's racing posters, the images of car and driver have been presented in so many forms and by so many famous artists, from Henri Toulouse-Lautrec to Walter Gotschke, that automotive art has virtually become a part of our culture.

As one might expect, since Daimler and Benz were the first automakers, the most abundant prints and paintings spanning the late 19th to early 20th century are of Benz, Daimler, and Mercedes motorcars. To depict every historic image pertaining to the marque would require a book unto its own, so we have selected the best-of-the-best from more than 100 years of Mercedes-Benz art by some of the world's greatest illustrators.

During the golden era of the motorcar, all of the illustrations were paintings; in fact, rarely were photographs used except for the occasional portrait of a winning race driver. Some of the most striking illustrations for Mercedes-Benz were done by the legendary Walter Gotschke in the late 1930s and originals of his work command very high prices today. Other noted Daimler and Benz illustrators are Henri Rudaux and Ludwig Homlwein (c.1908-1914), Hans Neumann (c.1920s), Charles Belser (1930s), and Hans Liska in the 1950s, who illustrated the great 300 SL and SLR poster series from 1952 to 1955, as well as many 1950's sales brochures, which have themselves become collectible art among Mercedes-Benz collectors.

Most of the early illustrations used for Daimler, Benz, and Mercedes-Benz advertising were signed by the artist and this too has added value to collecting these magnificent works of automotive art. All of the images in this chapter are from the DaimlerChrysler archives, and as such, all are original German advertisements.

Like music, art transcends cultures and borders, and Mercedes-Benz automotive art looks great in any language!

Center: Drama was the artist's inspiration for this c.1914 Mercedes advertisement which played upon the sports racing theme while incorporating the new Mercedes star in the steering wheel.
Top left: From the earliest years Mercedes played upon its racing successes in advertising. This poster from 1908 was illustrated by Henri Rudaux.
Bottom left: Rudaux was a popular illustrator in the early 1900s and was often commissioned to design Mercedes art, such as this example c.1908-1910.
Top right: Another early 1900's Mercedes poster subtly noting the company's manufacture not only of motorcars but aircraft engines as well. The illustration was done by Ludwig Hohlwein.
Bottom right: Rudaux created a variation of an earlier work to depict Mercedes passengers excited to see a Zeppelin powered by Daimler engines.

Top left: Benz & Co. (Benz & Cie.) was also involved in manufacturing aero engines and this c. 1914 advertisement displays both automobile and flugmotoren (flight motor) in a fashion similar to Daimler ads of the period.
Bottom left: Daimler had also been a leader in commercial vehicle manufacture since the turn of the century and occasionally depicted both cars and trucks in its advertising.
Center: In the period during World War I the dual images of motorcars and aircraft were frequently illustrated in Mercedes ads, this example c.1914 painted by Klusmeyer.
Top & bottom right: Two 1914 ads for Daimler's commercial vehicles.

Top left: In the midst of a world war Benz advertising displayed the company's involvement on land, sea, and in the air.

Bottom left: Peace made for better illustrations than war and in this whimsical 1921 ad the lovely fräulein is hugging her Benz, "My Benz!!" The style is similar to illustrations done by French artist Louis Icart in the 1920s.

Top center: Something Mercedes-Benz collectors might consider looking for, a DMG typewriter, one of many products built by Daimler after World War I.

Bottom center: The Castle Solitude was to play an historic role in Daimler and Mercedes history. This poster for the 1925 Solitude Motorrad-Rennen (motor race) would be the last year the two marques would compete against each other. Solitude became the backdrop for some of the most significant Mercedes-Benz photographs of the 1950s and 1960s, and is used even to this day.

Right: The June 1926 merger of Daimler and Benz was depicted in a variety of new advertisements, one of the most famous being this dramatic illustration from 1926.

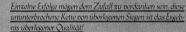

Top left: Competition had played a significant role in both Daimler and Benz history up to the 1926 merger, and this dynamic illustration signified the joining of the two great racing teams under the Mercedes-Benz banner.

Bottom left: Another famous illustration underscoring the merger is this ladies day out in a new 1926 Model K. The company often used women, rather than men, in their advertising.

Center: Mercedes-Benz quickly made a new name for itself in racing with motorcars like the 1927 Model S.

Top right: Another colorful Mercedes ad from 1928. Once again the artist chose a woman (and a rather strong one at that) to emphasize the brand. The illustration was done by Hans Neumann, who created a number of ads for Daimler-Benz in the late 1920s.

Bottom right: This c.1928 ad shows the Model S Mercedes as the vehicle of choice for a Maharajah. The luxury automotive market in India was, at the time, dominated by Rolls-Royce.

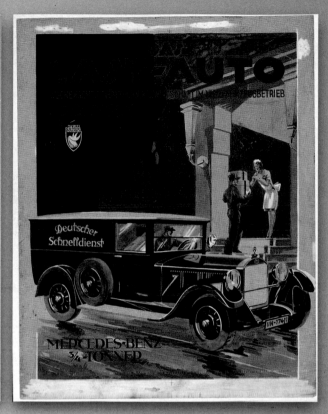

Top left: A 1928 illustration shows a lovely lady ready for a drive in her Model SS. No doubt there were many women owners and drivers of the sporty Mercedes S series cars.

Top center: This 1928 illustration shows an elegant limousine body style.

Top right: The commercial side of Daimler and Benz also flourished after the merger, as this 1928 ad illustrates.

Bottom left: To wish upon a star. This beautiful 1929 illustration by Hans Neumann is one of the most elegant of the early Mercedes-Benz ads.

Bottom center & right: One must remember that in Germany, and much of Europe before World War II, Mercedes-Benz was the equivalent of General Motors in size and manufacturing, with full lines of commercial vehicles including trucks, buses, tractors, and farm equipment.

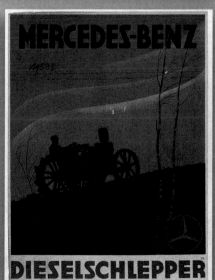

Rudolf Caracciola

stellt mit dem

Mercedes-Benz-Rennwagen

auf der Rekordstrecke des Königl. Ungar.
Automobilklubs Budapest am 28. 10. 1934
zwei Internationale Rekorde auf und zwar:

1 fliegender km = 317,460 km-Std.
1 fliegende Meile = 316,591 km-Std.

Dabei erreichte Rudolf Caracciola mit dem
nach der internationalen Rennformel gebauten
MERCEDES-BENZ-Schwingachs-Rennwagen eine

Spitzenleistung von 320,855 km-Std.

also die größte Geschwindigkeit, die jemals
auf normaler Straße erreicht wurde.

DAIMLER-BENZ A.-G. STUTTGART-UNTERTÜRKHEIM

Im schwersten Bergrennen
der Welt stellt

MERCEDES-BENZ

zum 10. Mal einen Rekord auf!

Caracciola fuhr auf dem neuen MERCEDES-BENZ-
Rennwagen im X. Internationalen Klausenpaß-Rennen
1934 mit 15 Min. 22⅕ Sek., rd. 83,9 km Durchschnitts-
geschwindigkeit, die beste Zeit des Tages und stellte
einen neuen Klassen-Rekord für Rennwagen auf.

Damit hält MERCEDES-BENZ
alle Wagenrekorde auf dem Klausenpaß,
also für Touren-, Sport- und Rennwagen!

MERCEDES-BENZ beweist
wiederum Höchstleistung u. Qualität

DAIMLER-BENZ A.-G. STUTTGART-UNTERTÜRKHEIM

Caracciola siegt
auf MERCEDES-BENZ
im Eifel-Rennen 1935!

1892 gefährliche Kurven
7700 m Höhenunterschied

stellten unerhörte Anforderungen an Fahrer und Wagen. Aus phantastischen Spitzenge-
schwindigkeiten mußten die Fahrzeuge in die Kurven gezwungen werden, mit faszinierender
Beschleunigung schossen die Wagen aber in die langen, dennoch aber heimtückischen Geraden.
Die Überlegenheit der mit Bosch-Kerzen und Continental-Reifen ausgerüsteten MERCEDES-
BENZ-Wagen kommt am deutlichsten dadurch zum Ausdruck, daß drei MERCEDES-BENZ-
Wagen rundenweise in prächtiger Fahrt führten, Caracciola in der 11. Runde mit 123,85 km/Std.
die **schnellste Zeit des Tages** fuhr, daß außer dem siegreichen Caracciola auch noch
die beiden MERCEDES-BENZ-Fahrer Luigi Fagioli und H. Lang den 4. und 5. Platz belegten
und daß schließlich auch in der großen Sportwagenklasse H. Berg auf MERCEDES-BENZ-
SSK-Wagen den Sieg eroberte.

MERCEDES-BENZ führt weiterhin in Leistung und Qualität!

DAIMLER-BENZ AG. STUTTGART-UNTERTÜRKHEIM

MERCEDES-BENZ siegt
überlegen im »Großen
Preis von Frankreich«
23. Juni 1935

Nach den prachtvollen Rennsport-Erfolgen zu Monte Carlo, in Tripolis, auf der Avus und beim Eifel-
Rennen siegte MERCEDES-BENZ in überlegener Form auch im »Großen Preis von Frankreich«. Mit
dem überragenden Stundendurchschnitt von 124,971 km meisterte Caracciola als Sieger
dieses phantastische Rennen. Den zweiten Platz sicherte sich von Brauchitsch mit nur wenigen
Wagenlängen hinter Caracciola. Als Vierter beendete Fagioli in hervorragender Fahrweise diesen
schweren Kampf. Diese ausgezeichneten Ergebnisse beweisen erneut die ausgeglichene Konstruktion
der MERCEDES-BENZ-Wagen, die Kurvenlage und
Bremsfähigkeit, die Durchhaltefähigkeit und vor allem hohe Fahrgeschwindigkeit des MERCEDES-
BENZ-Wagen unübertroffen ist. Die herrlichen Erfolge sind um so höher zu werten, als die Bahn zu
Montlhéry durch schwierige »Schikanen« unerhörte Anforderungen stellte, mußten die Wagen
doch aus den höchsten Geschwindigkeiten heraus plötzlich abgebremst, im Zickzack durch die
»Schikanen« hindurchgesteuert und sofort wieder auf Spitzentempo beschleunigt werden. Alle drei
gestarteten MERCEDES-BENZ-Wagen, mit Continental-Reifen und Bosch-Kerzen ausgerüstet, haben
sich bei dieser Zerreißprüfung glänzend bewährt. MERCEDES-BENZ triumphiert wie 1914 im Großen
Preis von Frankreich dank der Ausgeglichenheit der in jeder Beziehung überlegenen Konstruktion
und der bewundernswerten Fahrkunst von Caracciola, v. Brauchitsch und Fagioli.

DAIMLER-BENZ AG. STUTTGART-UNTERTÜRKHEIM

Top & bottom left: While business was making cars, trucks, and
other forms of motorized transportation, the heart and soul of Daimler-
Benz revolved around motorsports, and ads proclaiming the company's
success were quite popular. In these rather straightforward print ads,
the company proclaimed the victories of Rudolf Caracciola in 1934.
Center: Caracciola was in the spotlight once again in 1935 with a win
in the Eifelrennen.
Top right: Victory for the Mercedes team at Montlhéry in June 1935.
Bottom right: Another Mercedes sweep, with a 1-2-3 finish in the
1935 Spanish Grand Prix. Celebrated team drivers Rudolf Caracciola,
Luigi Fagioli, and Manfred von Brauchitsch finished in order.

22. September 1935:

Großer Preis
von Spanien

1. Rudolf Caracciola
2. Luigi Fagioli
3. M. von Brauchitsch

3 MERCEDES-BENZ-Wagen am Start!
3 MERCEDES-BENZ-Wagen beendeten, inklusiv
klug gefahren, eines der schwersten Rennen
der Saison, die 519 Kilometer lange Strecke des
»Großen Preis von Spanien«, siegreich in
neuer Rekord-Zeit. Sie setzen die unvergleich-
lichen MERCEDES-BENZ-Siegesserie dieses
Jahres fort: Es ist der 9. MERCEDES-BENZ-
Sieg der Saison, oder 6. Sieg des Deutschen
Straßen-Meisters Rudolf Caracciola auf

MERCEDES-BENZ
mit Continental-Reifen und Bosch-Kerzen

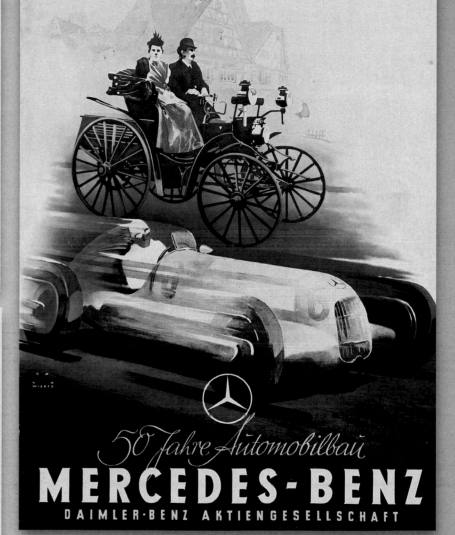

Top left: This ad was used to proclaim Mercedes 1935 Grand Prix victories.
Top center: Victory in the 1935 Swiss GP for Caracciola and Fagioli.
Bottom left: The two most popular and charismatic drivers of the 1930s, Rudolf Caracciola and Manfred von Brauchitsch, pictured in a rarely seen photographic ad from the 1935 season.
Bottom center: A 1935 victory ad for races won in Africa (Tripoli) and in Finland.
Above: The year 1936 was the first great milestone for Daimler-Benz as the company celebrated the first half century of the automobile and the 1886 Benz patent.

Top left: It seemed as though Caracciola and Mercedes could not be beaten and the cannonade across Europe and Africa brought victory upon victory in the 1930s. Here is the poster from the 1936 race at Tunis.

Top center: Hermann Lang, promoted from racing mechanic to company driver, reached an uncontested average speed of 261.7km/h (156mph) in the new W 125 at the Avus; the top speed of 380km/h (228mph) in this race was not to be exceeded until 1959! Lang won the Grand prix at Tripoli in 1937.

Top right: Caracciola was the European driving champion in 1935 and 1937. This again was one of the few Mercedes illustrations to use a photograph.

Bottom left: Caracciola won the 1937 German Grand Prix, with von Brauchitsch in second, Christian Kautz sixth, and Hermann Lang finishing seventh.

Bottom right: In 1938, Mercedes' domination of Grand Prix racing continued. The Silver Arrows would continue to do so until the start of World War II in 1939.

Top left: This c.1937 poster from the Swiss GP proclaims a first through fourth place sweep by the W 125 and Mercedes-Benz team, with Caracciola, Lang, von Brauchitsch, and Zautz finishing in order.

Bottom left: Three names kept coming up in rotating order throughout the last years of Grand Prix racing before World War II. In this 1938 poster by Gotschke, it is von Brauchitsch, Caracciola, and Lang finishing 1-2-3 in the 32nd GP of France.

Bottom center: Caracciola winning the 1938 Coppa Acerbo. The illustration again by Gotschke.

Top center: By the end of the 1930s, Hermann Lang was becoming a star, winning the last German GP before the war. The spectacular poster was illustrated by Walter Gotschke.

Above right: It was Lang in the winner's circle again in the 1939 Belgian Grand Prix.

Top left: The Three Musketeers of German Grand Prix Racing, von Brauchitsch, Caracciola, and Lang left their mark on the 1939 Eifel-Rennen with Lang adding another first place finish to his new career as a factory race driver.

Top Center: Lang and Caracciola took the top honors at the 1939 Grand Prix of Tripoli, and another striking Gotschke poster was created.

Bottom left: Lang was now the leader with another 1939 victory at Pau, followed by von Brauchitsch for a 1-2 finish.

Bottom center & above: With victories in the 1939 Swiss GP and the Höhenstrassen-Rennen, Lang had become a legend behind the wheel of the W 125. His career as a Mercedes team driver would continue after the war when the factory returned to sports car racing in 1952.

MERCEDES-BENZ

Der große Erfolg im 1000-Meilen-Rennen von Brescia

2. Preis: Karl Kling   4. Preis: Rudolf Caracciola

Kling, Gewinner des Preises „Coppa L'Aquila" und Schnellster auf der Strecke Brescia-Rom

AUF MERCEDES-BENZ „TYP 300 SL"

Dreifacher Sieg
der Sportwagen
MERCEDES-BENZ
im „Preis von Bern"

1. Karl Kling 2. Hermann Lang 3. Fritz Riess
auf Mercedes-Benz Typ 300 SL

Lang fuhr die schnellste Runde mit 2:56,1 = 148,825 km/Std.
und damit gleichzeitig einen neuen Rundenrekord

Überlegener Sieg
im Großen Jubiläumspreis vom Nürburgring
für Sportwagen

1. Hermann Lang, 2. Karl Kling, 3. Fritz Riess, 4. Theo Helfrich

alle auf Mercedes-Benz Typ 300 SL

Hermann Lang fährt die schnellste Runde mit

MERCEDES-BENZ

MERCEDES-BENZ

Nach harter Zerreißprobe
DOPPELSIEG
im 24-Stunden-Rennen von Le Mans
1. Lang-Riess
2. Helfrich-Niedermayr

auf Mercedes-Benz Typ 300 SL

Neuer absoluter Streckenrekord - 3733 km 780 m in 24 Stunden gefahren

III. Carrera Panamericana Mexico
Triumphaler Doppelsieg
1. Karl Kling 2. Hermann Lang

Im härtesten 5-Tage-Kampf siegt überlegen in neuer Strecken-Rekordzeit
der „Typ 300 SL", entwickelt aus den serienmäßigen Personenwagen von

MERCEDES-BENZ

Above: The 1952 Mille Miglia was the only race in 1952 that the Mercedes-Benz 300 SL team would not win. Karl Kling finished second behind Giovani Bracco driving a new Ferrari. Still, a 2-4 finish in the toughest race in the world with untried cars was worthy of a poster by artist Hans Liska.

Top center: After the Mille Miglia the Mercedes team never looked back. In the Grand Prix of Bern it was Karl Kling, Hermann Lang, and Fritz Riess finishing 1-2-3.
Top right: At the Nürburgring in '52 it was a first through fourth place sweep for the 300 SLs with Lang, Kling, Riess, and Theo Helfrich finishing in order.
Bottom center: In the 1952 Le Mans 24 Hours, the team finished 1-2 with drivers Lang and Riess in first and Helfrich and Niedermayr second. The haunting charcoal pencil illustration was by Hans Liska.
Bottom right: After sweeping across Europe the 300 SL team went to Mexico and won the Carrera Panamericana. Karl Kling and Herman Lang finished 1-2. The poster was another Hans Liska creation.

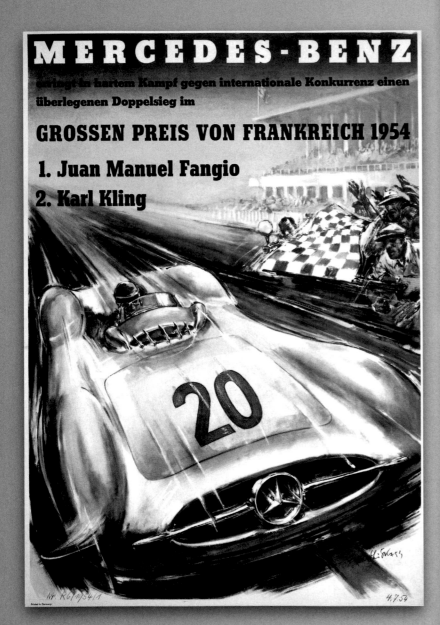

MERCEDES-BENZ

erlegt in hartem Kampf gegen internationale Konkurrenz einen überlegenen Doppelsieg im

GROSSEN PREIS VON FRANKREICH 1954

1. Juan Manuel Fangio

2. Karl Kling

MERCEDES-BENZ

gewinnt in hartem Kampf gegen stärkste Konkurrenz auch das schnelle Rennen um den „Großen Preis von Italien 1954"

1. Juan Manuel Fangio

4. Hans Herrmann

Und wieder siegt **MERCEDES-BENZ** mit seinen Silberpfeilen im „Großen Preis der Schweiz"

1. Juan Manuel Fangio

3. Hans Herrmann

Dreifacher Sieg! **MERCEDES-BENZ** gewinnt auch den „Großen Preis von Berlin" auf der schnellsten Rennstrecke der Welt

1. Karl Kling

2. Juan Manuel Fangio

3. Hans Herrmann

Top center: In the 1954 Italian GP it was Fangio in first and Hans Hermann in fourth, adding another notch in the Argentinean race driver's belt. This was another striking Hans Liska illustration.

Top right: The duo of Fangio and Hermann scored another victory for Mercedes in the Swiss GP with Fangio claiming another first place finish on his way to the world driving championship.

At left: Karl Kling bested his teammates to win the German Grand Prix in 1955.

Above: Mercedes skipped the 1953 racing season and came back in 1954 with the remarkable W 196 racecars. In the 1954 and 1955 seasons, the W 196 models won a total of 11 out of 14 races, with Juan Manuel Fangio collecting two world championships along the way.

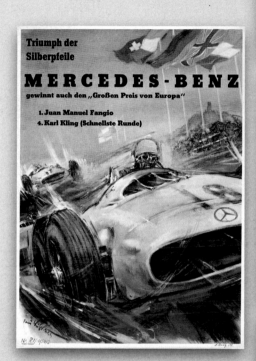

Triumph der
Silberpfeile

MERCEDES-BENZ

gewinnt auch den „Großen Preis von Europa"

1. Juan Manuel Fangio
4. Karl Kling (Schnellste Runde)

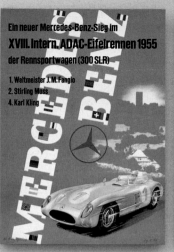

Ein neuer Mercedes-Benz-Sieg im
XVIII. Intern. ADAC-Eifelrennen 1955
der Rennsportwagen (300 SLR)

1. Weltmeister J. M. Fangio
2. Stirling Moss
4. Karl Kling

Überzeugender Sieg am Rio de la Plata
Großer Preis von Argentinien 1955

1. Weltmeister J. M. Fangio
4. Herrmann / Kling / Moss

Überlegener Mercedes-Benz-Sieg
XXII. MILLE MIGLIA 1955

Rennsportwagen (300 SLR)   1. Stirling Moss/Jenkinson
                                  2. Weltmeister J. M. Fangio
Seriensportwagen (300 SL)   1. Fitch / Gesell
                                  2. Gendebien/Bascher
                                  3. Casella
Dieselklasse (180 D)   1. Retter / Larcher
                                  2. Reinhard/Wiesnewski
                                  3. Masera/Cardinar

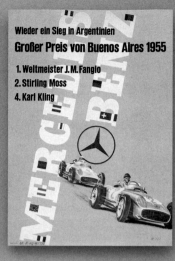

Wieder ein Sieg in Argentinien
Großer Preis von Buenos Aires 1955

1. Weltmeister J. M. Fangio
2. Stirling Moss
4. Karl Kling

Ein klarer Mercedes-Benz-Sieg im
Großen Preis von Belgien 1955

1. Weltmeister J. M. Fangio
2. Stirling Moss

Doppelsieg der Mercedes-Benz-Rennwagen
Großer Preis von Holland 1955

1. Weltmeister J. M. Fangio
2. Stirling Moss

Zwei Mercedes-Benz-Doppelsiege im
Großen Preis von Schweden 1955

Rennsportwagen (300 SLR)
1. Weltmeister J. M. Fangio
2. Stirling Moss

Sportwagen (300 SL)
1. Karl Kling
2. Erik Lundgren

The 1955 racing season
belonged to Mercedes-Benz
and the W 196. This series
of victory posters from races
around the world left no
doubt on any continent that
Mercedes-Benz was back.

Auch Sportwagen-Weltmeisterschaft gewonnen
Triumphaler Abschluß der Rennsaison
Sieg der Rennsportwagen auf der Targa Florio

1. Stirling Moss / Peter Collins
2. Weltmeister J. M. Fangio / Karl Kling
4. J. D. Titterington / John Fitch

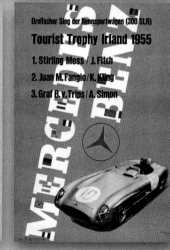

Dreifacher Sieg der Rennsportwagen (300 SLR)
Tourist Trophy Irland 1955

1. Stirling Moss / J. Fitch
2. Juan M. Fangio / K. Kling
3. Graf B. v. Trips / A. Simon

Entscheidender Doppelsieg im
Großen Preis von Italien 1955

1. Weltmeister J. M. Fangio
2. Piero Taruffi

Vierfacher Mercedes-Benz-Sieg im
Großen Preis von England 1955

1. Stirling Moss
2. Weltmeister J. M. Fangio
3. Karl Kling
4. Piero Taruffi

Index